Romantic Modernism

Romantic Modernism

Nostalgia in the World of Conservation

Wim Denslagen

Translated by Donald Gardner

Amsterdam University Press

The book has been written under the authority of the
Department of Cultural Heritage in the Netherlands
(Rijksdienst voor het Cultureel Erfgoed).

The translation has been made possible with a grant
from the Prins Bernhard Cultuurfonds.

Cover design: Geert de Koning, Ten Post
Lay out: ProGrafici, Goes

ISBN   978 90 8964 103 8
E-ISBN   978 90 4850 870 9
NUR   648 / 955

Contents

Introduction   7

Sentimentality and the City   9

The Rectangular Sickness   43

Romantic Modernists   75

Self-seeking Romantics   107

Bad-mannered Buildings   121

The Revival Styles and Time Regained   155

Nostalgia and Imitation   167

Notes   223

Bibliography   231

Index   255

Introduction

Starting a collection of vintage cars, antique furniture, historical monuments or old towns may be a sentimental or nostalgic activity, but such activities are very widespread and one presumes that they do not do very much harm. The phenomenon is generally tolerated, as long as it is conducted in closed institutions, such as museums. In the public domain, however, there is much less acceptance of the phenomenon. Generally speaking, it requires much more effort to preserve a historical town intact than it does to conserve a period room in a museum. This is understandable to an extent, because historical cities sometimes have to be altered to make way for modern amenities, for example by laying tram tracks, building a car park or a new hotel. It would of course have been much better to spare the few surviving historical city centres and to install the modern facilities required as far away as possible in the suburbs, because one can build as one wants there, unimpeded by historical monuments. In general, however, this is not what has occurred. From the beginning of the twentieth century, historical cities have been expected to keep pace with modern times. Businesses, banks and department stores preferred to keep their premises in the older quarters, and residential areas are mainly found on the outskirts of cities. Only when it became inevitable, when there was no longer room to expand, did businesses depart from the inner city with a heavy heart, leaving many scars in the urban tissue in its wake. To mention one recent example, between 2000 and 2002, Amsterdam lost 6,000 jobs due to business enterprises leaving the city. According to one Dutch newspaper, 'A good third of those leaving stated as their most compelling reason the limited possibilities for expansion.'[1]

In retrospect, one can mourn the fact that our historic cities have not been better preserved, but it is simply not possible to prevent every change from taking place. Even if all the residents of a city and all the businesses, not to mention the local government, might want it, it is virtually impossible to maintain a historical city as an open air museum; something sometimes has to give, and then all one can do is to resign oneself to the inevitable. This is true not only of the city centre, but also of historic interiors. A house full of period rooms is a wonderful thing to own of course, but there are not that many home-owners, male or female, who would renounce the conveniences one enjoys in a modern kitchen. In order not to clash with the rest of such a house, modern kitchens are furnished with old-fashioned cupboard doors in profiled oak, so that the modern equipment is kept out of sight as much as possible. Something similar also occurs in many old cities, with historical façades proving to be little more than stage sets masking modern office interiors. This is not entirely honest, and the question is whether city governments and their conservation departments should be involved with these sorts of half-truths. Should a governmental body be allowed to provide grants to restore old façades when virtually everything behind them is modern, with the exception perhaps of a few old beams, a rickety wooden staircase and, if you are lucky, a ceiling in the entrance hall with stucco ornamentation from around 1870? In the world of conservationists, doubts are growing about the value of preserving historical façades as pieces of scenery. Does a historical cityscape based on an architectural charade have any value? Most architects and conservationists are inclined to think not.

Where does this trend towards honesty and openness to the idea of integrating new architecture in historical surroundings come from? Perhaps it is a legacy of functionalism, in architecture, because the rules of functionalism held it to be morally reprehensible to erect any fake architecture.[2] It may be that functionalism, as part of the Modern Movement, had its origins in Romanticism, when architects turned their backs on academic formalism and strove to devise a new, rational form of building. Nineteenth-century rationalism may well have laid the foundations for a dislike of architecture that mainly aims to please the eye. And it is probably the case that functionalism has left its mark on the world of conservation. The Romantic aim of achieving sincerity in art is translated by conservationists into a renewed respect for the authentic work of art and a revulsion against historicizing restorations. Conservation thus became an ally of functionalism, with its dislike of false display. Hence a certain dislike emerged in the world of conservationists of the cultivation of a harmonious cityscape, because such an image is artificial, and thus false. A conservationist policy that aims for the restoration of a harmonious cityscape, then, is ignoring the course of history and that, too, is reprehensible, because it means that reality is sacrificed to a myth. Is this thesis correct, however?

Sentimentality and the City

Museumification

In an article of 1992 about the history of conservation in Holland, Kees van der Ploeg expressed his concern about the sentimentalizing of the city – his term for historicizing trappings of old cities. Historical inner cities, he argued, were being 'museumified' by the conservationists, and he did not see this development as positive. The image of the historical city, he wrote, is in danger of becoming 'a sugary-sweet backdrop' that 'bears hardly any real relation to normal urban activities'. He concluded that 'no answer has yet been found, including by the conservationists', for this problem.[1]

Conservationists have failed in this regard, and something will need to be done about this unsatisfactory situation. To come up with an answer, however, one must first understand what is actually involved in the problem. Kees van der Ploeg and many others like him are exasperated by the fact that historical city centres look increasingly like open air museums; they are reduced to tourist attractions. This development is considered deplorable, because the artificially historicized image of the city does not relate at all to modern life. Previously, the historical cityscape would be regarded as an authentic and living heritage from the past, but nowadays the historical city seems to be artificially put on ice. Conservation, the critics say, has taken a wrong turn by supporting this process of freezing the historical and, to an extent, historicized, urban scene.

Why however do these historical façades no longer relate to the modern age? According to critics such as Kees van der Ploeg, the world has undergone huge changes over the past century, whereas all those restored façades look so bright and new that they give us the illusion that we are still living in the eighteenth century. The preservationists do not allow them any chance of becoming genuinely old; at the first trace of dilapidation, they speed to the rescue, armed with funds and the proposals of experts, to make everything as good as new. The result is that the architecture of the historical city is no longer alive; instead, it is embalmed like a mummy to comply with the banal expectations of the hordes of tourists. This, more or less, is Kees van der Ploeg's criticism and, as just mentioned, he is by no means the only one to make it.

What the conservationists are charged with – rightly or wrongly – is that they are putting on ice an image that has grown historically over the centuries. The beauty of an old city, the argument goes, is the product of a long series of changes that occurred during the past, and for the sake of this specific beauty this process should be allowed to continue. Let us suppose that the image of a certain city had ceased to change after 1750, what would we say about it? Would we call it a historical fluke, a lifeless and vacuous open air museum? Presumably not. It is quite possible, for instance, that the average tourist cherishes a city like Venice exactly because most of the buildings don't give any impression of having changed with the times. The question remains then what conservationists should be aiming for. Should they nurture the illusion that time has stood still, or should they permit the city to evolve in relation to modern urban activities?

For various reasons, Kees van der Ploeg's criticism is not entirely correct. First of all, it is mistaken because for many years now the conservation movement in Europe has been doing its utmost to show that it does not see its task as putting any historical cityscape on ice. Preservationists proclaim to anyone prepared to listen that their concern is to ensure that new and modern architecture is integrated into the historical environment in a responsible fashion. Yet the popular image remains that the aim of preservationists is to keep the image of the city on ice. This is intrinsically interesting, because it means that many people regard conservation bodies as institutions whose purpose is to conserve our built heritage and that, by definition, they must therefore be opposed to modern architectural developments. This is why critics like Kees van der Ploeg see them as reluctant to change with the times.

But something else is also going on here. Perhaps preservationists are actually making the opposite mistake by fostering the integration of modern architecture into historical contexts. After all, there are many people who think that the task of conservation should indeed be to protect a valuable, comparatively intact historical environment as much as possible against new architectural experiments. It is undoubtedly the case, these people argue, that modern architecture can disrupt the historical image. Isn't this group of people perfectly entitled to express concern about the loss of historical urban images? And isn't it true that preservationists – in their zeal to be liberated from their conservative image – attach too much importance to integrating new architecture in historical cities?

One irritating incidental consideration is that those who want to leave a city intact in its former state usually have an irrational dislike of modern architecture. This isn't necessarily always the case, however. The image one usually has of conservatives as being insensitive to art is reinforced each time they lodge an objection to a new development in the historical city, even when the quality of the development in itself – independent of its context, that is – is not at issue. In contrast to what Kees van der Ploeg thinks, those who oppose change are getting less and less of a hearing in the world of conservation. This is because this world is in a state of panic about being regarded as backward both by public and private organizations. Preservationists no longer want to be associated with conservative fuddy-duddies who refuse to keep up with the times. For this reason, very few protests against new architecture in old cities are heard from this quarter, not even when it genuinely does encroach on the historic cityscape. Is there anyone who still remembers why conservation bodies were set up in the first place?

As governmental bodies, the departments for conservation were founded in a period that also witnessed the birth of the monster known as modernity which was threatening to wipe out the old world altogether. It is no coincidence that the building inspectorate and the various movements for nature conservation also emerged at this time. In other words, the rise of the idea of the conservation of historic buildings was intimately linked to a political aspiration that, while not new, only acquired a national dimension around 1900. Conservation is a historically determined phenomenon – that is, it emerged in a certain historical context. It should therefore be regarded against the background of the fear people felt at that time for the loss of their historical surroundings. The original aims of the conservation movement have remained more or less the same during the course of the twentieth century; these aims continue to be the social foundation on which conservation was built. These aims, however, have seemingly been forced into the background by those who claim that the beauty of the historical city, that is after all the product of a historical process, would not have come about if the government had blocked that process in the past. The argument goes that if there had been an idea of conservation back in 1750 which had put the historically evolved cityscape on ice, then the historical cities would lack the diversity they acquired in the nineteenth century in particular. It is precisely that diversity we admire so much today.

But there is a specific reason why it was not in 1750 but only in the course of the twentieth century that conservationists took measures to intervene in the process of change. Conservation bodies formed part of that historical process and there was good reason to institute them at that time. They were the product of the emergence of a broad public interest in the beauty of historical cities and landscapes. This interest was admittedly not new, but it took on a political meaning during the nineteenth century. As just mentioned, a broad basis of support emerged around 1900 for a policy aimed at protecting historical cities against the feared assaults of modernity. This historically determined basis for the conservation movement has not essentially altered since then. But the strange thing now is that many people in the world of conservation hold the view that this basis has been completely superseded by new ideas.

Before one can address these ideas however, a potential misunderstanding needs clearing up. It was presumably not Kees van der Ploeg's intention to complain about the fact that restorations often hark back to an older design, so that historical cities have come increasingly to look like open air museums. That is not what he wrote and presumably it was also not what he was talking about, however much this development may have distressed him. As said, he meant that the urban scene had become frozen so that it had the air of a stage set, with the result that there was no longer any 'real relation' between image and reality. What upsets him is the discrepancy between the historical urban scene and the world that has changed utterly. Presumably he must feel a similar discomfort at the sight of something like computers behind eighteenth-century sash windows. While it is possible to sympathize with him, a sight like this is not unreal. It is only truly unreal and even a little disgusting when this window was installed just recently in order to restore a situation that existed before it was altered in, say 1860. Once again however, this is not where the problem lies and we will thus not dwell on this popular form of 'retrospective restoration'. As far as this is concerned the damage has already been done and, it has to be said, it has occurred with the approval and support of the official preservationists for whom historical architecture came to an end around 1800.

Ugliness as an ideal

The above-mentioned imbalance between the historic image of the city and modern life is a form of torture not only for historians of architecture, but for many architects too. The idea that a historical environment is not allowed to change is greeted by them with disbelief. They think that those people who try to put a cityscape on ice are trying to do something which is impossible: to cause time to stand still. Even so, the question remains whether it is really in defiance of common sense to want to preserve a beautiful and universally admired historical city as much as possible in its existing state. Why should an aim like this be seen as nonsensical and im-possible? After all, so few ancient cities and landscapes have been preserved intact; why should those few square miles 'keep up with the times' with all the violence this implies? In most countries of Europe, little more than one per cent of the total built environment is protected by any legislation to preserve historic buildings. That is very, very little, so why do historians of architecture and architects complain about the fact that these few miserable remnants of our architectural heritage have not 'kept up with the times'? There are well-intentioned and critically minded people who feel noth-ing but scorn for the tourists on the tour boats in Venice and Amsterdam. They despise them, because they are stupid enough to get pleasure from an artificially preserved stage set.

After the Second World War it was possible to redress this imbalance between the old image and the living reality, at any rate where ancient cities had been reduced to rubble. It seems incredible, but the fact is that quite a number of city planners in Germany viewed the catastrophe as catharsis, an exceptional opportunity to design a modern form of planning on this *tabula rasa*.[2]

As late as 1949, the publisher of *Baukunst und Werkform*, Alfons Leitl, was indignant about the opportunities that had been missed. There were, he wrote, many planners who thought that 'die Vernichtung der Häuser den Weg freigemacht hätte für grundsätzliche Neugestaltungen' (the destruction of homes has made the way free for radically new structures). In reality, however, their ideals had also been reduced to rubble, because they saw that 'Frei gewordenen Flächen in Wirklichkeit keineswegs frei sind, sondern dass sie überwuchert sind mit einem Gestrüpp von Grundbesitzrechten' (Spaces made free are not free at all, because they are overgrown with a thicket of property rights). In the magazine *Die neue Stadt* of 1948, an article on German reconstruction was published with the title 'Ein Unglück ja – aber auch eine Gelegenheit' (a tragedy but also an opportunity).[3]

It has been argued that it was easier for Germany to say goodbye to its historical cities, because there the past was tainted by two world wars. This may be so, but virtually all Modernists, German or otherwise, disliked historical cities. Modernist planning actually originated in this distaste. Part of the legacy of Modernism is the continuance of the functionalist idea that a city must adapt to meet changed circumstances. It cannot be reduced to a splendid stage set or a pretty picture. This idea is also found in the work of the renowned British architects, Alison and Peter Smithson. In their eyes the historical cities were not suitable for the modern city dweller, 'seeing that the social reality they represent no longer exists'.[4]

It is perhaps with this idea in mind that the Smithsons were unaware that the nineteenth-century St. James's Street in London may have been an artwork of urban planning in itself and that its historical character might be ruined by their office complex. The Smithsons had no eye for the street's architectural qualities, because architecture wasn't a pretty picture for them, but a function. They were convinced that their Economist Building, which has stood in St. James's Street since 1964, represented a good use of the city. Both architects had already described in 1957 how a hole in a street can be exploited to intensify the use of the urban space. In their view 'the problem of building the three houses in an existing street is one of finding a way (whilst still responding to the street idea) to chop through the old building face and build up a complex in depth, of providing a suggestion, a sign, of a new community structure.'[5]

The Smithsons called a complex like this a *cluster*, and they built their first example in St. James's Street, a street of some distinction with a variety of eclectic architecture from the last decade of the nineteenth century. In her study of the work of these architects, Helena Webster wrote that the success of this design was mainly due to the tact with which the immediate surroundings were treated: 'The success of the design lays in its particularly sensitive response to context.' Admittedly, she continued, the tradition of the closed block was disrupted, but in its use of materials, its scale, height zoning and street-lines, 'the scheme responded to and respected its surroundings.'[6] Besides Helena Webster, Kenneth Frampton also admired the block, calling it a 'work of studied restraint'. In his view, the way that it

1   The Economist Building by Alison and Peter Smithson in St. James's Street in London (1964)

ROMANTIC MODERNISM

was slotted into the street was done 'very tenderly indeed'. Vincent Scully joined in the chorus of praise, describing it as 'one of the most important buildings of the decade'.[7]

These statements were definitely not intended as ironic, although those who love the nineteenth-century character of this London neighbourhood and think that the Smithsons' skyscraper disrupts the urban harmony of this street may find this hard to believe. The Smithsons gained enormous prestige in the 1950s, partly due to their receiving the stamp of approval from an influential figure such as Reyner Banham, the author of *The New Brutalism. Ethic or Aesthetic?* This book, published in 1966, tells of a group of young architects who emerged in the early 1950s who aspired to a new architecture that would be purely functional and liberated from such notions as art and beauty. It was an architecture that was 'entirely free of the professional preconceptions and prejudices that have encrusted architecture since it became an art'. According to Banham, what was involved was 'an utterly uninhibited functionalism', entirely uncorrupted even by 'the machine aesthetic' of the 1920s. Alison and Peter Smithson also belonged to this strict functionalist trend, and in this connection it is maybe also worth mentioning that not only were they 'utterly functionalistic' and deliberately 'anti-aesthetic', but that they also displayed a liking for everything that looked ugly and neglected. That can clearly be seen for instance in the collection of photos they chose in 1953 for an exhibition at the Institute of Contemporary Art. The organizers of this exhibition took pride in the fact that the most repugnant images had been selected, because it was their intention to present the ugly side of life. One of the photographers who had contributed to the show, Nigel Henderson, wrote later, 'I feel happiest among discarded things, vituperative fragments, cast casually from life, with the fizz of vitality still about them.'[8]

A revulsion against everything that looks beautiful and a preference for squalor – sentiments like this were fundamental to the work of the Smithsons, as they also inevitably were of that of the host of pupils and admirers of the famous couple. They associated the notion of 'beauty' with a mistaken kind of bourgeois sentimentality.

From Nigel Whiteley's biography of Reyner Banham, we learn what the author of the famous 1960 book, *Theory and Design in the First Machine Age*, thought about the protection of the familiar urban scene. In as much as he ever paid any attention to something as inferior as the preservation of architecture from an age not yet fortunate enough to have machines, he saw it in the first instance as resulting from the vulgar material self-interest of home owners. According to him, people like this misuse the notion of 'culture' to get the authorities to protect their properties. In his view, this protection involved 'dwellings (or rents) of the rich on the grounds that they are Georgian, and therefore priceless monuments of our heritage of blah, blah, blah … but because it is in Belgravia or Bath, it is safe from the replacement on which any sane society would insist. Men of good will are being fooled into defending privilege disguised as culture'. Banham believed that conservationists were not so much concerned with preserving buildings as class distinctions. Furthermore, he saw historical architecture as an obstacle to progress. In a 1963 article, *The Embalmed City*, in which he deploys his full arsenal of literary fireworks to expose the 'preservationists' as ridiculous, he wrote that, 'The load of obsolete buildings that Europe is humping along on its shoulders is a bigger drag on the live culture of our continent than obsolete nationalisms or obsolete moral codes.'[9]

In the eyes of some Modernists, the desire to preserve a familiar living environment is already enough to make one suspect, as it may form a fertile soil for racism. *Heimatsarchitektur* is dangerous and must be resisted, according to Alexander Tzonis and Liane Lefaivre in the journal *Architecture and Urbanism* (1990). They argued that critical regionalism was 'one of the most interesting directions in contemporary architecture', because it offered an alternative to a whole range of architectural pornography. They were attracted by critical regionalism, because it sought a relation with local architectural traditions while not imitating them slavishly. Architects should respond critically to regional styles. They shouldn't be allowed to erect any cheaply sentimental pastiches, or nostalgic imitations that would form 'a suitable setting for xenophobic, neo-tribal and racist hallucinations.' Tzonis and Lefaivre are allergic to any architecture that reinforces narcissistic sentiments about one's own region, or *Heimat*, or which creates a backdrop for a self-satisfied complacency. What was needed if one was to avoid a frighteningly romantic form of regionalism was a degree of critical distance. The sentimental link that the complacent consumer may have with the familiar architectural setting can only be broken by a form of dislocation, by wrong-footing the consumer and getting him to think for himself. The building should engage in 'an imagined dialogue with the viewer'. The viewer must not be made to feel too comfortable with familiar images, because, as just said, these can form a fertile soil for undemocratic behaviour; instead he should be confronted with a 'sense of displacement' that would raise him to 'a metacognitive state'. Tzonis and Lefaivre are profoundly suspicious of the unconscious adoption of forms from the past just because they are all-too familiar.

Their fear may well have been prompted by the history of Nazism or other, more recent forms of xenophobic behaviour, but their conclusion that all traditionalism is suspect by definition is perhaps taken to something of an extreme. Why should the residents of a modern experimental housing estate be less susceptible to racism than those of a fake farming village? Does a sloping and overhanging glass front have a more favourable impact on human feelings than a seventeenth-century style stepped gable? Why should non-critical regionalism or any clinging to local architectural traditions be in conflict with normal humane behaviour in every case?

Frustrated creativity

A certain timidity prevails among architects about an approach to conservation that aims only to preserve the existing and which therefore has an inhibiting effect on creativity. The famous Austrian architect Karl Schwanzer put it as follows in 1975: 'Das Bestreben der heutigen Zeit, Baudenkmäler als historische Monumente zu würdigen, diese zu erhalten, zu pflegen und auch zu revitalisieren, muss jeden Architekten primär erfreuen' (The fact that efforts are made today to appreciate, maintain and restore historical buildings as ancient monuments should be welcomed by every architect). Nonetheless, he saw any uncritical adoration of historical buildings as misguided, because their function was then lost sight of – 'Auf einmal tritt die Bedeutung der Funktion und des Nutzen, jene Begriffe, die unsere heutigen Bauaufgaben gesellschaftpolitisch vorrangig beherrschen, zurück, wenn es um das Bewahren historischer Bauwerke geht' (If what is involved is the preservation of historic buildings, the significance of their function and use are straightway set on one side, although these notions are of the greatest social importance in today's architectural world). It is a mistake for architects to despise the functional aspects of architecture and to go along too passively with the nostalgic desires of the general public. 'Architekten von heute sollten der Mumifizierung der Städte nicht tatenlos zusehen. Sie brauchen den Denkmalschutz generell als Mobilisation des Bewusstmachens der Baugestaltung als historische Aufgabe unserer Zeit' (Architects today must not submit to the mummifying of our cities without a fight. Generally speaking they need the notion of conservation in order to understand that architecture is a historically determined task). People appoint themselves as champions of the revitalization of everything old out of a sense of inferiority – something that Schwanzer sees as a typical weakness of our times.

The quotations from Schwanzer occur in a remarkable book from 1977 by Gerhard Müller-Menckes, *Neues Leben für alte Bauten. Über den Continuo in der Architektur*. It deals with a great many instances of modern infills in historical environments, most of which are accompanied by admiring comments. Why the projects selected are regarded as so exemplary is sometimes hard to understand. In what regard was Dieter Oesterlen's museum plan of 1963 that replaced the former Zeughaus in Hanover supposed to be so instructive for conservationists? The text accompanying the illustrations of this museum remarks that in designing the façade on the Burgstrasse, the architect had taken into consideration the half-timbered houses on the other side of the street, which had been entirely reconstructed after the Second World War: 'Die massstäbliche Eingliederung des Neubaues wird unterstützt durch eine plastische Durchformung der Fassade' (The incorporation of the new development was supported by the plastic design of the façade). According to the commentary, the façade was designed in such a way that the result could be described as a success: 'Alt und Neu durchdringen sich in einer Synthese, die beglückt' (Old and new converge here in a happy synthesis). It is not immediately obvious what it is that is so happy here. We see new archi-

2   *The Historical Museum in Hanover, designed by Dieter Oeserlen (1963)*

3   *The new town hall building in Bensberg, designed by Gottfried Böhm (1976)*

tecture juxtaposed with reconstructions of historic houses. I can imagine that the architect must have felt tremendously challenged by the commission and that the result must have been thought rather striking, but in the context of what stood on this spot before the war, it amounts to little more than a game with forms. It is possible that the architects did their best under the circumstances, but that hardly justifies this example being praised to the skies or being called an interesting example of conservation. The whole thing was born of need and the solution opted for is a monument of architecture coming to terms with a guilty past. The design is thus in the first instance tragic – the torn past of Germany is actually drawn attention to by the big gestures of the modern museum façade. The author of the book *Neues Leben für alte Bauten* was apparently so enchanted by his subject that he overlooked the question of whether everyone else was equally charmed by the examples he praises. His judgement, for instance, on the new town hall of Bensberg sounds apodictic, to put it mildly: 'Die meisterliche Lösung kann generell ein Beispiel dafür geben, wie sich moderne Bauten in alte Ortskerne einfügen und dabei die Kontinuität der Stadtgestalt weiterführen können'(The masterly solution can be used generally as an example of how modern buildings can be fitted into historical villages, in such a way that the shape of the city is continued). The author of this eulogy meant that the new building, based on a 1967 design by Gottfried Böhm, had put an end to the useless existence of the romantic ruined castle. In this sense, a domain that until then was thought 'dead' was given a new life. The architect has provided his design with something of the wildness and inaccessibility of the old stronghold. There should, one would think, be little to complain about, apart from the fact that the new building has done away with the magic of the medieval ruin and that the site has been supplied with a new meaning – melancholy has been cast out by modern concrete. The book does not address the question of what this transformation has actually meant for the romance of old castles, once so vital a theme in Germany. This presumably comes from the fact that the author deemed creativity far and away more important than any romantic fixation on the architectural vestiges of a distant past. It is a pity he didn't take the trouble, however, to explain why the new development in Bensberg is called an improvement – something of greater value than the ruin.

A comparable viewpoint can be discerned in *Neues Bauen in alter Umgebung*, the catalogue of a 1978 exhibition organized by the Architektenkammer of Bavaria and the Staatliches Museum für angewandte Kunst in Munich. In the catalogue introduction, Friedrich Kurrent argues that, in the age of Max Dvořák, the most important task of conservation consisted of rescuing monuments from ruin, because around 1900 there was still a great danger that they would be demolished to make way for the headlong advance of modernity. But by 1978 the situation would appear to have changed radically. According to Kurrent: 'Die wichtigste Aufgabe scheint mir heute, zu verhindern, dass derartige Bauwerke oder ganze Stadtteile durch den Schutz, den sie geniessen, in Isolation geraten, dass die als Denkmal isoliert werden' (The principal task today would seem to me to be to prevent buildings like this, or entire inner city areas, from becoming isolated as monuments by the protection they receive). Manfred F. Fischer takes this thesis a stage further, pointing out that the image of a historical building or town is not something static but is constantly subject to change: 'Das Erscheinungsbild eines Raumes, eines Gebäudes, eines Ortsbildes, einer Stadt is kein statischer Begriff, sondern ein Prozess, also das Ergebnis einer sich stetig vollziehenden Wandlung. Die Denkmalpflege muss dieses Naturgesetz akzeptieren, wenn sie glaubwürdig bleiben will' (The shape of a space, a building, a village or a city is not something static, but a process, the result therefore of continuous change. Conservationists must accept this law of nature if they want to remain credible). Some years later this seemingly profound idea was entrusted to paper – though admittedly in slightly different wording – by a planner from Delft, Rutger A.F. Smook, in a dissertation with the pregnant title *Binnensteden veranderen* (Changing city centres). In it he put forward the thesis that the purpose of conservation was not reconcilable with common sense, because the preservation of historical architecture meant that 'certain elements are removed from the natural process of change'. Furthermore he also considered that 'removing things from certain processes of transformation is essentially unnatural'.[10] Diseases are also natural processes, but no one would dare draw the conclusion from this that medical intervention is 'essentially unnatural'.

In the context of thought processes like this, it will no longer come as a surprise that the contributors to *Neues Bauen in alter Umgebung* make statements that are difficult to grasp, not just for the general public, but presumably also for the interested layman. Take for instance, the account of the Diözesanmuseum in Paderborn, built by Gottfried Böhm in partnership with Franz Kilian and Hans Linder in 1975 next to the cathedral. While admitting that this new building forms a contrast with its surroundings, the contributors also think that this 'monolithischer Block geht mit seiner grossflächigen Gestalt rücksichtsvoll auf die Plastizität der Umgebung ein.' (monolithic block with its great volume fits into its surroundings with due respect). The square on the south side of the cathedral had also previously been built upon and, according to the clients, this was a convincing argument for allowing a new development to be erected there. In his book on the work of Böhm, Wolfgang Pehnt remarks that in Paderborn there had initially been some criticism of the fact that the new museum blocked the view of the cathedral, but he did not respond to this criticism, confining himself to pointing out that 'auch die zerstörte Vorgängerbauten den Dom eingefasst hatten'[11] (the view of the cathedral was also blocked by the demolished buildings that had stood there before). It is understandable that the author of a work about a famous artist does not want to enquire too deeply into matters that might detract from his reputation. Nonetheless it is hardly surprising that the residents of Paderborn were appalled by this huge lead-grey hulk that had been erected on their cathedral square. The whole building is clad in lead, like an arsenal or a nuclear physics research laboratory. Wolfgang Pehnt does no justice to history by failing to take such understandable reactions seriously, whether they come from special-ists or from the general public. The development that had stood on this square had been demolished during the war and perhaps it wouldn't have been a bad idea to restore the situation to its previous state. This approach was rejected, however, apparently in the expectation that new architecture might heal the wounds. But why did the restoration make no reference to the architecture that formerly stood here? What reason was there for such a curious choice? The architects, I think, must, I think, have opted for a modern design like this to demonstrate that modern architecture is in no way inferior to its historical counterpart. The self-aware volume of the new museum has something provocative about it. It is as though it is telling the churchbuilding, 'Look at me, I know a thing or two about architecture my-self'. The cathedral doesn't reply, but maybe it is muttering to itself, 'What a show-off'.

It could be argued that one has no reason to get upset about a bit of architectural contrast; after all, isn't every historical city an example of ar-chitectural diversity, due to the different styles of the various historical pe-riods? Shouldn't our own age have just as much right as another to leave its mark on the ancient city? Moreover, one shouldn't forget that the siting of this church museum, next door to the cathedral, is not unreasonable – one might even argue that it makes sense, especially if one bears in mind that the site was also built on in the past. One might find fault with Gottfried Böhm's design, but it's a known fact that major art works are not always understood straight away. It is quite possible that the next generation will judge his design positively – a point that is often made. The idea is that the next generation will be in a better position to judge, that the quality of an artwork does not have to be plain for all to see directly, that in the past too many buildings which are now historical monuments weren't appreciated at first.

This line of argument is not entirely correct, however, because it implies that artists are the only people in a position to assess works of modern art and that the general public normally only catches up with them later. It is based on the myth that an artist is a kind of visionary. But apart from that, one should bear in mind that architectural commissions are usually not given by the artists themselves, but by clients or patrons who might in a sense be counted as belonging to the general public. At any rate, they don't normally belong to the artistic elite. In Padernborn, the public was furious with Gottfried Böhm, but, properly speaking, it should have blamed the client (and the local authorities) for putting up the ugly grey monster next to their cathedral.

In the 1970s in particular many unqualifiedly enthusiastic accounts were written of new developments in old cities. In 1975 Manfred F. Fischer and a number of his colleagues published the book *Architektur und Denk-malpflege. Neue Architektur in historischer Umgebung*. In the journal *Monu-mentum* of 1975, B. Monnet contributed an article, 'L'Architecture con-temporaine dans les monuments et ensembles historiques en France'. In

4   *The cathedral square in Paderborn in 1938*

5   *The Diocesan Museum in Paderborn, designed by Gottfried Böhm and Hans Linder (1975)*

ROMANTIC MODERNISM

it, he states that renowned historical environments were not served by an architecture of adaptation; what they needed was a modern architecture of outstanding quality: 'la présence d'une architecture ancienne de qualité, qu'il s'agisse d'un monument isolé ou d'un ensemble urbain, apelle, non le pastiche déguisé sous le nom d'architecture d'accompagnement, mais une architecture de qualité qui soit de notre temps, de manière que nos matériaux, de la technique et de la recherche plastique contemporaines.' In 1988 the famous architect, Mario Botta, even took this idea a stage further with the remark that 'the old needs the new in order to be recognizable and the new needs the old in order to engage in a dialogue with it'. He went on to say, 'I see no reason why an architectural creation should be subordinated to existing values, as though these were more powerful. Architecture must be an expression of the age in which it is built and I think that a dialectical confrontation of the old and the new is the only way to treat the past with the proper respect.'[12] What he seems not to realize is that this is a typical nineteenth-century notion. The quest for an architecture in keeping with the *Zeitgeist* was the great architectural project of the nineteenth century, but it was one that failed, because people were incapable of designing anything contemporary and thus remained stuck with imitation old architecture. In the next century, the quest stopped, but oddly enough, the complementary, if bizarre, idea that every age requires its own style was not abandoned, at least not by Mario Botta and some of his colleagues.

Ground to dust

In his famous 1995 book, *S, M, L, XL* – a book that could be called weighty in more than one sense, Rem Koolhaas wrote that historical cities suffer from international concern for their refurbished history to such an extent that they end up being caricatures of themselves. Everyone wants to live in them and they are inundated by ever-growing numbers of tourists. The conservation departments provide ever more funds for made-to-measure historical décors, resulting in empty, hollowed-out, unreal cities. Due to the constant emphasis on the 'typical' they eventually lose whatever identity they had – in Koolhaas's words, these cities are being ground into 'meaningless dust'.[13]

Rem Koolhaas was probably saying the same thing here as Kees van der Ploeg. Both authors think that the artificial preservation of historical façades is symptomatic of a mental illness suffered mainly by planners. There are enough people who would agree with them, but, generally speaking, the residents of the restored houses and the tourists have a different opinion. The question arises then of how much notice conservationist bodies should take of this kind of criticism that always comes across as a bit naive and even slightly prim. The critics act as though conservation was formerly an honourable activity that at one time guaranteed the pure process of handing down our architectural heritage. They behave as though historicizing restorations are typical of our times, the age of mass tourism. This is simply not true. Restoration activity has been a feature of every age, and every historical building of any significance has been subjected to it, often in drastic form. By the end of the eighteenth century, most medieval buildings only displayed a superficial resemblance to their original condition. The nineteenth century then embarked on the restoration of all these old medieval edifices, something that usually boiled down to new additions in historicizing forms. The twentieth century gave all this work another going over, only what was involved then usually amounted to undoing what had been done in the nineteenth century. Today, the critics of architecture appear on the scene letting us know how inauthentic our historical cities have become.

Charges like this, however, can do serious harm. There are people in the world of conservation who refuse to have anything more to do with reproductions of historical forms and think that the only task left to them is to protect the authentic. It is easy to understand this, because in previous periods, conservationists had no problem if what was involved was an imitation of historical architecture. In 1969, the National Department for Conservation ordered a wing to be built on the Broederplein in Zeist that was once planned around 1750 but which was never implemented. That is, until the Department had it built after all, in order to use it as its own office. This wing isn't even a monument that has been 'ground to dust'; instead, it is a ghost. Although made of brick, it is as unreal as the music that the Dutch composer Ton Koopman composed for the missing parts of Johann Sebastian Bach's *St Mark's Passion*. Koopman stated that he behaved as though he was 'one of Bach's pupils', endeavouring to 'remain as close as possible to the eighteenth-century style and the musical language of Bach'. He was perfectly happy to admit that Bach would have done a much better job of it.[14] It may have been a falsification of history, but at least it was a melodious one. Nor is the imitation eighteenth-century wing in Zeist out of place, because in the original project the wing had already been drawn, making this case of rewriting history rather disarming. The fact that the Netherlands Department for Conservation decided to complete this architectural composition without any thought that it might be bad for its image is in itself quite odd. If a governmental body commissions imitation historic buildings for its own use, how can it ever accuse anyone else of falsifying history? That neither the Department nor the Ministry of Culture, of which it is a part, saw this piece of anachronic architecture as a problem does, however, display a certain insouciance.

Rem Koolhaas, however, is not one to complain about the rewriting of history. What he does criticize is the lack of passion in architects who allow themselves to be forced into a certain aesthetic straitjacket, for instance that of a historic urban environment. The fact that the Kunsthal on the Westzeedijk in Rotterdam designed by Koolhaas in 1992 makes no attempt to be beautiful expresses his view on of architecture. According to one specialist, a building should, in Koolhaas's view, be able to proclaim 'subversive messages as well'. 'Why, after all', says Bernhard Colenbrander, 'should a building have to convey a humanistic cheerfulness by definition? As long as it doesn't get in the way of its functioning, a building may speak the coarse language that has long belonged to possibilities of the other arts in the modern age.'[15] He was probably referring to the visual arts that, according to some artists, don't necessarily have to be beautiful. Artists regard it as beneath their dignity to be obliged to make something that looks beautiful.

'I don't want people only to think of my works as beautiful', said the Dutch artist Lydia Schouten in 1993, 'I also want to provoke other reactions, such as anger or laughter. I want to get people to think.'[16] She once made an installation for the Arnhem Gemeentemuseum that consisted of dolls hung from strings in a number of disturbing ways. Her aim was for the installation to be a symbol of child abuse. The artist wanted to wake up the settled bourgeoisie, a class that has the reputation of being extremely complacent, and get them to think. Those people who think that art is for their own aesthetic enjoyment have got it all wrong. 'What the work of art looks like isn't too important', the famous theoretician of conceptual art, Sol LeWitt, once said. Maybe something like this is Rem Koolhaas's aim, too – to get people to think by designing ugly buildings. But what are we supposed to think about? The Dutch architecture critic Bernhard Hulsman recently wrote that many people have been impressed by Koolhaas's coded language. As an example, he mentioned Harm Tilman in the journal *De Architect*: 'Tilman reacts like most of Koolhaas's critics. They are afraid of not understanding his strategies and being exposed as idiots by the sagacious guru.'[17]

Another Dutch architecture critic, Max van Rooy, also seems to find these things beyond his comprehension. This is evident from his analysis of Koolhaas's Byzantium development that fronts on the Vondelpark in Amsterdam. It is situated just next to the clumsy-looking Marriott Hotel and together they form a new, contemporary cityscape. Max van Rooy described Byzantium as 'barren and uninteresting'. He said that the façades had been given 'ugly little eyelets, and little flat aluminium windows', the terror of 'every urban renewal project in Amsterdam'. In short, it was a monstrosity.[18] According to Paul Vermeulen, writing in *Archis*, however, Byzantium is 'an effective example of innovatory urban architecture'. He explains that the 'architectural strategy by which the Byzantium building aims for the opposite urban qualities of anonymity and variation is the collage.' He says that the heterogeneous fragments of the composition preserve 'a degree of autonomy and become involved at their own expense in the urban theatre, thus partially doing away with the complacent isolation of the tower block.'[19]

Byzantium is a collage – it reminds you a bit of a cut-out and it also looks a bit like the way Dutch cartoonist Joost Swarte depicts architecture. Perhaps it is therefore somewhat irritating as a whole, because in a sense it looks a bit childish, like a child assembling pieces of a puzzle. However that may be, the last thing this building aspires to be is easy on the eye. It aims for something more, but what that is, is hard to say, despite Paul Vermeulen's explanation. Today's art connoisseurs regard designing something that looks beautiful as being completely dated; apparently a deep-rooted dislike of the harmonious image has also had its influence on conservationists. In the eyes of many architects, an old city that treats its monuments like stage sets is a ridiculous and obtuse phenomenon. They consider it both backward and cowardly to protect a harmonious cityscape by concealing new developments behind old façades, or designing a façade that contributes to a harmonious urban scene.

The tradition of Modernism considered it suspect to pay too much attention to the aesthetic aspect of the design. In 1980 the Amsterdam architect Herman Herzberger warned his colleagues against the sin of pursuing beauty. He did this in his article, 'De traditie van het Nieuwe Bouwen en de nieuwe mooiigheid' (The tradition of Dutch functionalism and the new prettiness), and the first sentence reads, 'At present we are plagued internationally by the misconception that what architecture is about is mainly forms, lines and proportions, that overawe people with their prettiness.'[20] Designing a charming modern architecture, in the style, say, of Richard Meier, is condemned by an influential group of architects. Their disapproval extends to the artificial freezing of historical cities in their existing condition, because this too only serves outward appearances.

Bruges and Rio de Janeiro

Even in Bruges, where from about 1870 onwards it was architectural policy to promote the Gothic Revival style at the expense of all others, and particularly those of Classicism and Modernism, the criticism of historicizing redevelopments became increasingly deafening. In Bruges today, people want to rid themselves of the clichéd image of a dead city as depicted in Georges Rodenbach's novel of 1892, *Bruges-la-Morte*. The campaign to restore the image of the medieval city began even before then, and was described as follows in the magazine *La Plume* of 1872: 'conserver à notre ville ce caractère en respectant les anciennes constructions et en poussant l'architecture dans la direction que nos ancêtres avaient su lui imprimer'. The Gothic style was to reconquer the city, with neo-Classical stuccoed architecture as the great loser. Today in the early twenty-first century, the image of the city is much more medieval than it was around 1850. This is evident on the Markt, where the Halle and the Belfort are the only authentic medieval structures left. The other façades on this square in the centre of Bruges are romantic imitations, of which the neo-Gothic Provincial Courthouse of 1889, by Louis Delacenserie, is the most important. The row of façades on the opposite side of the Markt is a nice example of the architectural costume ball: the Gothic front of the Huis Craenenburg (Markt 16) dates from 1956 and was designed by Maurice Vermeersch on the model of a historic façade on the Academiestraat (number 1). This Gothic Revival façade of Craenenburg replaced a stuccoed cornice front, the 'face' of Craenenburg since 1822. The house next to it, De Maene (Markt 17) dates from 1947 and was designed by Luc Viérin. De Maene also had a stuccoed cornice front from the beginning of the nineteenth century. Next to it is the broad façade of the bank building, designed in 1924 by Joseph Viérin (the father of Luc) in partnership with Lucien Coppé. This design is a free copy of the Gothic façades in the Jeruzalemstraat 56-60. The blue limestone façade next to it is from 1971 and is an enlarged copy of the bell gable demolished in 1912. In this row of façades on the Markt in Bruges, everything is recent, and there have been plenty of protests against it. In the journal *Brugge Die Scone* (number 1, 1990), Jaak Fontier wrote that famous city historians such as A. Janssens de Bisthoven and Luc Devliegher had spoken out against this sort of historical sham as early as 1959. At the time this was thought rather strange, because most people still assumed that historians of all people ought to have applauded the return of the past to the city scene. This, however, proved not to be the case and Jaak Fontier explains why these historians were right: 'Their position was based on the conclusion reached through study that every period in a historical city like Bruges can be recognized in its high-quality architecture, and that architecture only possesses quality when it is conceived in the spirit of its age and when as a consequence it is an expression of the way of life, mental climate and modes of behaviour, thinking and feeling of that time.'[21]

There is perhaps something else worth adding to Jaak Fontier's analysis. First of all, it would be reasonable to suppose that historians in particular would speak out against the deliberate destruction of the authentic Bruges, and hence also of the neo-Classical city. The correction by generations of twentieth-century architects of the neo-Classical image of Bruges was indefensible. Secondly it is difficult to maintain that all the neo-Gothic architecture in Bruges is lacking in quality, just because it was not 'conceived in the spirit of its age'. What style in the nineteenth century really would have suited the spirit of that age? What Jaak Fontier perhaps overlooked is that that age may not have had any special 'spirit', and that there might not be one today, either. Perhaps the whole idea of a spirit of an age is a fiction. What is certain, however, is that since around 1870, Bruges's architectural policy has been to pursue the Gothic Revival style and this has remained the case until the second half of the twentieth century. Some creative-minded people have had a problem with this and anyone who takes a look at the medieval fabrication at Vlamingenstraat 40 will be inclined to agree with them. This house was built in 1963 by the well-known local architect A. Dugardyn. It is an imitation of a house depicted by Pieter Pourbus in 1551 in his portrait of Jacquemyne Buick, and also draws upon the shape of the house in Marcus Gerards' map of the city (1562).[22] It is a dolls' house, a piece of child's fretwork that easily lends itself to the purposes of a cheap kind of mass tourism. There are more of this sort of recent medieval Revival style buildings in Bruges that have a childish atmosphere because of the pedantic application of a knowledge of architectural history. If they were

6   *Markt 16-20 in Bruges (2003)*

7   *Vlamingstraat 40 in Bruges by A. Dugardyn in 1963 (2003)*

ROMANTIC MODERNISM

replaced by a rebuilding of what was there previously, the urban landscape of Bruges would probably be none the worse for it. The medieval Revival façade of Spinolarei 10 is a good example. The present façade was designed in 1926, and before then the house had a plastered cornice front from 1833. The harmony of the Spinolarei would presumably not be encroached upon were this nineteenth-century façade to be rebuilt. But it seems that there is no one around who is prepared to advocate such an action, although one could easily imagine something like this as a reaction to the fashion for medieval Revival architecture that has driven out the plastered cornice fronts.

Creative spirits and the more progressive residents in Bruges are arguing for something quite different, namely the acceptance of new architectural designs. A good example of this can also be seen immediately opposite Spinolarei 10 at Spiegelrei 8-10 and its architect is E. Vanassche. According to Gavin Stamp the design belongs to the postmodern trend, 'that with its whimsical references to tradition and its delight in using different materials and colours, actually suits Bruges very well'.[23] His opinion, however, is not shared by everyone in the city. While one could well find fault with this somewhat contrived play with forms, a more important issue here is why architects should feel the need to experiment with modern or postmodern architecture in Bruges of all places, with its exceptionally harmonious urban environment. What would have been wrong with a policy of strict consolidation in this unique city? Two nineteenth-century stuccoed cornice fronts stood on the site of Vanassche's postmodern building until the 1980s. Would it really have been so difficult to have them restored? Why did some postmodern object have to be erected here? People seem to have gone from one extreme to the other – one is either neo-Gothic or postmodern.

The complaint of progressive critics such as Kees van der Ploeg takes on an almost grotesque character, if one thinks that almost no city can rival Bruges in preserving so perfect a historical cityscape through encouraging a policy of architectural imitations over a long period. This policy too deserves to be respected and protected against medieval Revival style or postmodernist excesses. According to the progressive camp, a conservative approach like this is only interesting to tourists. They think that in saying this they have exposed the depravity of this policy, because tourists are almost always stupid and they certainly haven't a clue about architecture. That is evident from the places and buildings they visit, as they always go to spots where time has 'stood still' and never to contemporary cities. They stand and gawp at the Pantheon, but they never visit Rem Koolhaas's buildings – the only people to do that are a bunch of super-critical students.

The notion that a city shouldn't be a historic stage set is one held by Paul Meurs as well. In his doctoral thesis *De moderne historische stad* (2000) he argues for a 'progressive concept of conservation' rather than the 'cultivation of a historic cityscape'. We read in his study that his concept is drawn from the Brazilian architect Lúcio Costa, who died in 1998, for whom 'the preservation of historic buildings was anything but a romantic or conservative task'. According to Meurs, one only needs to visit Rio de Janeiro to see

8   *The Dutch Indies Discount Company, Keizersgracht 573, Amsterdam by J.A. van Straaten in 1909 with, on the right, the high outline of the Nederlandse Handelmaatschappij building on the Vijzelstraat by K.P.C. de Bazel (1923)*

9   *Herengracht 115 by H.P. Berlage (1890)*

ROMANTIC MODERNISM

what he meant. Those historic buildings that still remain in Rio stand like cherished fragments of the past in between the many skyscrapers of that city. In Brazil, 'the creative recycling of existing buildings and structures has been raised to an art form' and. in Meurs' view, that is better than cultivating a 'homogeneous urban image', which he sees as uninspiring. In his view, new buildings may acquire 'their own scale, aesthetic taste, function and shape unashamedly ... without the designers having to go through all kinds of complex manoeuvres for their creations to adapt spatially to an environment where they often have nothing to do functionally, aesthetically and historically.' The word 'unashamedly' reminds one of Lydia Schouten's frightening dolls or Rem Koolhaas's deliberately ugly Kunsthal building.

Paul Meurs thinks that endeavouring to preserve a harmonious urban image is too easy an option, but he does not explain why the examples of unashamed new development in a historical city are better than the bettermannered option. In his book he discusses the work of C.B. Posthumus Meyjes, the architect of the Bank of Java on the Keizersgracht in Amsterdam, built in 1936 as a strapping example of an eighteenth-century mansion. The architect opted for this exterior in order not to infringe on the urban image. He spoke of his approach as 'conservative modernisation', modern times in an old guise. After its completion, however, a Modernist like Albert Boeken dismissed it as being only interesting to 'timorous aesthetes' and Meurs shares his criticism, because he too rejects the timid preservation of a harmonious urban image. His dissertation ends with the following complaint, 'historical buildings lost their self-evidence in the city and turned into attractions – for the residents and for the tourists.' This complaint strongly resembles that of Rem Koolhaas quoted above and this is not a coincidence, because that is the mindset of everyone who believes that art is intended to get people to think.

At least Rio de Janeiro's conservation policy is honest, according to Meurs. Historical buildings are properly maintained, while new ones may be built as well. Surely this gives an honest picture of the real relations between the two. Moreover, isn't it repulsive to gloss things over? Was C.B. Posthumus Meyjes a liar, a forger, or a fascist? Perhaps it makes more sense to see his work as a continuation of that of his nineteenth-century predecessors, among them I. Gosschalk, A.N. Godefroy, W. Poggenbeek, W. Hamer and, above all, A.L van Gendt and his two sons, J.G. and A.D.N. van Gendt with their enormous production of Renaissance Revival architecture in the heart of Amsterdam. But if all Renaissance Revival architecture was removed from Amsterdam's canals, the city would be a shadow of what it is today. This is why Vincent van Rossem argued some time ago that the urban image of Amsterdam has, to a large extent, been determined by nineteenth-century architecture.[24] On closer inspection, Amsterdam's famous historical city centre is anything but the miracle of urban planning that the tourists admire; it is a nineteenth-century evocation of a seventeenth-century city, a typical case of the 'invention of tradition'. Even the man who later became famous for breaking with nineteenth-century style imitations,

H.P. Berlage, built a house in 1890 in the traditional old-Dutch style at Herengracht 115, in imitation of what was then a generally accepted form of architectural propriety. Albert Boeken's 1939 tirade against the Bank of Java by C.B. Posthumus Meyjes, which denounces it as the product of a timorous aesthete, is not just arrogant, but also unthinking, as though it was a stupid thing to take account of the architectural style of one's neighbours. In the conviction that the picturesque beauty of Amsterdam was more important than freedom of expression, the previous generation aimed to serve what it saw as the public interest. Shortly after 1900, however, a generation came on the scene that wanted no more truck with bourgeois ideas of art like this.

In 1923, when neighbourhood residents complained that the new Nederlandsche Handelmaatschappij building in the Vijzelstraat in Amsterdam was far too large and tall, the architect, K.P.C. de Bazel, replied that the picturesque was something for artists to bother about, implying that it couldn't be the departure point for an architectural plan: 'I haven't used any picturesque features as a motif; but have concentrated solely on essential architectural values and mathematical certainties such as measurements and proportions; seeing that the picturesque is not a cause of these but the result.'[25] But for a modern-thinking planner such as Dirk Hudig, then director of the Netherlands Institute for Public Housing and City Planning, this colossal edifice did harm to one of the most beautiful spots in Amsterdam, the bend in the Herengracht. In the house journal of his institute, Hudig wrote that this bend was 'robbed of its finest glory through the cruel outline of a broad edifice on the Vijzelstraat … The arid, unbroken line of the huge building spills violently across its whole width, its rigidity clashing with the curved line of the canal itself.' Hudig was angry. So were others, especially after Hudig's reprimand of Karel de Bazel was published by A.W. Weissman in his magazine, *De Bouwwereld* (1 August 1923). De Bazel's defence, with its appeal to mathematical certainties, was pretentious nonsense, since it was perfectly clear that what was involved was a disruption of existing proportions. It reminds one a little of the way that the educationalist Thomas Gradgrind in Charles Dickens's 1854 novel, *Hard Times*, tried to root out every form of aesthetic awareness in his pupils, because the only thing that mattered was facts. The first sentence reads as follows: 'Now, what I want is, Facts. Teach these boys and girls nothing but Facts. Facts alone are wanted in life. Plant nothing else, and root out everything else.' Thomas Gradgrind was 'a man of realities. A Man of fact and calculation. A man who proceeds upon the principle that two and two are four, and nothing over, and who is not to be talked into allowing for anything over'. A wallpaper depicting horses, he taught his pupils, conflicts with reality, because who ever heard of 'horses walking up and down the sides of rooms?' You should not want anything that doesn't exist in reality, hence the proposition: 'What is called Taste, is only another name for Fact.'

Modern artists regarded it as entirely beneath their dignity to preserve old façades because they were a suitable subject for calendars. The architect

Willem Kromhout, for instance, had no understanding at all of the criticism of De Bazel's bank building, as one can see from his remarks on 25 July 1923 in the Dutch daily, *De Telegraaf*.[26] He thought it was nonsense to turn every city into a 'ville morte' – a reference to the title of Henri Havard's famous 1874 book, *Voyage aux villes mortes du Zuiderzee*, that was a eulogy to the picturesque character of those towns and which opened the eyes of many Dutch people to a sort of beauty they had not always appreciated. The reduction of a city panorama to a pretty picture – this was something that Modernists could never take seriously, as it was against their functionalist principles. In the course of the twentieth century this dislike of the harmonious cityscape was increasingly subscribed to by architects, including those who rejected functionalism. The rationalist legacy of architects such as Eugène Viollet-le-Duc continued to play a role. As is well known, his legacy includes the idea of functionalism, and for some reason, functionalists continue to have a problem with the notion that a city may be beautiful in the sense of being picturesque – a city, that is, as painters depict one.

Listed sites in town and country

There is a dramatic gap between tourists and conservationists with regard to the protection of listed urban and rural sites. The instrument for the protection of these sites in Dutch legislation owes its existence to the desire to protect the historical image of a city, but strangely enough, in implementing this article, it was the use of the buildings that was regulated and not the image. What the legislators had in mind can be found in the Explanatory Memorandum of the Historic Buildings Act of 1961. It declares that 'it is in no sense the intention that such listed urban and rural sites be frozen in their present state.' The legislators went on to stipulate that 'necessary changes' should not infringe on the appearance of the protected area. In practice, this formulation allows a greater deal of freedom to the bodies responsible for assessing each particular situation. In the world of conservationists, the word 'necessary' in the Explanatory Memorandum doesn't carry much weight, because a large percentage of the official specialists seems to adhere to the view that conservation is not only about protecting the old, but that it also has a task in cultural policy. The argument runs that, given that the Department for Conservation falls under the Ministry of Culture, it should not in any case stand in the way of new architectural quality. This argumentation is incorrect, as the Department for Conservation became part of the Ministry of Culture more or less by chance. It could also have been included as a department of the Ministry of Planning and the Environment, although it has to be admitted that in the Planning Department, too, the prevailing opinion is that quality takes precedence over age.[27]

In 1996, in a book published to commemorate the tenth anniversary of the Netherlands Department for Conservation with the subtitle *Dyna-*

mism in conservation – surely no coincidence – Peter van Dun explained the new task of the Department for Conservation in the area of architectural quality. According to him, conservation had formerly been too one-sidedly concerned with the care of the historic buildings as separate objects in the built environment. Presently, however, he wrote, there was a question of 'a harmonious fusion of cultural management (conservation) and cultural innovation (new architecture and urban planning).' He argued for a strengthening of this fusion: 'To prevent cultural decline, the power of both cultural history and the new architecture and the urban planning that is inspired by it with the aim of attracting new businesses, must be given greater political emphasis and be propagated as an instrument of policy.'[28] His article betrays an undertone of dissatisfaction about the reluctance of many residents to accept new architecture in their traditional surroundings, and he appealed to politicians and policy makers to rid the world of this reluctance. To stress the urgency he used the little word 'must'.

With regard to the latter, he didn't need to worry, because the mood in the world of culture purveyors had already started heading in the direction he wanted, with the support of the highest authorities. This is evident amongst other things from an earlier article where the notion of 'dynamic preservation' cropped up. This article was published in 1984 in the journal *Wonen TABK* by Niek de Boer, who sat at the time on the National Committee for the Preservation of Historic Buildings in his capacity as an urban planner. One finds a statement in it that must have sounded like music to the ears of many architects: 'A protection that is purely concerned with the preservation of forms ignores the passage of history'. According to De Boer, the core activity of conservationists, namely that of preserving historically important architecture and urban areas, was in conflict with the course of history, because time never ceases to advance and as far as we know there is no way of stopping it. The entire enterprise of preserving forms was, in his view, meaningless and stupid. On top of that, he declared, every generation has the right to 'express itself culturally with its own forms' in architecture and planning. In his thesis, this has the character of the inalienable right in the civilized world of architects to be allowed to build, even in the very small areas – not much more than one per cent of the entire Dutch built environment – that after a century of fuss and bother the Department for Conservation has succeeded in protecting. The degree of protection, moreover, has always depended to a large extent on the goodwill of local authorities. Niek de Boer had no time at all for the imbalance on the one hand between the considerable spatial and visual consequences that the artistic rights of the modern artist may have in these small and always vulnerable surroundings and, on the other hand, the complex and inadequate legislative instruments that have been drafted for conservation. This is odd, certainly for someone who was a member of the National Committee for Conservation.

In the world of conservation, in the Netherlands as well as abroad, however, his message was all too familiar. Some years later, in 1987, it could be heard loud and clear in the journal *Monuments Historiques*, which was devoted to the subject of the creative contributions by modern art to the historical environment. In his contribution to the debate, Jean-François Marguerin declared that 'Faire pénétrer l'art contemporain dans les monuments historiques, c'est contribuer à leur garantir un avenir. Le passé pour appartenir au futur doit affirmer son lien avec le présent.'

This viewpoint is also frequently found in the world of local building inspectorates. What experts really think remains a great mystery to most people, because the task of the building inspectorate is purely to advise the local authority and it is not answerable to the public at large. Sometimes, however, as in cases where there is a disagreement over a specific application for a building permit, one gets a glimpse of something of a notion or viewpoint. This was the case in the application filed in order to build a new Tuschinski cinema on the Vijzelstraat in Amsterdam, diagonally opposite the Nederlandse Handelmaatschappij building. For some years now, a postmodern façade, designed by the French architect Christian de Portzamparc, is to be seen there. In the design drawing, this façade looked totally delightful, but once it was built in a dull grey brick, the applause fell silent. The façade does its best to be challenging, but falls flat, as it were, giving one the uncomfortable feeling of a comedian who is no longer funny.

Why was this renowned architect from France invited in the first place? It seems that the client required a celebrity in order to impress the Planning Authority. The City Council had initially rejected a high-tech design for the façade, and this led to an impasse. To get around this, the client turned to the French master. According to Jaap Huisman, writing in the Dutch daily, *De Volkskrant* (11 September 1997), the Amsterdam Municipal Planning Authority played a crucial role here; in its view, the architect 'did not necessarily have to make a building that was in harmony with the surroundings'. Huisman jotted down the following statement from a spokesperson of the committee, 'It could very well be a gesture of this age just as the former Tuschinski Theatre was one in its day.' As long as it is a gesture of this time, no one is going to grumble about the loss of the two nineteenth-century houses in a Renaissance Revival style, which had stood there for more than a century.

What is wrong in fact with the notion that the preservation of the old *must* go hand in hand with the development of new architectural qualities? The average citizen who cares about his historic town or village takes it for granted that the legal instrument for preserving listed sites in city and country was set up to preserve his beautiful surroundings for the future. He or she has no idea that the legislator meant something else, nor does he realizes that specialists in the field of both modern and historical arts are anything but opposed to the erection of modern architecture in historical towns. The considerable difference in perception here gives rise to many misunderstandings in practice.

10 Utrecht town hall extension (Enric Miralles, 2000)

Good and bad manners in architecture

There are advocates of new developments in historical cities, such as Jean-François Marguerin and Mario Botta, who respect historical architecture – in theory, at any rate. That cannot be said of all architects. Architects want to build and they find it extremely irritating if a number of out-of-date buildings stop them from doing so. This is logical and completely understandable. When the president of the Netherlands Royal Society for Architecture, Carel Weeber, said something of this sort in an interview of 1992 with H.J.A. Hofland, the latter was not in the least surprised. Weeber complained that it was regrettable that in the Netherlands, 'the inclination exists historically and traditionally to consolidate the inner cities, in terms of their shape as well.' This inclination has given rise to a crisis that one doesn't find in other countries, 'where one is quicker to replace the inner cities with new developments.' In Brussels, many new developments are allowed, something that can hardly be said of Amsterdam: 'If we weren't so attached in Amsterdam to historical forms, tourism and other cultural considerations, you would of course build all those things in the city centre that now have to be erected on the IJ Plein.' Hofland then asked whether Weeber had certain districts in mind. He said that he didn't, but went on to add, 'Let me put it this way: history, the importance we attach to history, costs us an appalling amount of money. What it amounts to is preserving this historical city, with all its shortcomings, in a fashion that is totally artificial.'[29]

Carel Weeber was expressing concerns here about the budget for the restoration of monuments, but there was absolutely no need for him to worry about that, because the amounts set aside have always been paltry. Presumably what tormented him was not worries about money, but all those old obstacles listed as historical buildings. Some years prior he had already let it be known that his first love did not lie with the historical cities. On page 58 of his 1986 pamphlet, *Hoog Haags*, Weeber, who held the post of chief architect for the Dutch government, says the following, 'You shouldn't fall in love with the existing image, because things can always get better. In fact, I think it is a danger for the city if you base yourself too much on reinforcing an image.' In Ed Taverne's study of this architect, we learn that he paid no special attention to the 'aesthetic significance of architecture'. For Weeber, architecture was a matter of engineering and he had no desire to get bogged down in the question of whether his work did anything to serve the greater happiness of humanity. This cynicism, that Taverne describes with incredible composure, has led to the world becoming even uglier than it already was, and we owe a debt of gratitude to the good manners of the residents of, say, the unsightly Zwarte Madonna in The Hague (a residential block designed by Weeber in 1980) that they haven't collectively turned to crime.[30]

Unlike Ed Taverne, Carel Weeber has no experience in the field of conservation, but his notions are widely concurred with, as is evident in the built environment, and even in historical neighbourhoods. Though a cynic, Carel Weeber is by no means unfriendly and he is definitely not a boastful man. He does not shout from the rooftops about the ugliness of his own edifices, nor does he make a cult of ugliness. For anyone viewing these new developments, however, it may not matter much whether the designer is a cynic or a braggart, but for the historical city, the boastful variant is much more dangerous than the cynical one. No right-thinking person is going to admire a tower block by Weeber for its outward form, because what you see is what you get – one huge block. It is utterly without pretensions. But there are also buildings that are deliberately ugly, that are meant to impress one with their ugliness, with the claim that ugliness is a form of art. The greater danger is that people tend to admire this ugliness as a form of high art. Take, for instance, the new extension of Utrecht's Town Hall, which is based on a design by the Spanish architect Enric Miralles. His exterior is untidy on purpose, with fragments of architecture stuck onto the façade as if to draw attention to the mess he has made. In artistic circles one hears smart talk of deconstructionism and scorn is cast on those who don't understand why artists can't do their deconstructing somewhere else, for instance in a waste lot outside town, where no one would have to see it.

In the cultural sector and, consequently, in the world of conservation as well, consolidating the existing image – I repeat Carel Weeber's words – is out of favour. Anyone who wants to consolidate is thought to be lacking in both ambition and artistry. It is not just artists who think like this. In the Amsterdam daily, *Het Parool* (11 March 2001), there was a report of a public debate about the legal basis for listing Amsterdam's historical city centre as a

11 Projected high-rise development on the Dommel designed by Winy Maas in 2000

12 The Dommel Valley in 2002

ROMANTIC MODERNISM

national monument; on this occasion the architectural historian Koos Bosma apparently made a plea for the demolition of large parts of the city centre, allowing new buildings to be erected on the sites that became available in this way. According to the article, this statement by a member of the Planning Department caused great consternation.

The views of Weeber and Bosma may be somewhat extreme and, in general, they are not shared by policy makers in the field of conservation. Where the authorities are united, however, is in their approval of the policy of confrontation of someone like Mario Botta. His approach finds support at top governmental levels. An interview by Flip ten Cate in April 2002 with the Secretary of State for Culture, Rick van der Ploeg, makes this clear. The latter argued for 'conservation through development'. This is the core idea of his white paper, entitled *Belvedere*, regarding the protection of valuable man-made environments. As one example of how he wanted to protect historical landscapes, the Secretary discussed new developments along the Dommel River, in the vicinity of Den Bosch. He explained that 'a bitter debate was being waged' about this ancient fluvial landscape, where some parties 'embraced a fairly traditional way of opposing encroachments from the outside world.' Van der Ploeg was referring here of course to those people who wanted the landscape to be left as it was. He himself felt that this was by no means a proper strategy, because 'you are then always forced onto the defensive'. He preferred the designs of Winy Maas: 'On the bends of the meandering Dommel River, Maas has erected hypermodern high-rise buildings, thus actually emphasizing the historic character of the Dommel.' Somewhat shocked by this statement, Ten Cate asked, 'Isn't it a bit meaningless to say that an assault on the old actually highlights the historic character of a site? After all, plenty of confrontational objects have been built in historical environments.'[31]

Despite the predominantly urban character of Holland, there are still some old rural areas that have not been rationalized by land reallocation schemes. The valley of the ancient Brabant river, the Dommel, is one of this small group of extremely rare well-preserved historical landscapes. One would expect a Ministry of Culture, that has issued a number of white papers declaring its intention to preserve landscapes of cultural and historic importance, would discourage modern high-rise buildings on the banks of the Dommel River. One would be naïve however, to think so, because the experts in modern art and architecture don't primarily view a historical landscape, whether urban or rural, as a beautiful environment that evokes memories of the paradisiacal fluvial landscapes, such as those painted by Johannes Weissenbruch, for example. Instead, they regard it as a background that can serve as a source of inspiration for developing new art and architecture. In the eyes of many architects and policy makers, the historical Dutch landscapes appear old-fashioned and dated. Landscapes, too, are expected to keep up with the times. In the field of nature conservation there is sufficient counterweight, but in the cities, the opposition is still too weak.

According to Bernhard Hulsman, the building of Ben van Berkel's glass office complex on the Nieuwezijds Voorburgwal in Amsterdam (1996) represented a turning point in this policy after which traditional architecture became more accepted. This glass office looks like a huge ship forcing its way into the old fabric of the city: people were simply shocked by the sight of it. As an example of the changed attitude, Bernhard Hulsman mentioned the extension of the Anne Frank House on the Prinsengracht. The architects Jan Benthem and Mels Crouwel had initially come up with a Modernist plan, but, Mels Crouwel explained, 'under pressure from the local authorities, the Planning Department and neighbourhood residents, we fell back on our alternative plan. We have interpreted the traditional Amsterdam style of architecture without allowing it to be dowdy.' He also told Bernhard Hulsman that he was extremely satisfied with the result and that it was sensible to approach the historical city with a degree of caution: 'Previously a few good modern buildings have been put up in the city centre, but most modern infills have been mediocre. The problem with these modern infills is that when they are mediocre, they immediately stand out as a blot on the cityscape. A mediocre traditional infill at any rate escapes notice.' [32]

Unlike Mario Botta, Mels Crouwel acknowledges that modern architecture can be dangerous or even downright disastrous for the historical city. He is even open to the idea of a traditional infill. This statement is mainly important here because it is made by a well-known Modernist. What is more it is an isolated one, since most Modernists would see it as blasphemy.

In Mario Botta's artistic circle, former architectural conventions appear to have surrendered to the pressure of a new form of bad manners. It is difficult to understand exactly what the advantage was of modern aggression over former conventions, such as the Classicist rule of *conformità* and the nineteenth-century norm of respecting the character of the city. For instance, the report of the judges of the 1884 Stock Exchange competition in Amsterdam prescribes that the architecture of the new Exchange Building should fit in with the existing cityscape of Amsterdam. According to the report, the panel of judges 'has decided that the architectural concept of the whole should not conflict with the picturesque appearance of the city and its own unique character'.[33] The influential nineteenth-century architect and theoretician of architecture, Gottfried Semper, thought that experimenting with new styles of architecture might even do harm to the beauty of the city; he argued that tradition was something to be prized in architecture and that it would even be a sign of arrogance to want to invent a new style of architecture like a new language.[34]

In the twentieth century, notions like this have been driven out by the triumphant march of the Modern Movement. The question remains, however, in what way the Modernist viewpoint of Mario Botta is better than that of a Classicist such as Gottfried Semper. There have admittedly been some figures who have continued to defend architectural good manners against the general trend of Modernism, but they have remained more or less marginal and unread. One such figure was A. Trystan Edwards, the author of *Good and Bad Manners in Architecture* from 1924.

Where does the idea come from that new architecture in a historical context decidedly does not have to submit to the character of that environment? How can this idea be accepted by the world of conservation and the buildings inspectorate? To answer these questions one should ask oneself how the different viewpoints have developed. What we now regard as the truth may well be based on an erroneous tradition. So-called abstract arguments may be less useful than an analysis of what people formerly thought and held true. At least this was Michel Foucault's idea. In a lecture at Stanford University in 1979 on his historical study of power structures, he said, 'I wouldn't go as far as Hermann Hesse, who says that only the constant reference to history, the past, and antiquity is fecund. But experience has taught me that the history of various forms of rationality is sometimes more effective in unsettling our certitudes and dogmatism than is abstract criticism.'[35]

The Rectangular Sickness

Postmodernism

Today it is old-fashioned to want to be modern. At the beginning of the twentieth century, the word 'modern' had threatening and revolutionary implications. Modernists rejected nineteenth-century bourgeois culture, arguing that a new age required new approaches. The word had an ominous sound for all those who did not believe in the blessings of progress. During the course of the twentieth century, however, it has lost its negative meaning. Gradually Modernism has come to be accepted, annexed and perverted. In the jargon of the new avant-garde of the 1970s and 1980s, it has finally ended up as a term of abuse.

This new, postmodern vanguard has deposed Modernism. In almost every area of art and culture, the old ideals of the Modernists have been denounced and rejected; this is especially true in regards to Modernist architecture. The postmodernist assault on the seemingly efficient-looking and functionally intended work of the 1920s was somewhat crude and by no means always correct. The way it was launched and, above all, its vehemence, suggests suppressed feelings of hatred towards an older generation of architects. This generation, which embraced the principles of the Modern Movement with heart and soul and was prepared to defend them to the death as eternal architectural truths, had apparently forced its pupils into a straitjacket of dogma from which they have struggled to free themselves since the early 1970s. The Modernists had a doctrinaire approach to architecture and they spent much of the twentieth century claiming to be the true representatives of the architectural culture of that age. Today these claims are laughed at, with a laughter that sometimes amounts to downright mockery. In 1991, Alain Paucard even wrote a pamphlet, *Les Criminels du Béton*, in which he compared Le Corbusier with Robespierre. With communism, according to Paucard, one could still claim that the theory was good, even if it had lost its way in practice; modern architecture, however, had no such excuse: 'l'architecture contemporaine est à condamner en bloc' – its theory is petty and criminal and its practice hideous. Just as Lenin invented the gulags, modern social housing in tower blocks was the invention of Le Corbusier and the Bauhaus.[1]

The downright hatred with which some postmodernists denounced the modern architecture of the 1920s seems to have much in common with the distaste the public at large has always felt for it, especially in the 1930s. Now it is the postmodernists' turn, and they are giving the battered victim an extra kick for good measure. Have they forgotten the diatribes of the national socialists of the 1930s? They probably have, and it is therefore worthwhile to refresh their memories. The scorn currently heaped on the Modern Movement is in some respects richly deserved, but now and then it leaves an unpleasant aftertaste. This is so when criticism strikes a triumphal note and ridicules indiscriminately everything that recalls the Modernists. It is hardly witty anymore to dismiss the Cubist façades of Gerrit Rietveld's Schröder House in Utrecht of 1924 as superficial ornament, as Tom Wolfe did in his satirical book, *From Bauhaus to Our House*.[2] The composition of façades cannot of course be deduced in a purely functionalist way from the layout of the interior. The design was not intended to demonstrate the rightness of some Functionalist theory, as Wolfe supposed, but it is a paragon of the new style in architecture. Tom Wolfe seems to find the notion that architecture might be admired for its *style* laughable. He thought that the height of stupidity was reached by the 1932 book, *The International Style*, by Henry-Russell Hitchcock and Philip Johnson, in which they described the new architecture of the 1920s as a new style.[3] According to Wolfe, these authors were stupid enough to draw a distinction between architecture and construction, in the naïve assumption that they were employing objective, scientific categories 'after the manner of Vitruvius some two thousand years before.' It is possible that Wolfe would also have thought Vitruvius stupid, or outdated, or both, but in any case it seems to him absolutely unscientific or worthless to identify and explain historical styles in architecture. In his view, the generations of art historians who have done so might have found better ways of spending their time. The latter is not impossible, but before we let ourselves be persuaded by Tom Wolfe, we should first ask him to explain what he has against style in architecture, and how he pictures an architecture without any distinguishing stylistic features. Questions like this are something that Wolfe ducks, rather than allow his triumphalism to be diluted by doubt. His verdict on Hitchcock and Johnson was that their book was an example of 'forced labor or gun-at-the-temple scholarship ... notorious for its sophistry, when it isn't patent nonsense'. Compared with the words of another hater of the Modernists, however, Wolfe sounds positively benevolent.

In 1977, the famous historian of architecture, Charles A. Jencks, stated that, on reflection, the German National Socialists were not entirely mistaken in their criticism of the modern architecture of the Weissenhof Siedlung in Stuttgart of 1927. Why, he argued, should people's homes look like mass-produced articles and be painted white like hospitals?[4] The gangster element in European culture is invoked here to give this experimental housing estate of the Deutscher Werkbund a parting shot – something that was quite gratuitous of Jencks, because the project had already been declared stone dead by the National Socialists when they sent the architects into exile in 1933. The model homes of this international housing exhibition were treated as a form of 'degenerate art' and the estate was referred to as 'Little Jerusalem'. It was only long after the Second World War that the Weissenhof Siedlung gained renown as an admirably successful experiment of the Modern Movement, associated as it was with names such as Ludwig Mies van der Rohe, Le Corbusier, Walter Gropius, J.J.P. Oud, Victor Bourgeois, Josef Frank, Hans Scharoun and Mart Stam.[5]

It is hardly surprising that Jencks's remarks rubbed some people the wrong way. Julius Posener, a great connoisseur of modern trends in architecture, expressed his outrage at the thought of anyone sharing the National Socialists' hostility towards anything.[6]

Jencks's criticism is nonetheless interesting, because it touched on a vulnerable spot in the Modern Movement, namely, the question of aesthetics. In doing so, he chose the side of the anti-Modernists, to which, by chance or otherwise, the *Heimatschutz* also belonged. Not only did the latter denounce the modern architecture of the Weissenhof in the 1930s; it did so again in 1956, when the authorities proposed that the remaining houses should be protected as historic monuments. The principle target of this sort of aggressive anti-Modernism was – and still is – the new aesthetics. It was this that understandably caused Wolfgang Pehnt to complain that, 'Not even in the domain of aesthetics, where the movement was pre-eminently competent, did Modernism, compromised as it was, achieve success. With a few exceptions, it retained its pariah status. Historians have always admired it more than the actual users.'[7]

His conclusion is corroborated by recent figures. Of the roughly eight million houses built between 1924 and 1936 in England, Germany and France, not more than 0.5 per cent can be attributed to the Modern Movement.[8] In France, all the members of the *Union des Artistes Modernes* founded in 1929 were systematically rejected for public commissions during the 1930s.[9] Le Corbusier's evenly plastered Cubist 'machine à habiter' didn't stand a chance in the housing market, and the same was true of all the other functional and Functionalist designs of the 1920s and 1930s. 'When you've been working the whole day,' wrote Elizabeth Mock in the exhibition catalogue *Built in USA Since 1932* (New York, 1945), 'you're in no mood to come home to even the most beautiful "machine à habiter". Call it escapism if you will.'[10] This is a candid and interesting remark, because she was saying what many other people thought but didn't dare to say, namely, that the pure beauty of functional architecture was an exhausting form of art. While it richly deserved admiration, it was preferably confined to an educational exhibition, and didn't belong in people's homes, where what mattered was warmth and cosiness.

According to the German historian of architecture, Wolfgang Pehnt, the explanation of the failure of the functional domestic architecture of the Modern Movement is to be found in Thorstein Veblen's 1899 book, *The Theory of the Leisure Class*. According to Veblen, most people aspire to

13 *The housing estate of Pessac in Bordeaux by Le Corbusier in 1926 (photo, 1990)*

a higher social status. Poor people, for instance, are keen to identify with the well-to-do and are thus reluctant to live in houses specially designed for workers. They want to be surrounded with the luxurious-looking forms of the wealthy. No one chooses of his own accord to live in accommodation that looks like social housing, because poverty is humiliating. What was true in Veblen's times still applies today, more than a hundred years later. There are still people who associate white stucco with social housing.[11]

A notorious example in the history of social housing is the estate of Pessac in Bordeaux, built by Le Corbusier in 1926. The opposition to the azure blue, golden yellow, jade green, creamy white and chestnut brown block-shaped houses was so universal it was almost impossible to get anyone to live in them. One resident explained in 1966 'it was simply too modern ... d'you know what I mean, people didn't like it, no ... it felt like a Moroccan village to them! Yes! because that's what people said, they're Moroccan houses, in a Moroccan style ... .' She had gone to live there shortly after the estate was completed. On the 40th anniversary of the estate, Corbusier's client, the industrialist Henri Frugès, said that he reckoned that 55 per cent of the general public in 1926 thought he was crazy to build modern architecture like this.[12]

The general public never liked the Modern Movement. In certain influential architectural circles, however, it enjoyed enormous prestige right up to the 1970s, when views underwent a radical change. And the curious thing about this change was that adulation turned into its exact opposite – contempt. What was the explanation?

ROMANTIC MODERNISM

In 1990, a leading Dutch architectural critic wrote that the recipes for the *Nieuwe Bouwen* movement – the Dutch variant of Functionalism – had aridified into a formal tradition. Modernism, once so challenging a concept, 'had been hung up as a trophy over the cosy hearth of social acceptance and professional common sense'. This self-satisfied reliance on principles deemed unassailable was deadly for creativity; this critic argued instead for an architecture that relied less on pedantic certainties and in which the unpredictable and uncertain were to play a greater role in the design process.[13]

This was the central theme in the postmodern debate – namely that Modernism has proved a failure, that it has outlived its time and has become arid. The ideals of the beginning of the century have produced monsters, and this is true not only of totalitarian social systems, but also of totalitarian architectural and planning systems. The blame for the boring, soul-destroying uniformity of modern housing estates was laid at the door of the rationalism and functionalism of the Modern Movement. According to philosophers like Michel Foucault, Jacques Derrida and Jean-François Lyotard, the blind acceptance of the supremacy of technology has lent legitimacy to an abuse of power. Ideologues are totalitarian by nature and sooner or later this expresses itself in legally enforced intolerance. This is why such systems should be dismantled everywhere, or 'deconstructed', to use the postmodern term.[14]

The philosopher Wolfgang Welsch accused the International Style architects of opting for uniformity as a design principle – they designed for an anonymous, cosmopolitan public that really only existed in their own imagination; their architecture was based on precepts that they tried to impose on society at large. Postmodernism, by contrast, tries to not to prescribe anything, but to communicate instead – something that Welsch perceives as progress. His most important criticism concerns the *Trabantenstädte*, or satellite cities, of the 1960s, for the creation of which the Modernists are partially responsible – witness, for example, the plan that Ludwig Hilberseimer designed for a *Hochhausstadt* in 1924. Welsch calls this plan 'totalitär, uniform und gespenstisch' (totalitarian, uniform and spooky).[15] He must have been delighted to learn that Hilberseimer, four years before his death in 1967, had admitted that his design looked more like a necropolis than a metropolis. He confessed that he must have produced designs like this out of a hatred of the city.[16]

Welsch is not the only one to have made this criticism of monotonous giant housing complexes and office blocks.[17] What is new and typically postmodern, however, is his attempt to lay the blame for all these architectural atrocities on the pioneers of the Modern Movement of the 1920s. In doing so, he ran up against the Functionalist doctrine that he ascribed, perhaps a little too hastily for his own good, as the essence of the Modern Movement. Welsch warns the advocates of the Modern Movement that they will get short shrift if they appeal to him. Because his mind is made up that every advocate of Modernism is 'unweigerlich ein Traditionalist'

14 *Hochhausstadt by Ludwig Hilberseimer in 1924*

(inevitably a traditionalist). Postmodernism on the other hand is 'die zuku-nftsweisende Transformation der Moderne (the future-looking transformation of the modern).'

The term *traditionalism* was a favourite swear word among Modernists. In their triumphal advance, the advocates of modern art reserved their deepest contempt for those who clung to traditions. Traditionalists were enemies of progress; they were petty bourgeois, reactionary and authoritarian. They were deaf to the magnetism of an open society where the rigid barriers of class structures had been removed and where everyone had the same opportunities. Welsch adopted the Modernists' swear word without qualifying it at all; nor did he wonder whether it retained the same meaning in the postmodern debate.

Presumably it didn't, because it was the postmodernists who denounced the Modernist myth about the opposition between progress and tradition. In the myth invented by the Modernists, the traditionalists were invariably depicted as a backward, narrow-minded and conservative type of human being. This image has very properly been corrected. Modernists are no longer regarded as the saviours of twentieth-century culture, and the traditionalists are no longer all treated as National Socialists; nor are they portrayed any longer as the great losers in this debate. One result of all this has been the gradual emergence of an appreciation of traditionalist trends in twentieth-century architecture.

The postmodernists have brought about the downfall of Modernist ideology, but their iconoclastic victory dance has not always testified to good taste. Some postmodern architects started displaying a great deal of 'attitude' about paradoxes, kitsch and glamour. They have suddenly rejected all ethical codes and embraced the mechanisms of the market, dismissing all debate about principles and cultivating ambiguity instead.[18]

The glee with which the postmodernists have launched their assault on the Modernist ideology has made them suspect to some. One such doubter was Jürgen Habermas, who went so far as to call postmodernism a form of neo-conservatism.[19] The essence of the Modern Movement as he saw it lay in its social commitment, its endeavour to create decent housing free of all historicizing ornament which only served to conceal appalling living conditions. He wrote that the nineteenth-century Revival styles belonged to the 'Baukunst der Verdrängung'(Architecture of Suppression). A beauty that doesn't extend beyond the façade does not deserve to be called architecture. Blocks with tiny ill-lit rooms lacking in decent facilities and concealed behind imposing neo-Renaissance façades were the acme of hypocrisy. Habermas also condemned the postmodernists because they reintroduced the separation of function and form that the Modernists' great achievement had been to reconcile. Habermas's attempt to defend the Modern Movement against the attacks of the postmodernists would, however, have been more persuasive if he had attached less credence to the doctrines of the Modernists.

It must be admitted that the Modernists had a strong sense of social engagement, but they did not have a monopoly on this. The question also remains whether the Modernist housing estates of the 1920s and 1930s can be called more successful in a social sense than those designed by more traditionalist architects and planners. The latter, too, were often inspired by social motives, for instance, if they saw their commission as based on Christian ideals. Furthermore, it was the Modernists who let themselves be carried away by futuristic and megalomaniac urban master plans, not the traditionalists who frequently warned against such dreams. Maybe Habermas did not fully appreciate that there was a great difference between the well-meaning aims of the Modernists and actual social reality. In the field of social housing, for instance, they have left hardly anything of permanent value. As for their social commitment – this has sometimes proved counterproductive, because it often amounted to imposing their schemes on residents in a way that was patronizing and coercive.

As for Functionalism, Habermas was still clinging to an exhausted myth, because there has never been such a thing as a perfect unity of form and function. Different forms can be invented for every function and attitudes to style always play a role in the choice. That form should solely be dictated by function and not by something like style was the dream of technology worshippers; in the domain of architecture it is hardly relevant.[20] By no means all Modernists believed in the fairy tale of Functionalism, but despite all attempts to demonstrate that it is untenable, it has somehow acquired an established place in history textbooks. Perhaps the fairy tale cast its spell on *homo technicus* who, finally liberated from vague aesthetic theories, could henceforth devote himself to the exact science of architecture.

It is presumably no coincidence that those who dismiss the concept of 'style' as a superficial craze believed in a mystical union of form and function, while at the same time regarding nineteenth-century eclecticism as inauthentic. Habermas also belongs to this group of the faithful, because – in imitation of the Modernists – he saw Revival styles as inauthentic and deplored the separation of form and function. He attributed a negative meaning to the notion of 'stylistic questions', arguing that such questions always concealed other more important, social issues. Political problems were thus obscured by discussions about style and were thus removed from the 'öffentliches Bewusstsein' (public awareness). He saw the Modern Movement as a humanistic and rationalist project. In theory at least, it was indeed intended as such, but what Habermas did not realize was that this theory was actually a form of superstition.

Functionalism and the Absence of Style

Jürgen Habermas's faith in a reconciliation of form and function, in combination with his rejection of style as an independent phenomenon, originated in the conceptual armoury of the Modern Movement. For the Functionalists in this movement the artistic form of a building should never be the goal of the design. Function was the criterion and beauty of form was its logical result, because what is practical is always beautiful. This in short is the underlying theme of Functionalist theory. It has often been disputed, but here and there it has held its ground for a long time. For some people it was clear right from the start that modern architecture was more a style than a programme. Shortly before his death, Hermann Muthesius saw this immediately on his visit to the Weissenhof Siedlung in 1927. In his account of this housing fair he wrote, 'Anyone who takes the trouble to pursue the matter to its core, should understand that the thing that most preoccupies this movement at present is the new form. *The new form*, that has such an influence on it that all other viewpoints are driven under ... it is the new form that dictates that roofs must be flat and is willing to put up with the many, not yet entirely known drawbacks associated with them. It is the new form that leads to the unwarranted *excessive lighting of living quarters* ... to the abolition of overhanging roofs, to the exposing of exterior walls to wind and weather – Alle diese Dinge haben weder mit Rationalisierung, noch mit Wirtschaftlichkeit, noch mit Konstruktionsnotwendigkeit irgend etwas zu tun. Es handelt sich um reine Formprobleme.' None of these things have anything to do with rationalization, or with reality, or with structural necessity. What is involved is purely a problem of form.[21] Purely formal problems were, in Muthesius's view, superficial and thus objectionable.

A year later, Peter Meyer discussed this question in greater detail. Fortunately, he wrote, in his now virtually forgotten pamphlet, *Moderne Architektur und Tradition*, Classicism with its monumental compactness, its external pomp concerned with outward show and the display of power has been overcome; anyone who still builds in the Classical style is as ridiculous as someone who still wears a wig or carries a sword. The Modernists replaced this obsessive façade architecture by adopting the internal layout of the rooms as the starting point for their designs. The neo-Classicist, Friedrich Ostendorf, Meyer argued, was in a cul-de-sac, while Frank Lloyd Wright had produced pioneering work. The neo-Classical house was a closed block in a formal garden; Wright had abolished this egocentric constraint by breaking the façades open and 'dissolving' the rooms into the surrounding landscape. Peter Meyer thought that nothing in architecture was as contemptible as empty appearances. The excessive enthusiasm for modern forms was also 'seien wir doch aufrichtig' – a reprehensible aestheticism. And with it, he also condemned the work of Henri van de Velde, Erich Mendelsohn and everything that smacked of Expressionism or Jugendstil, including the Amsterdam School.[22]

Then, as now, a number of the Modern Movement's supporters have shared this negative attitude towards the aesthetics of modern architecture. An example is Manfred Bock, who wrote in 1982, 'As has often been stated, Functionalism is not a style', because 'the common denominator does not lie in any formal idiom, but in the notion of the architect's task, in the interpretation of commissions and the method used for solving problems.'[23]

Why should the architecture of the Modern Movement, unlike that of any other architecture, not deserve to be called a style? Is it because Mies van der Rohe said in 1924 that form was the result of an objective analysis of the architectural task? 'Wir lösen keine Form-, sondern Bauprobleme, und die Form ist nicht das Ziel, sondern das Resultat unserer Arbeit.'[24] Marcel Breuer said as much in 1935 when he wrote, 'Whoever supposes that our preference for flat roofs ... can be labelled as a 'style', has entirely misunderstood our object.'[25] The founder of the Bauhaus and upper-case abolitionist, Walter Gropius, said in 1934: 'das ziel des bauhauses ist eben kein *stil*, kein system oder dogma, kein rezept und keine mode!'(the aim of the Bauhaus is not a style, not a system nor a dogma, not a formula nor a fashion!)[26]

From all this it is clear that the Modernists still associated the word 'style' with nineteenth-century eclecticism, with adding ornament in a specific historical style or – in the Netherlands – with the decorative brick of the Amsterdam School. This pejorative sense of the term was later adopted by opponents of the Modern Movement to explain its failure. Sir James Richards used it in 1972 for instance when he wrote that the Modern Movement had 'degenerated into a mere style'.[27]

This is precisely the opposite of how the architecture of earlier periods was described. Then, one spoke of a 'fully developed or mature style' when one wanted to refer to the finest artistic achievements of a particular trend. The negative meaning of the term 'style' is confined to the mental world of the Modern Movement. Everywhere else it just means a form of design. James Richards appeared no longer to recognize this ordinary meaning, when – perhaps unintentionally – he betrayed the fact that he had based his ideas on the Modern Movement.

This negative, anti-eclectic sense that the Modernists had given the concept also survived unimpaired in Lewis Mumford's famous essay of 1962,

'The Case against Modern Architecture'. In it he wrote that the Function-alist principles of modern architecture were unfortunately 'dominated by a superficial esthetic, which sought to make the new buildings *look* as if they respected the machine, no matter what the materials or methods of construction'. According to him, this was the 'superficial esthetic' of the International Style of Johnson and Hitchcock. He argued that things started going off the rails with modern architecture the moment that Mies van der Rohe began to make use of the typically modern materials of glass and steel for their own beauty – 'to create elegant monuments of nothingness', buildings derived from a mental world of pure shapes without any relation to their surroundings, which paid no heed to the wishes of the users.[28]

Anti-Modernists

The criticism levelled at the Modernists was not restricted to matters of style. A number of people also cast doubt on their claims about the central role of industrial construction techniques. Well before the Second World War, the American engineer, Richard Buckminster Fuller, was persuaded that Walter Gropius's Bauhaus was only capable of producing token architecture of 'secondary rank', because of its deliberate refusal to explore innovations in technical installations and building materials. For this reason, all it could achieve was somewhat superficial stylistic adjustments: 'It peeled off yesterday's exterior embellishment and put on instead formalized novelties of quasi-simplicity, permitted by the same hidden structural elements of modern alloys which had permitted the discarded *beaux-arts* garmentation.'[29] The best retort to Buckminster Fuller came from his fellow countryman and colleague Philip Johnson, who wrote in 1960, 'He was, and is, quite right. *All* architecture is more interested in design than in plumbing.'[30] Unlike Buckminster Fuller, Johnson was an admirer of the new architecture (he was co-author of *The International Style* of 1932). But later on, in a 1959 lecture, he said that he had grown tired of what he had come to regard as a superfluous dogmatism. He was particularly critical of the designs of Mies van der Rohe that were always based on three departure points, namely finance, science and technology. Van der Rohe was, of course, entirely right, said Johnson – 'It's just that I am bored. We are all bored.'[31]

The American architect Robert Venturi made exactly the same point in the 1960s. He said that he was fed up with the puritan morality of modern architecture. He replaced the motto 'less is more' with 'less is a bore'. The Modernists' great mistake, in his view, was that they did not realize that in reality Functionalism was a style – it was a symbol of technology, and not technology itself. For Venturi, this mistake was their downfall. Due to their neglect of problems of form, an unconscious formalism took on a dominant role, leading to buildings without any character.[32]

In the 1970s the anti-Modernist trend that, as said above, had already begun to make itself felt, suddenly started to take on the rabid character of long-repressed emotions. While Johnson and Venturi merely felt bored with the predictable straight lines of Modernist architecture, others were almost incoherent with rage. Brent C. Brolin is a case in point. He vented his anger in 1976 in *The Failure of Modern Architecture*.[33] He was determined to raze the Modern Movement to its foundations. 'After fifty years of indoctrination', he began, 'the majority of the public remains indifferent or hostile to the modern aesthetic. The predicted universal acceptance of modern architecture has never come to pass.' This ominous opening sentence is followed by a merciless settling of the scores, suggesting an exasperation long held in check. To judge by his examples, however, his anger appears to have been directed mainly at recent large-scale new developments for which he held the Modern Movement of the 1920s and 1930s responsible. The author is so eager to persuade his readers to share his hatred of modern architecture that one ends up feeling a bit embarrassed by his lack of any sense of proportion. While there were many similarities between the Modern Movement of the 1920s and the modern architecture built after the Second World War, it is not quite fair to ascribe all the architectural disasters of the latter period to a heterogeneous group of experimental architects of the interbellum years. A second objection to Brolin's book has to do with his verdict on the style of modern architecture. Like Venturi, he is convinced that Functionalism was more a symbol than a reality, but instead of assessing it as a form of art, he denounces it as a con trick. The so-called functional, economic methods of construction that were supposed to emerge from new materials and building techniques 'are simply rationalizations for style preferences'. According to Brolin, there wasn't any practical need to apply modern forms – a 'functional' aesthetics is in no way better than a traditional one.

In fact, all his criticism amounted to was that the Functionalist doctrine was absurd (a flat roof does not function in any way better than a sloping one, not even in terms of building technology) and that, in the end, stylistic motifs had gained the upper hand. 'So we see that ultimately the modern criteria of excellence are stylistic rather than functional.' This criticism shows that he too saw the phenomenon of 'style' as an inferior one. Possibly without realizing it himself, Brolin was attacking a notion that had long amounted to little more than an obscure superstition with little credibility. His attack was therefore aimed at a secondary matter and not at the much more important aesthetic aspects. What is wrong with *style*? Brolin fails to tell us.

In 1977 the Modern Movement was dealt a serious blow by the book *Form Follows Fiasco* by Peter Blake.[34] 'I had never thought I would write this book', Blake confesses in his first sentence. He had after all been a great admirer of the Modern Movement and was the author of a famous book about Le Corbusier, Mies van der Rohe and Frank Lloyd Wright.[35] When someone accused him of having adopted a position diametrically opposed to that which he had held previously, he replied that he was perfectly aware of that and that it might well be held against him – 'but only if the facts correct me'.

And it is true that the facts don't really correct what Blake wrote in 1977, because his diagnosis of the weak points of modern architecture and city planning was right. Where one might object, however, is that he had turned history upside-down. He said that the Modern Movement begun as early as 1850 and that it ended in the 1960s: 'From its inception in the mid-nineteenth century, the Modern Movement was preoccupied with the urge to catch up with the Industrial Revolution.' This faith in the technical sciences, he said, has led to inhumane high-rise developments and cities that are frightening. He was still prepared to acknowledge the finest architectural achievements of the Modern Movement, such as Robie House by Frank Lloyd Wright, Mies van der Rohe's Barcelona Pavilion, the Villa Savoye by Le Corbusier and the John Hancock Tower in Boston by I.M. Pei and Harry Cobb. Apart from these exceptional masterpieces, however, he saw the Modern Movement as a failure and blamed this on what he described as a series of errors or fictions.

Functionalism was a fiction, because historical buildings often proved perfectly able of serving functions other than those for which they had been built. The 'free floor plan', that is, the possibility of having communicating interior spaces, was a fiction, because it did not take into account the need for privacy. The smooth, tautly finished and unadorned exterior of the architecture of the International Style was also a fiction, because there was not yet any material with which one could make these geometrical forms (plaster is a traditional building material that soon loses its machine-like exterior). Technology was a fiction, because competitive relations in the free-market economy get in the way of any total standardization of prefabricated elements. High-rise developments, the symbol *par excellence* of the Modern Movement, are expensive; they terrorize the city and bring with them a host of unresolved technical problems – for instance, in the domain of climate and fresh-air management, wind and especially fall winds, not to mention the psychological problems they inflict on the residents. Modern urban planning based on the principles of Le Corbusier's *Ville Radieuse* of 1933 has resulted in miles of boring suburbs. Zoning was a fiction, because the separation of functions has caused gigantic traffic jams between the different zones. Large-scale housing developments in the form of *Siedlungen*, as were built in Germany, were a dangerous fiction, because they formed an instrument of coercion for the authorities, to the benefit of industry and bureaucracy.

According to Peter Blake, these fictions brought about the downfall of the Modern Movement. It was a 'devastating tragedy' for all those who subscribed to the essentially honest intentions of this movement, that these intentions was almost always greeted by the populace at large with 'fear and loathing', to use Marshall Berman's phrase that Blake quotes.

Form Follows Fiasco is a powerful indictment of the failed architecture and planning developments of the 1960s, but Blake is less convincing when he ascribes all the failures of the post-war period to pre-war theories and experiments. His viewpoint here is no different from Brolin's. His polemical theories were sometimes deliberately one-sided, not to mention intransigent. Virtually everything that the Modernists produced was reprehensible in his eyes. While this exaggeration may have been effective at a rhetorical level, it also arouses suspicion. One could also describe Functionalism more positively, for instance as a reaction to nineteenth-century eclecticism, as a 'stilschaffende Bewegung' (style-inducing movement), to use Julius Posener's term, and as an artistic movement that had the beauty of the functional form as its motif.[36] Some architects of the Modern Movement were also of this opinion and had little time for a rigid, anti-aesthetic form of Functionalism. Le Corbusier was a case in point, as one can see, for instance, in his contribution to *The Studio* of 1929. In it he wrote that he was opposed to the dogmatic character of the *Neue-Sachlichkeit*: 'Because architecture is destined to come about in the creative moment when the spirit, entirely preoccupied by material needs, is suddenly raised to another level by a higher desire, in order to display that lyrical power that energizes our spirit and makes us happy'.[37]

As for the 'fictions' of the Modernists, Blake was perhaps too hasty in passing judgment. The 'open floor plan' can also be seen as advantageous, due to the technical possibilities of concrete structures, allowing for more variations on the ground plan layout. The purism of geometrical forms is perhaps not easy to sustain when they are implemented in plaster, but should an aesthetic ideal be rejected just because the technology cannot yet realize it?

The Modern Movement expected a great deal from modern technology, which proved a chimera according to Peter Blake. What is wrong, however, with hoping for a more advanced construction industry? There is nothing against high-rise buildings as such. It was of course a mistake to employ high-rise in council housing. Peter Hall is instructive here: 'The sin of Corbusier and the Corbusians thus lay not in their designs, but in the mindless arrogance whereby they were imposed on people who could not take them and could never, given a modicum of thought, ever have been expected to take them.'[38] High-rise development was one of the *idée-fixes* of the Modernists; it was part of the romanticism of futurist technology. This was also true of someone like J.B. van Loghem, the pioneer of the *Nieuwe Bouwen* movement, the Dutch variant of Functionalism, who submitted a plan for twenty-four sixteen-storey high tower blocks for a competition for cheap working-class dwellings in Amsterdam in 1934. Single-family homes with little gardens front and back, the ideal of the garden city movement, was in his view 'not in harmony with the spirit of this age ... it is the ideal of the good citizen who after his toils are over goes and sits in his little garden with the paper or who rakes his paths ... the collective spirit, breaking new ground in every direction and forming the foundation for a great emerging culture, is opposed to all this pettiness.'[39] Things have turned out differently in Holland for the collective spirit that Van Loghem dreamed of in 1929: there are of course plenty of high-rise developments – admittedly only on a large-scale in the period from 1960 to 1975 – but no one can say they have been a success. This wave of high-rise development mainly involved housing in the public sector during the period when there was a major housing need and a typical sellers' market – a situation where tenants didn't really have any choice. When, in the 1980s, there was more choice once again, they moved *en masse* to single-family homes, where they could sit in their gardens and read the paper or rake the paths.[40]

Zoning is not an invention of the Modern Movement; it had already been studied early in the twentieth century by planners such as Joseph Stübben.[41] Blake may have described the *Siedlungen* in Berlin and Frankfurt of the 1920s by architects such as Bruno Taut, Hans Scharoun and Ernst May as 'rows upon geometric rows of concrete slabs into which were fitted more or less ingenious shoebox apartments', but he failed to mention that the urban layout for these estates owed more to the garden city movement than to the CIAM, the *Congrès Internationaux d'Architecture Moderne*, founded in 1928.[42]

The 'devastating tragedy' brought on, as Peter Blake saw it, by the Modern Movement, occurred mainly after the Second World War and, if there were any guilty parties, they were to be found among the architects of the 1950s and 1960s.

How responsible were the Modernists of the 1920s? One can forgive them their ideology, Conrad Jameson wrote in 1977, in his bitter attack on the Modernists, but can they ever be excused for the surroundings they have bequeathed us?[43] Didn't Jameson realize how implausible it was to blame all the planning disasters of the 1950s and 1960s on the small group of Modernist architects of the 1920s and 1930s? The building of mistakes like these was of course in the first place a political choice. The negative verdict of Jameson and his like would seem to stem from blind hatred, because it is perfectly possible to point to successful examples of housing estates laid out according to the principles of the Modern Movement.[44]

A New World

It has been said that architecture is frozen music. This may be true of the Acropolis or Chartres Cathedral, but in our big cities it is noise, not music, that prevails and the streets are often filthy and full of traffic jams. Behind the main thoroughfares it is dark because of the densely packed blocks and in the low-rise dwellings there is always an unpleasant smell. Neighbourhoods like these were formerly to be found in every city of any size and here and there we still find them, especially outside Europe. São Paolo is an example, as we read in one of the 'Brazilian Letters' of the Dutch author and Portuguese translator, August Willemsen: 'this sweltering, monstrously oversize, too-rapidly expanding city that is demolished as fast as it is built, this absurdly crowded, filthy, dusty city with its honking traffic jams and impassable pavements ...'.[45] Whole families still live there in wretched hovels, similar to those Friedrich Engels saw in Manchester and other industrial cities in England in around 1840.[46] People lived in slums until well into the twentieth century, and housing needs still prevail in almost all the metropolises. In Moscow, hundreds of thousands of people still live in *kommunalkas*, or communal dwellings. The Dutch journalist Laura Starink described a home of this sort on the Moskvin Street, consisting of six rooms, a glory hole, one toilet and one bathroom. The occupants comprise five families – a total of nineteen people, including nine children. That amounts to six square metres of living space per person – still a metre over the official minimum permitted norm.[47]

Social misery in Western Europe at the beginning of the twentieth century was even greater. One of the most distressing reports of housing conditions in Amsterdam was that of Louis Hermans. On a visit to Passeerderstraat 26 in Amsterdam, he met an old couple who occupied a partitioned-off room in the attic. It was on the second storey and the ceiling was 1.95 metres high. No drains were connected to it, although there was a tap and a sink. This sanitary fitting, however ,was located on the first floor on a very small landing and was used by six families, four of which lived in the attic. In the Doove Albertsgang on the Brouwersgracht, Hermans met a decrepit woman who had just recently acquired an old armchair. One of its arms was missing and the seat had broken and had been patched up in a fairly primitive fashion, but 'she never stopped talking about the comfort she gets from this chair'.[48]

Conditions like this persisted until the 1930s, but today, in 2009, they definitely belong to the past, at least in Western Europe. Anyone, however, who wants to understand the history of the Modern Movement must make an effort to picture these outrageous circumstances. The socially responsible architect, J.B. van Loghem, visited the slums of Rotterdam to describe and photograph these abuses: 'this work doesn't exactly lift one's spirits, given that the result is one huge indictment of our society.'[49] Architects who are aware of their social task, according to Van Loghem, should no longer use their professional expertise solely to serve beauty, but should also do their utmost to improve these degrading living conditions.

Some architects expected salvation from a communist society in which private property was abolished and people lived communally. In 1930, Alexander Schwab, an expert in social housing, visualized a future society dwelling in communal blocks that would even have a central, communal kitchen, with everything based on the most modern designs of the Modern Movement. In his idealized image of a new industrialized and functionally organized society, these single-family dwellings with individual gardens were immediately made redundant. Ornament would also disappear, because unnecessary decoration could only exist in a capitalist society.[50] It is ironic to note, when one rereads what Schwab wrote in 1930, that, in the places where his communist ideals were put into practice (Eastern Europe and the former Soviet Union), it was precisely those artistic features for which he had such high hopes that were omitted. The Modernists who travelled to the Soviet Union with such enthusiasm only to realize their ideals in the promised land, returned disappointed, above all because the style they propagated was viewed as belonging to an elitist Western aesthetics.[51]

The Modernists' sense of outrage was directed not only at the widespread poverty, but also at the blatant wealth of the well-to-do. The emphasis that progressive planners placed on a purposeful and sober design should probably also be understood as a revulsion against the unbridled display of luxury by the rich. This aspect of late-nineteenth-century society is also something we don't experience at first hand any more and this makes it difficult for us to understand the anger of those who strove for more just social relations.[52] On top of that was the contemptuous attitude of the upper classes towards everyone who didn't belong to the aristocracy. In her book, *The Edwardians,* which begins by announcing that none of the characters is entirely fictitious, Victoria Sackville-West gave a picture of the class consciousness of the five sisters of Lord Roehampton. 'Their solidarity was terrific. They had a way of speaking of one another which reduced everybody else to the position of a mere petitioner upon the doorstep'. The way their house was furnished recalled the 'unhappy confusion of an earlier day'. It was overcrowded, and crammed full of 'little silver models of carriages and sedan-chairs, silver vinaigrettes, and diminutive silver fans, tiny baskets in silver filigree ... palms stood in each corner of the room, and among the branches of the palms nestled family photographs ... there were too many chairs, too many hassocks, too many small tables, too much pampas grass in crane-necked vases, too many blinds, and curtains looped and festooned, about the windows – the whole effect was fusty, musty, and dusty. It needed destruction, it needed air.'[53]

Such were the interiors of the wealthy upper class, to the great irritation of the intellectual avant-garde that had embraced the artistic lot of the lower orders and wanted to protect them against decadence like this.[54] The well-meaning efforts of this intellectual vanguard had little impact, however, because their notions about what a working-class interior should look like were quite different from what the workers themselves wanted. The intellectual classes could, of course, afford to do without the paraphernalia of wealth without any loss of face. The situation of ordinary workers was different; indulging in the elitist contempt for inexpensive kitsch was beyond their means. What they wanted was a posh interior; they had no desire to 'restrict themselves to the bare essentials in their furniture', as the socialist E. Kuipers, writing in 1919, would have liked.[55]

Social abuses that the upper classes generally ignored, acts of anarchist violence, nationalist fanaticism, and an epidemic lust for war – these ingredients fuelled the European conflagration of 1914, which more or less burned out by itself in 1918 due to general exhaustion, and after roughly 23 million deaths. None of the problems that caused it were resolved and historians still disagree about what it was exactly that needed resolving. This war that dwarfed all previous ones was started by a generation that did not see the warning signs, but which regarded democratic movements as a real threat, because, as Lord Salisbury put it, in a democracy 'the rich would pay all the taxes and the poor make all the laws'. According to him, it was the calling of the aristocracy to govern, 'to which they have every right that superior fitness can confer.' Lord Salisbury himself was appointed Prime Minister in 1895.

Waging war was the right of nation states, declared the German historian Heinrich von Treitschke, or else, as the philosopher Henri Bergson wrote, war was necessary for progress. As for the German kaiser, Wilhelm II, he couldn't wait for war to break out.[56]

For the younger generation that had suffered the senseless carnage of the First World War, European civilization as it had previously existed had come to an end and everything that displayed the outward forms of this 'civilization' was regarded as suspect and treated with ridicule. The nineteenth century remained a dirty word until well into the twentieth century – it was seen as a period of moral decline, of hypocrisy, of a dishonest masking of reality behind appearances and a claustrophobic atmosphere – 'ungesund stickigen, mit parfümierter Schwüle durchsättigten Luft', as Stephan Zweig wrote of his childhood during the last years of the Austro-Hungarian dual monarchy.[57]

The younger generation would change all this – a new world would rise from the ruins of the old. In contrast to the existentialist cynicism that was so typical of the generation after the Second World War, certain progressive circles displayed an optimism after 1918 with regard to a new, modern, more just and peaceful world that seems almost naïve today.[58]

In the expectation of the idealists, this world was already on its way. Not only that – in Russia it had already appeared in 1917. According to the Dutch architect Jan Wils, writing in 1919, 'It is as clear as daylight that today or tomorrow Communism will also celebrate its advent in our country.' He did not omit to add that he too was a 'Communist in heart and soul'.[59] Robert van 't Hoff gave up designing villas for well-to-do private individuals, because after the revolution only mass housing would be needed. I am trying, he wrote in 1919, to prepare everything for the implementation of this Soviet government after the upheaval. In 1923, when it became clear that the proletariat wasn't going to gain power immediately, he went to England and joined a group of anarchists. Others went to the Soviet Union to help with the construction of new towns as provided for by Lenin's New Economic Policy. J. B. van Loghem, who worked in Russia between 1926 and 1928, explained his enthusiasm for Soviet communism as follows, 'I must return for a moment to the war years when the old world was preparing its own downfall, a downfall that was experienced by artists of every nation in an exceptionally intuitive manner ... impulsive as artists are, they have pictured the new world that was to rise out of the chaos of the war as an entirely different one, a world in which production and the division of labour would undergo a general change. The resulting, totally transformed society would free the artists from the outdated and exhausted respect for forms, that despite the dynamic energy of a few advocates of genius, still plays such a suspect and crucial role in social life.'[60]

According to the German architect, Bruno Taut, the forms that existed prior to the First World War were finished, because, 'This period was regarded as the cause of all the suffering and because everything from this period was more or less complicit in the origins of that war.'[61]

'Communism', Arthur Koestler wrote, 'seemed to be a logical product of the progressive humanistic tendencies of Western history, a fulfilment of the Judaeo-Christian tradition, of the liberalism and ideals of the French Revolution.'[62] Koestler was also one of those intellectuals who had worked in Russia out of idealism, but he returned disillusioned and, in 1940, he wrote *Darkness at Noon*, his famous indictment of state Communism.

Sometimes idealism was overshadowed by a hatred of the bourgeois character of the nineteenth century, as was the case with the Futurists. The *Futurist Manifesto* of Filippo Tommaso Marinetti of 1909 was a far-fetched hymn to modern technology. A fast car was more beautiful than the Nike of Samothrace and Italy should be liberated from all the museums that fill the country like so many cemeteries. Nothing was superior to war, the Futurists proclaimed, and they saw women as inferior because they couldn't fight! In 1912, Marinetti fought in the Balkan War and enjoyed it too. The same was true of Guillaume Apollinaire in the First World War. In 1915 he wrote from the trenches, 'War is definitely something marvellous and despite all the dangers, the exhaustion, the shortage of water and many other things ... I'm having a great time here.'[63] The old world had to be destroyed and nothing therefore was more beautiful than the sound of exploding grenades. Marinetti survived the war, Apollinaire died of his wounds two days before it ended. The movement for innovation in the arts during this epoch sometimes displayed totalitarian traits.[64]

This was the background to the emergence of the Modern Movement. In the domain of architecture, the great expectations ended in disappointment – that, at least, was the verdict of the postmodernists. Society has evolved in a different direction than some of the socially committed architects of the early twentieth century had anticipated. Their hopes for a new, international architectural culture have not been realized, because the general public did not embrace them and, finally, it should be stated that the anti-aesthetic Functionalism of the dogmatists among them lent legitimacy to the development of dreary, uniform housing estates. Has the Modern Movement then produced nothing of any value?

The International Style

Perhaps there was never such a thing as a single movement for architectural innovation, but one can discern a common background one can denote as 'modern', in the sense of the total rejection of all historical styles. The Functionalists no longer wanted to use the term *architecture*, because the notion could easily be associated with the fine arts. *Building* was the new buzz word.

According to Theo van Doesburg, the study of historical architecture had become a meaningless pastime. The attempt to conceive of building as an art form was, in his view, 'the great error of all great epochs'. 'During the Renaissance and the Baroque period in particular', he argued, 'such an important place was attributed to the decorative element, that it was a very long time (until the end of the nineteenth century), before it occurred to the brightest spirits, the genuinely architectural temperaments, to treat architecture as a problem of building, housing and traffic in an organic and functional fashion and to resolve it in these terms.'[65]

Adolf Loos, the writer of the famous essay 'Ornament und Verbrechen' (Ornament and Crime), was preaching almost the same gospel in Vienna: 'Instead of the fantastic forms of previous ages, instead of the lavish ornament of the past, the time has come for uncompromising and pure construction. Straight lines and right angles – this is how a craftsman works, with material and tools, never deviating from his goal.'[66] In 1910 when Loos omitted the obligatory ornament in his building for the company of Goldmann & Salatsch on the Michaelerplatz, the Viennese bourgeoisie was dumbfounded, even if it was adorned with a monumental portico with four Tuscan columns of green marble from Greece. A writer in the *Deutsches Volksblatt* spoke of an 'abstossende Kahlheit' (repulsive bareness) and compared it with a factory or a prison – to think of something like that standing in such a distinguished street as the Herrengasse, opposite the Hofburg! A critic from the *Wiener Montags-Journal* wrote, 'The beauty of the Opera building is debatable; this however cannot possibly be said of the structure on the Michaelerplatz. If buildings like this are to be representative of current architectural ideas, it would be better not to propagate any ideas at all than such stupid ones.'[67] Anyone seeing this building today would find reactions like this hard to relate to.

There is something else that is also almost unimaginable today – namely the horror that architects such as Loos felt at the sight of the nineteenth-century stylistic imitations. Something of this revulsion can be seen, for example, in the 1916 book that Cürlis and Stephany wrote as an indictment, *Die künstlerischen und wirtschaftlichen Irrwege unserer Baukunst*, that speaks of the 'völlige Zusammenbruch' (total downfall) of architecture after 1870, when Germany was inundated with 'jener internationalen Welle, die in sinnlosen Taumel die "Renaissance aller Stile" mit sich führte, und deren Abschaum wir in jeder Stadt auf dem Erdball sehen'.[68] The authors advocated an art that was pure, honest and functional, produced in the same way as motorboat engines, submarines or a 42-cm mortar – 'Ihr Stil ist die absolute Zweckmässigkeit und verkörperte Sparsamkeit' (Their style is one of absolute functionality and the embodiment of economy).

According to them, architecture was in the throes of a profound crisis and they didn't see any way out of it. They appeared not to know that a new architecture was about to be born, so that their book is an authentic document of architectural despair.

The birth of the new architecture of the Modern Movement had in fact already taken place in 1911 in Ahlfeld on the Leine with the construction of a shoe last factory after a design by Walter Gropius. According to Sigfried Giedion, this was the first time that a reconciliation between building *technology* and architecture had been achieved: 'The break between thinking and feeling which had been the bone-sickness of European architecture was healed', he wrote in *Space, Time and Architecture* in 1949.[69] Gropius's renowned building was shaped like a glass shoebox – simple, plain and functional. Its construction was supposed to be indistinguishable from its artistic expression. The unfortunate distinction between technology and art was, in Giedion's view, the product of the nineteenth-century mistake of including architecture as a faculty in the *Ecole des Beaux-Arts* (founded in 1806 by Napoleon) and civil engineering in the *Ecole Polytechnique*, founded in 1794. Giedion, as is well-known, saw the nineteenth-century Revival styles of the *Beaux Arts* solely as obstacles in the way of 'the real spirit of the age', which lay in the development of building technology. The false nineteenth-century spirit, according to him, could be seen in everything that was intended to pass as *art*. It was thought incorrectly that *artistry* had to do with ornament and historical stylistic conventions. This mistake was not confined to architecture, but also had an impact on the fine arts, which were almost entirely worthless in his age: 'The entire output of official painting was a transitory fact of that period, almost wholly without significance to the present day.'[70] According to Giedion, the 1911 Ahlfeld factory originated in nineteenth-century building technology, but was implemented in a new form that expressed the true spirit of the twentieth century – a concrete structure encased in non-structural glass walls.

However outdated his notion of history, with its belief in a *Zeitgeist*, may be, Giedion succeeded with a great sense of drama in explaining the motives of the advocates of the Modern Movement.[71] Modern architecture was no longer to be subordinated to the whims of artistically minded clients, but should serve the community as a whole. Architecture was no longer a question of art but of morality.

The question of which year the Modern Movement started is, however, somewhat beside the point. It depends on how you define it, and it is hardly surprising that different people have had different ideas on the subject. According to Henry-Russell Hitchcock and Philip Johnson, Gropius's 1911 factory still contained too many traditional features to be counted as belonging to the new style (the division of the façade into bays, visible brick columns, the symmetrical layout).[72] They saw the reconciliation between civil engineering and architecture as taking place some years later, in 1921, with Le Corbusier's design for a *machine à habiter*, the Citrohan House. The plaster model was exhibited in 1922 at the Salon d'Automne in Paris and in 1927 it was built in the Weissenhof, the Deutscher Werkbund's housing exhibition in Stuttgart.[73]

Hitchcock and Johnson argued in 1932 that the 'International Style', as they called the style of the Modern Movement, was born with this design, which was a synthesis between Gropius's factory and the aesthetics of J.J.P.

Oud's Rotterdam housing estate in Oud Mathenesse. The Citrohan House is the automobile (the Citroën) among houses: a taut and functional rendered block on pillars, with horizontal window bands and a roof terrace.

For Giedion, then, Gropius's shoe last factory built in 1911 was the beginning of the Modern Movement, while Hitchcock pointed to Le Corbusier's Citrohan House of 1921. The difference largely boils down to the fact that Giedion employed a moral criterion, while Hitchcock was more concerned with style criteria. These two totally different approaches can be discerned at every point in the history of the Modern Movement.

Giedion identified three criteria for the Modern Movement: the rejection of historical styles, functionality and honesty. By the latter, he meant the rejection of the architecture of appearances, of a false monumentalism. In this approach, stylistic conventions are, in theory at least, unacceptable. Building is primarily the solving of technical problems on behalf of humanity.

Hitchcock spoke of 'a single new style' that had conquered the world – a new style for the entire human race. That this new style could develop, despite the Functionalist departure point of the Modern Movement, was explained, he said, by the fact that a building is virtually never determined solely by technical or economic factors. Strictly applied, Functionalism ought to lead to stylistic diversity. Architects always have to make specific choices of design and form, so that one can never entirely dismiss aesthetic considerations – 'whether they admit it or not is beside the point'. Hitchcock realized all too well that modern architects would be reluctant to admit that they were influenced by a certain style. Anyone who compares the *Declaration of La Sarraz* of 1928 (the Modern Movement's famous statement of principles) with what the signatories of this declaration of faith of the Modern Movement built then and continued to build for a while afterwards, has to acknowledge that, in practice, they could hardly sustain their professed distaste for aesthetics. Amongst other things, at this first international congress of the Modern Movement in La Sarraz, the participants required 'of the consumer, the person who orders or lives in the house, a clarification of his requirements in the sense of a far-reaching simplification and generalization of living habits. This means a retrenchment in the present overestimated individual requirements, which are inflated by certain industries, in favour of the most general and widest possible fulfilment of the present neglected needs of the vast masses.[74]

A year later, in 1929, one of the signatories, Le Corbusier, built a spacious country house in a park – the luxurious Villa Savoye in Poissy-sur-Seine. It is a spectacularly beautiful house, but far from simple and with little relevance for social housing in general. 'The Villa Savoye could have been built only by a master', Peter Blake wrote in 1961.[75]

The *Declaration of La Sarraz* was an attempt by architects to safeguard their profession by provisionally taking the side of the anticipated triumphs of industry. Hence, perhaps, their exaggerated rejection of aesthetics, because anyone who wants to compete with economically functioning industry, has to serve function and not aesthetics. It is probably in this light that one should view their statement about city planning, that it should 'never be determined by aesthetic considerations but only by functional conclusions'. With declarations like this they appeared to submit entirely to the notion of 'the most economically effective production', because one had to take account of 'general sharpening of the conditions of life'.

Notwithstanding statements like this, however, it was possible to achieve an unprecedented beauty of the pure line and a totally new approach to spaces and compositions. The technical traditions in architecture in the sense Giedion gave them, seem to have been continued in fields such as aviation rather than in the architecture of the twentieth century. The white-plastered stereometric houses of the 1920s *symbolized* modern technology rather than belonging to it. This was Reyner Banham's conclusion in 1960 and he added that architecture was possibly something entirely different from technology – a conclusion that totally sabotaged Giedion's thesis.[76]

After some initial successes, the moral renewal of architecture, the task of building unpretentious and financially reasonable public housing was defeated by recession. And due to the popular dislike of seemingly functional housing with flat roofs, the movement never recovered. The International Style became the style of a limited elite. This was in fact already the case with the Weissenhof in Stuttgart, where the rent for the cheapest four-room homes was 150 marks a month, way beyond the means of most workers. Later housing developments where simplicity was taken to an extreme, such as those designed by Walter Gropius in 1929 in the district of Dammerstock in Karlsruhe, were in fact affordable, but since all possible expenses were spared, they looked more like a barracks than a housing estate.

The Modern Movement is a generic term for a wide variety of innovatory trends. The unity proclaimed in La Sarraz was a hollow pretence. The first designs for a new architecture had hardly left the drawing boards before the Modernists were at each others' throats. This was already evident in 1923 at the De Stijl exhibition in the Parisian gallery L'Effort Moderne, where the architectural models of Theo van Doesburg, C. van Eesteren and Gerrit Rietveld were savagely criticized by their colleague, Le Corbusier, who thought that they were superficial, that they slavishly followed fashion, and that their composition was too complicated. He preferred simple, self-contained, basic forms. Van Doesburg, for his part, regarded Le Corbusier's villas as being 'crude and lacking in any character'. In 1926, J.J.P. Oud said that Van Doesburg hadn't 'the slightest notion of building', and that his statements about architecture 'have done a lot of harm to the work of serious modern architects ... and I know that Perret and Le Corbusier feel the same way as I do on this subject'.[77]

In the Netherlands, the Modernists were only capable of maintaining their partnership for four years. In 1932, the Rotterdam group Opbouw merged with the Amsterdam group De 8. Now known as De 8 en Opbouw, the two groups were joined in 1934 by Groep '32. This collaboration ended in 1938, due to quarrels over how far architects in the group should comply with the traditionalist wishes of clients. The members of Groep '32 stuck to the principles of Functionalism, while rejecting its style. The most important spokesman of this group, Albert Boeken, referred to this style in 1930 as 'a rectangular sickness', a 'fashion of nickel-plated furniture on which people can hardly sit, of white lamps that blind you instead of shedding light, of captions without capitals, etc., etc.'. In 1936 he wrote, 'The period from 1920 to 1930 is over and done with, and belongs to the distant past. The formalists of international architecture have had their day.'[78] The break of 1938, it seems, was not only caused by differences in political approaches, but also by the pronounced hostility of the members of Groep '32 for the taut, geometric style of the 1920s.

The International Style was already history in the sombre years prior to the Second World War; in many people's view, it had failed because the essence of modern architecture lay in technical advances and not in a specific type of design, not in a *style*. In this way, the artistic inspiration that gave rise to the Modern Movement was driven under. J.J.P. Oud has recalled this development on more than one occasion. He had just been looking for a new approach to design, something other than the 'natural attractiveness of the raw material, the brokenness of glass, the vitality of the surface, the cloudiness of colour, the curdled quality of glazes, the weathered character of walls, etc.' What he wanted to achieve was 'the clarity of glass, the gleaming and round quality of the surface, the gloss of paint, the glow of steel, the sparkle of colour, etc.'[79]

The purist, geometrical architecture of the International Style originated in the Modern Movement, but was also destroyed by it. The strange thing about this history is that not only have the traditionalists distanced themselves from this style, but many Modernists have done the same – J.J.P. Oud, for instance, with his office building (1938-1942) for the Batavian Import Company in The Hague and Le Corbusier with the *béton brut* of the *Unité d'Habitation* in Marseille (1948-1954).

Why did the Modernists reject this geometrical style? Because it was too provocative? Whatever the reason, it was rejected by some Modernists because architecture as they saw it had to serve society, to conform to economic and social existence and not dance to the tune of elitist art lovers. For a rationalist and realist like W. van Tijen, the designer of the Bergpolder Flats in Rotterdam (1934), the aesthetic of *De Stijl* was too artistic and he saw this as an obstacle to the healthy development of architecture. In a letter to Dick Apon in 1952 he acknowledged, 'I understood how Mondriaan, Rietveld and Oud created the basis for modern architecture during those years, but this only amounted to a theory about form; it wasn't modern architecture as realistic concrete art.' Van Tijen clung to his role as engineer of social housing, even late in the 1950s when he astonished a client for a luxury villa by drawing a kitchen that did not differ much from the normal council house type. What was not strictly necessary, in his view, was reprehensible excess and waste.[80]

An interesting example of this realistic civil engineer's approach is found in *Architectuur, een gewetenszaak* by J.P. Kloos (1985).[81] Kloos was closely involved in the Modern Movement; for instance, he worked on Jan Duiker's Zonnestraal sanatorium between 1926 and 1928. He remained faithful to the principles of Functionalism all his life and his interpretation of architectural history strongly resembles that of Sigfried Giedion. With both of them one can speak of an evolution where the development of architecture is brought into relationship with social and economic developments. Anything that doesn't fit in with this development is reprehensible because it blocks progress. Kloos, for instance, couldn't find a good word to say about the Jugendstil, not even as late as 1985. This was because he saw the lavish forms of this architecture as nothing but 'empty show'. 'In the play of forms – that was supplementary to the structure – the social and economic factor was lacking, something that would a short while later start insisting on its rights.' For precisely the same reasons he also rejected the architectural models of the De Stijl group. Admittedly, he recognized that *De Stijl* had made a contribution to the development of new notions of beauty, but he also thought that it had become bogged down in outward appearances: 'We have to liberate ourselves from the ill-considered submission to the outward charms of a design. We must explore critically whether this formal idiom is suited to contemporary tasks and to the matter of structure which is fundamental to architecture – and if so, to what extent.' By this Kloos meant that the construction had to be integrated in the design. 'This integration', he argued, 'is essential. It depends on this whether the object in question can be called a work of architecture.' Apparently Kloos didn't see it as a problem that this Functionalist stance would exclude virtually every building from the Renaissance right up to nineteenth-century eclecticism. He felt nothing but contempt for useless beauty and he dismissed all criticism of this Functionalist principle out of hand.

Geometrical Aesthetics

Geometrical aesthetics meant nothing to either dyed-in-the-wool Functionalists or the general public, and the purist, stereometric style of the 1920s therefore remained a marginal phenomenon.

Let us leave the Functionalist principles of the Modern Movement aside for a moment in order to reappraise the pure forms of the International Style as a 'rational poetry'. According to Arthur Drexler this was the approach taken by Eisenman, Graves, Gwathmey, Hejduk and Meier, the five leading New York architects of the 1970s. They were, he said, no longer impressed by 'brutalism, the architecture in blue jeans and other effete mannerisms of proletarian snobbery'. And they were still less impressed by the 'elegant, but arbitrarily pure structure' of Mies van der Rohe. The five architects 'picked up where the 1930s left off' and continued the architecture of 'rational poetry' that had been interrupted by the Second World War.[82]

They were fed up with the wearisome debates about the moral foundations of architecture, concentrating shamelessly instead on the beauty of white geometrical forms.

All this paved the way for a reappraisal of Mies van der Rohe. An American architect, J. Brownson, expressed his admiration for the Lake Shore Drive Apartments in Chicago (1948-1951) as follows: 'Walk in – no dark, smelly apartment house lobby, no fake plants, you feel good. Light, air, life, nature! And what makes you feel so good – an economy of means. The spiritual space of Mies van der Rohe.'[83] Brownson's words from 1986 relate to the style of these buildings, the pleasing atmosphere created by their pure lines, their openness and tautness and the absence of inessential additions. Who needs all that fuss about something as banal as 'functions'? Mies van der Rohe never did. But the *Prinzipienreiter* among the Functionalists were merciless towards aesthetes. Back in 1923, Adolf Behne warned that the younger generation of German architects were far too strict: 'Die junge Generation der deutschen Architekten stellt sich auf den Boden einer strengen Sachlichkeit.' Anyone who rejects aesthetics, he said, is cutting off the branch he is sitting on. He argued for an architecture in which function was elevated to an artistic form, just as J.J.P. Oud had written. Behne's book, with the predictable title, *Der moderne Zweckbau*, ends with a quotation from Oud. In modern architecture, according to Oud, it is the construction itself which is raised to the level of aesthetics: 'über ihre materielle Notwendigkeit hinaus zur ästhetischen Form'.[84]

The remarks of Behne and Oud made little impression on this younger generation, more open as they were to the numerous seemingly scientific arguments of people like Walter Gropius who could 'demonstrate' that architecture meant solving problems of construction and had nothing to do with aesthetics. According to Gropius, the Dutch *De Stijl* movement fizzled out in a Modernist romantic mode: 'der stijl brachte starke propagandistische wirkungen, übertonte aber zu sehr formalistische tendenzen und gab den anstoss dazu, dass die kubische bauform modisch wurde. heute [1934] beginnt die konstruktive auffassung langsam die romantisch-Modernist zu verdrängen'.[85]

No one in the younger generation was more orthodox than Hannes Meyer. When he succeeded Gropius as director of the Bauhaus in Dessau in 1928, he immediately drew up a new curriculum. It opened with these words: 'alle dinge dieser welt sind ein produkt der formel: (funktion mal ökonomie)/ alle diese dinge sind daher keine kunstwerke ...' (everything in this world is the product of the formula: (function times efficiency)/ this means that all these things are not works of art). Note the use of totally irrelevant brackets and slashes, a typical feature of those who worship abstract formulas. Meyer hoped to deal with matters root and branch and in the case of housing he did this by splitting family life into twelve separate functions – 'geschlechtsleben, gartenkultur, körperplfege, kochbetrieb, bedienung' (sex life, gardening, personal hygiene, cooking, services), and so on. Further enquiry into these functions can lead to a 'funktionsdiagramm'. After that, relations between residents and visitors, such as the postman, neighbours, burglars, doctors, and so on, could be enquired into, with attention being also paid to 'wechselwirkungen zwischen menschen, haustieren und insekten' (interaction between people, pets and insects). All of this of course was not the business of architect. What function did he still have then? 'He used to be an artist, but now he was a specialist in organization.' Architecture is organization and that was that; above all, it had nothing to do with art. These were the views of the director of the art institute that later became world-renowned.[86]

In the Netherlands, too, opinions differed when style was at issue. J. Duiker, the brilliant artist of rational architecture, did not permit himself any aesthetic experience that wasn't functional. He thought art for art's sake an asocial idea that was beneath his professional dignity even to consider. With the severity of a Calvinist he pronounced that the only thing that counted in an architectural assignment was to discover 'the perfect eco-nomics', because one would then automatically come up with the best and neatest solution. Duiker felt morally obliged to take a stance against his he-retical colleague, J.J.P. Oud, who had written in the magazine *8 en Opbouw* that even in 'the most functional engineering work' there was always some latitude in the design, so that 'even with those architects, who maintained this "functionalist" viewpoint, the theory was virtually never converted into practice, but a work was almost always produced possessing an aesthetic value over and above the functional.'[87]

One encounters the same ideological fixation on the economic aspects of architecture and the accompanying distaste for the notion of 'style' in the writings of the architect J.B. van Loghem. In his celebrated 1932 book, *Bouwen, bauen, bâtir, building*, Van Loghem wrote that Cubism preceded Functionalism, but that few people had understood that Cubism was only intended as a phase in the evolution of architecture. This phase had admit-tedly produced something new, but 'life had not been sufficiently experi-enced in its dynamic vigour. The excitement that should have provoked the new architecture to express the fluidity of life, led in Cubism to rigidity ... .'[88] Cubism was a style and Van Loghem saw styles as 'forms of rigidity' that belonged 'to the dark ages of humanity when the fear of death was still all-powerful.'[89]

That the new aesthetics of Cubism were not exactly welcomed by the general public is well known. Less well known, perhaps, is that there was even a trend in the Modern Movement – one that still flourishes here and there – that combated this geometrical aesthetics on theoretical grounds. This severe Functionalist trend originated in the rationalist theories of nineteenth-century architects like Henri Labrouste, Eugène Viollet-le-Duc, Auguste Choisy, Gottfried Semper and A.W.N. Pugin. Their theories were mainly based on the primacy of efficiency in architecture, to which aesthetics had to be subordinate. Henri Labrouste never failed to remind his pupils that 'in architecture form is always subordinate to function'.[90]

William Morris, considered one of the most important pioneers of the

Modern Movement, felt a profound contempt for the many forms of style imitation so popular at the time. 'Honesty and simplicity' was his mottos. At home it was his principle to dine at a table without a tablecloth, something exceptionally unusual in his day. He had a similarly negative view of art: 'Let us make up our minds which we want, art or the absence of art' and it didn't take him long to choose. 'Learn to do without' – that was his motto.[91] As early as 1826 the editors of the *Monatsblatt* announced that, 'Nichts ist schön, was nicht zugleich zweckmässig ist' (Nothing is beautiful that is not also functional).[92]

This attitude towards aesthetics continues to influence many Modernists. A recent case occurs in the philosopher Roger Scruton's 1979 study. His thesis is as follows, 'The value of a building simply cannot be understood independently of its utility'.[93] One can of course see a building solely as a work of sculpture, but that is 'to treat buildings as forms whose aesthetic nature is conjoined only accidentally to a certain function' – a notion that he regards as nonsensical. The idea that architecture was primarily a matter of form, with function subordinate to image, is something that Scruton rejects, while taking it for granted that it must have also been seen in this way in the past. The implication of his thesis is that all architecture that doesn't comply with this is based on erroneous principles, as if there were such as thing as a timeless architectural principle. Scruton's supposition is unhistorical and erroneous. Prior to the rise of rationalist theories of architecture in the eighteenth century it was unusual for the prevailing classical façade layout to be made subordinate to the internal organisation of the building. It was for this reason that a rationalist like Eugène Viollet-le-Duc thought Classicism so reprehensible. Classicists required that a façade should automatically be ordered symmetrically, regardless of the functions of the rooms behind it, while rationalists saw this as illogical. A good example of what they thought was nonsensical can be found in *A Complete Body of Architecture* by Isaac Ware (1756). This advocate of the Palladian style argues that the enfilade, or series of linked rooms, was in practice inconvenient, but that its application in designing villas was an 'unanswerable rule'. While seeing the lack of logic, Ware did not regard it as sufficient argument for violating the rules of Classicism.[94]

The Fear of Modernism

Although protests were still made against modern art and architecture after the Second World War, they were no longer experienced as a threat. Attacks, such as that of Hans Sedlmayr in 1948, no longer had much impact. In his *Verlust der Mitte* he wrote that a 'radikale Gleichmacherei' (radical uniformity) dominated the Modern Movement and that while functional design may have been suitable for kitchens, bathrooms and hospitals, it was not so for the 'whole' man. The new style was inspired by machines, ships, airplanes and cars and Sedlmayr saw this as typical of the new culture, in which people had become nomadic once again and only wanted to live in temporary housing.[95]

Before the Second World War however modern art, as said above, did form a potential threat. On the occasion of the founding of the monthly magazine *De Stijl* in 1917, Theo van Doesburg received a number of letters from readers who were worried about the direction that modern art had taken. He didn't feel any need, he wrote in the first volume, to fill his new journal with all the objections that were normally made of modern aesthetics; he made an exception, however, for Edith Pijpers, a well-known painter at that time, because her views were fairly representative.[96]

Modern art, she wrote, is without love or feeling; it is scientific, cerebral, cold and rigid. The quest for elemental forms is a kind of vivisection, a dissection, a murder and plundering of nature. Modern art is bare and empty. Reticence in the face of beauty is replaced by impudent research. 'We no longer kneel' she said, 'but stand on our two legs and argue. Primitive art was carefree, but in modern art deliberate experiments are conducted. For this reason it arouses our hatred.' The cinema, incidentally, was also a target of her hatred, because it only provided superficial entertainment for the 'insensitive'. Today the regressive voices of that time sound somewhat shortsighted, narrow-minded and needlessly fearful of the new aesthetics and technology. Primary forms and colours, according to Pijpers, were not considered ugly as such, but became so due to their association with a robotic and uniform society. What was more, the Modernists were ferocious in their opposition to the older architecture – 'archaic pottering', was Van Doesburg's phrase for it. That older world that people like Edith Pijpers were brought up in appeared to have been shattered into pieces.

Moderate opponents of the new Functionalism in architecture did in fact think that the Modernists had too high an opinion of themselves. According to the architect T.H. Zwiers, in a much-debated article of 1933, they lent too much faith to rationalism, that is, to 'the belief in exact, tangible causality and logically constructed systems.'[97]

In the opinion of another architect, Jan Gratama, all architectural styles had a relationship with nature until around 1920. The adherents of the new Functionalism wanted to break with this by devising a style that was as ethereal and immaterial as possible. He gave as an example the Van Nelle factory in Rotterdam (1926-1930) by J.A. Brinkman and L.C. van der Vlugt, and the work of Jan Duiker.[98] Gratama argued that the new style displayed a 'marvellous serenity', but that its machine-like character was essentially inhuman. He saw it as an architecture of intellectual arrogance, of an opposition to the 'eternal forces of God or Nature', in conflict namely with 'tradition that is logical and healthy'. He concluded his essay by declaring that there is 'growing doubt about the positivism of science', so that the 'values of intuition, of the soul, of feelings and senses that have been repressed for so long by science, are now emerging stronger than ever.' This backlash could also be seen in the increased interest in romantic waltzes (opposed to modern dance), in Anna Pavlova, in Johann Strauss (as against jazz) and in long dresses that are 'the opposite of the new functionalist, practical short skirts'. Gratama also informed his readers that he considered the *Untergang des Abendlandes* of 1923 by Oswald Spengler to be 'a book of genius'.

In the wave of fear about the downfall of Western civilization, everything that was new appeared threatening and people sought security in traditions. Johan Huizinga thought Spengler's famous book erroneous as a work of scholarship, but acknowledged its enormous contribution to the widespread 'sense of living in the midst of a stormy cultural crisis where downfall threatened'.[99] Communism, that today feels hopelessly old-fashioned, was considered a modern movement in the period prior to the Second World War. In reactionary and religious circles the new Functionalism in architecture was equated with the 'red peril'. In the *Rooms-Katholieke Bouwblad* of 1934 it was described as 'an expression of Bolshevism and Marxism', that is fortunately increasingly being driven out by 'a healthy native architecture', especially in Germany.[100]

As early as 1892, modern art was classified by Max Nordau in his notorious book *Entartung* as a form of pathology, thus fuelling the fear of everything that diverged from the familiar.[101] The origins of all these anxieties about the degeneration of German culture have been wrested from oblivion with remorseless accuracy by Richard Hamann and Jost Hermand in their study *Stilkunst um 1900*. The fear of a modern society that would wipe out traditional values and bring about the downfall of German culture led to a flight into mythical fantasies about a racially pure 'folk', a Teutonic state from the River Meuse to the Black Sea and the Baltic to the Tirol. Paul Lagarde foresaw a future German Empire way back in 1878. Houston Stewart Chamberlain followed in his footsteps, advocating a racially pure German state free of 'internationalism, Jewish Socialism, large cities and the Roman Catholic Church.' These theories were taken a stage further after 1900 by figures such as Ludwig Kuhlenbeck (*Rasse und Volkstum*, 1905), Albrecht Wirth (*Volk und Rasse*, 1914), Ludwig Wilser (*Die Überlegenheit der germanischen Rasse*, 1915), Ludwig Schemann (*Die Rasse in den Geisteswissenschaften*, 1927) and Hans Günther (*Rasse und Stil*, 1926).[102]

Racial purity played a role in art and architecture too. Paul Schultze-Naumburg wrote in his 1928 book *Kunst und Rasse* that, '... the downfall of cultures is the consequence of the decline of races.' [103] He was shocked by the increasing degeneration of German architecture. It was, he wrote, as if people no longer attached much value to planning their surroundings. He, too, found a deeper explanation for this in the degeneration of the German race. Strangely enough, he argued, we do not apply what every stockbreeder knows to our own race – namely that a pure breed deteriorates when mixed with an impure one. This at least was Schultze-Naumburg's hypothesis – one that was not particularly original, since it was inspired by a collective fear of the loss of the familiar *Heimat*.

This fear became more widespread in the 1890s, especially among the middle classes. Socialism was seen as the greatest threat, because it spelled the end of independent entrepreneurship. It was seen as a diabolical movement, since it was opposed to religion, nationhood, traditions and family life. There was also a danger from large-scale industry and financial institutions that would force the traditional professions out of the market and reduce craftsmen to a modern form of slavery. This fear again led to a hatred of Jews, liberals and intellectuals, as the chief proponents of socialism, capitalism, urbanization, secularization and democracy.[104]

This cultural discontent was propagated by prophets, almost forgotten today but who had a great following at the time. One such was Julius Langbehn, the author of *Rembrandt als Erzieher*, written in 1890, who blamed academic studies above all for the approaching decline of German culture.[105] For Langbehn and his cronies, there was only one acceptable type of human being – the German farmer.

In 1933 this fear manifested itself in hysterical aggression. The National Socialist Bettina Feistel-Rohmeder urged the new government of Germany to remove all 'weltbürgerliche' and 'Bolshevist' art from the museums.[106] Less aggressive campaigners exorcized their fears of the future with an emphatic sort of traditionalism. 'He who operates in conflict with the profound meaning of tradition', the architect Paul Schmitthenner wrote in 1933, 'is committing a crime against history and thus against the roots of the national character.'[107] He saw Modernist architecture as forming a threat to humanity: human life was in danger of being trampled on by cold-blooded calculations and collectivism. His 1932 book about German homes was intended as an appeal to protect the German landscape against Modernist architecture, which he saw as originating abroad. It was not his intention constantly to imitate the old, but rather to 'keep alive and continue what was essential'. According to Schmitthenner, the essential lay in traditional construction that had unfortunately stagnated totally in around 1870 with the rise of modern technology and industry: 'after which people fell back on the great German past helplessly and with a lack of understanding of the tradition, thus giving rise to a bombastic, simulated architecture.'[108]

The only good thing Paul Mebes's famous 1908 book, *Um 1800*, had to say about the Modernists was that they also resisted this 'Talmikunst', this masquerade of nineteenth-century styles. But why, he wondered, was it necessary always to be designing new things? Hadn't architecture reached a state of perfection with Classicism? There was only one way out of this Babel of conflicting styles without being overwhelmed by the anonymous mass production of the Modernists, and that was to return to the period around 1800, when architectural traditions were still a living reality.[109]

The aim of Mebes's book was to restore peace to the chaos into which architecture had fallen by introducing a new historicizing style. It was one that would make all other styles redundant, and that is just what it looked like. His ideal was a 'timeless' architecture dating from before the nineteenth-century stylistic chaos, preferably implemented in brick and with an abundance of white-painted wood, mostly consisting of bars in sash windows and massive hipped roofs. Despite all the dull bourgeois primness that this architecture exudes, it still has something comforting about it. In the face of turmoil and revolution, its value was medicinal and therapeutic.

Paul Mebes wanted to draw on the myth of tradition to exorcize the crisis in architecture. Unlike the German architect Alexander von Senger, he didn't feel any need for a frontal assault on the Modernists. Von Senger was driven by a strange fury and succeeded in conveying people's fear of modern architecture in the sharpest possible terms. There is, he wrote in 1928, a great deal of fuss about the new aesthetics, but 'what is so special about the fact that some people prefer houses that would look good on the moon, rooms like operation theatres and chairs that appear to be based on the electric chair?' You may, however, get upset about this, Von Senger argued, and still fail to see the real dangers. He thought that something else lay concealed under the surface of this aesthetics and that the promoters of Modernism were a dangerous sect in search of absolute power. They were not interested at all in art; all they were was a group of bullying missionaries who wanted to transform human nature with their sectarian fanaticism. What Le Corbusier and his colleagues of *L'Esprit Nouveau* were really after was a Communist society with people reduced to slavish automata, creatures totally lacking in initiative, only able to obey their animal instincts and entirely alienated from their intellectual faculties – 'that is why some of these newfangled movements in painting, literature, music and architecture combine amorphous passions with a chaotic intellectualism ... .' It is no surprise, Von Senger went on, that those Europeans who had come down in the world got on so well with the half-Asiatic hordes of Russia, a country that even before the war was notorious for its pathological decrepitude. Von Senger didn't mince words. For him and many others, the new aesthetics symbolized a dangerous assault on our familiar surroundings, on traditions and on German culture, which is organic and 'erdverwurzelt' – rooted in the soil.[110]

This fear was fuelled further by the fact that the Modernists did indeed start displaying an interest in the Communist utopia. In his vision of the future, the painter El Lissitzky already foresaw homes that would have no kitchens, because in the new world order the community would have precedence over the individual. The 'Einzelküche' was thus replaced by the 'Kochlaboratorium', where food was to be prepared for the 'Hauptmahlzeit in öffentliche Speiseanstalten' (main meal in public dining institutions). Walter Gropius already had plans ready in 1929 for a 'Grosshaushalt', a communal dwelling for industrial workers. According to him, in the future society 'individual activities would be at the service of the community' and family ties would automatically dissolve.[111]

The fear of Modernism was not just a typical Dutch or German phenomenon. In England, too, there was a powerful anti-Modernist traditionalist movement. W.R. Lethaby and Reginald Blomfield were the most important defenders of 'the English scene', a new sort of religion that started becoming popular in around 1900, according to David Watkin.[112]

Blomfield wrote a diatribe against the spectre of Modernism that, borrowing a phrase from Hilaire Belloc, he described as a 'cheap short cut', adding that what was involved was 'the getting of an effect without the trouble of research'. Most people are aware that this is the truth, he said, but no one dares to open his mouth.[113]

In England, anti-Modernism was reinforced further by a horror at the devastation of the countryside resulting from the growth of the great industrial cities. Urban development, Lethaby wrote in 1922, is a matter of civilization and of 'civic pride', 'town planning' is necessary, but there is something we need even more and that is 'a general cleaning, tidying, and smartening movement, an effort to improve all our public and social arts, from music to cooking and games.'[114]

The complaint that the great cities were impossible to live in, which first emerged in the nineteenth century, led to the utopias of the Modern Movement such as that of Le Corbusier. The horror at the inhumane scale of the metropolis and of the resulting disintegration of social relationships and rise in crime has undoubtedly been the greatest of all the anti-modern influences mentioned above, and nothing has been done to date to prevent its increase.[115]

After the Second World War, architectural historians concentrated more on the Modern Movement than on traditionalism.[116] This had presumably to do with the inevitable association of traditionalism with conservative, right-wing and even National Socialist movements. Modern art, on the other hand, was associated with the defeat of the dark forces that had brought about the downfall of Europe. In Germany, 'everything that Hitler had forbidden was welcomed after 1945 with an enthusiasm prompted by curiosity and guilt feelings', wrote Hans Sahl in 1955. In 1954, Alois Melichar asserted in his fanatical pamphlet, *Überwindung des Modernismus*, that, after the 'catastrophe' of 1945, 'every opponent of atonal racket and abstract kitsch was automatically labelled a Nazi.'[117]

In the post-war period, America became the symbol of Modernism, bringing with it all the dangers of jazz and film for young people in the concrete jungle. Nothing could resist the appeal of American mass culture. 'Any kid worth his salt has only 1 plan now – to get to the U.S.A. as soon as possible', wrote Jan Cremer. Dutch Prime Minister G. van der Leeuw's efforts to protect the younger generation of the postwar period from Modernism and all things American by fostering pursuits such as folk dancing and folk singing were of no avail.[118] As a result, traditionalism in the arts and in architecture was slowly but surely driven under. In professional circles, traditionalism has still not received the recognition it deserves. When it comes, we will have to acknowledge that the traditionalists were not always wrong, except in their rejection of the aesthetics that the Modernists developed in the 1920s.

Romantic Modernists

Science, Art and Nostalgia

In 1994, the Amsterdam weekly paper, the *Amsterdamse Stadsblad,* contained a report on the City Council's plan to cut down a third of the trees in the large wooded park on the edge of Amsterdam, the Amsterdamse Bos, and to replace them with a layout for a primeval forest complete with a herd of Highland cattle. 'We will all have to get used to the sight of trees that have fallen over or that have grown crooked', the council spokesperson said. He admitted that it wouldn't look pretty, but added that 'it will give us a feeling for the prehistoric landscape that is in danger of vanishing from the face of the earth.'[1]

The Amsterdamse Bos was laid out in the 1930s as a romantic landscaped city park. From the point of view of the conservation of historical sites, the layout should have been respected, and planting a 'prehistoric forest' put an end to that. Why did Amsterdam pick this park to create a version of primeval nature? One reason is that an ecological approach to nature conservation has gained broad political support in recent years. In the farming community, however, ecologists are not exactly loved. This was evident in 1998 from the opposition of a number of farmers in Gaasterland to the government's plans to convert a cultivated landscape into a wilderness. The local farmers argued that the scenic landscape of Gaasterland was already rich in natural beauty and that the government would do better to subject the arable lands of northern Friesland to natural conservation. On top of that, they criticized the authorities because the planners of the *Ecologische Hoofdstructuur*, a network of 'green' areas, did not count livestock as part of 'nature'.[2] The ecologists don't regard chickens as belonging to 'nature', only the foxes that eat them. The farmers in Gaasterland thought that they were in as good a position as anybody to say what should be called nature and that they didn't need any advice on the subject from ecologists in the ministries of The Hague. The struggle between the civil service departments involved and the farmers was particularly bitter and their difference of opinion in fact came down to the question of who actually decided what 'nature' was – the ecologists or the farmers.

In 1995, an interesting book was published by Jozef Keulartz with the title, *Strijd om de natuur* (The Struggle for Nature). The book exposes how undemocratic ecological conservation is, because there are a variety of ways of experiencing nature, and the approach of the ecologists is in no way superior to that of a day tripper.

The conservationists of historical monuments should really concede that the people of Gaasterland are right, because the region is a traditional man-made landscape and, as such, it is of cultural and historical importance. The Netherlands Department for Conservation is thus in serious conflict with ecological conservation. And if what is involved is the reconstruction of the past, the public bodies representing these different interests have diametrically opposite agendas. While there is hardly any longer any support among historical conservationists for the reconstruction of original architectural forms, nature conservationists plead for the reconstruction of indigenous prehistoric nature. That is strange and also hard to understand if one remembers that both branches belonged to the same department not so long ago.

In his study of the history of nature conservation, Henny van der Windt explains how nature conservancy in the Netherlands came under the influence of biologists who, with the rise of ecological concepts, succeeded in causing a volte-face in government policy. According to Van der Windt, the love of the countryside has been replaced by theories about self-regulating ecosystems. In ecologically correct landscapes, where an idyllic harmony of virgin primal nature prevails, there is plenty of room for sand drifts, moorland, marshes, reptiles, birds of prey and European bison, but almost none for human beings. The ecologists bar civilized man from any return to paradise, because he has sinned against nature. Human beings have been guilty of slash-and-burn activities against nature and have downgraded the countryside to a terrain for agricultural production. This viewpoint is legitimized by recent scholarly studies and has therefore been granted a head start over other forms of experiencing nature. Scientific theories, however, do not always have to be socially acceptable. Science and scholarship may come in conflict with democratic codes of behaviour, as proved the case in 1976 when the *Landelijke Werkgroep Kritisch Bosbeheer* – the national study group for critical forestry – brought its scientific ideas about restoring the primeval forest as an ecosystem into practice by pulling trees down here and there with a view to using the dead wood to instigate a 'self-regulating ecosystem'.[3]

The role that ecology plays in nature conservation can perhaps be compared with that of Modernist architectural theory in the conservation of historic buildings. Just as ecologists, according to Van der Windt, were able to an extent to dictate environmental policy, Modernist architects have probably had an influence on approaches to historical conservation. Just as biological studies have succeeded in cleansing government policy of the nostalgic approach to nature, Modernist theories about art and architecture have done the same for historical conservation.

An early example, from 1920, of the influence of the Modernists on the policy for the preservation of historic monuments is the question of the rebuilding of the Wijnhuistoren in Zutphen, a structure dating back to 1640, that had been destroyed by fire. The National Historic Monuments Commission (*Rijkscommissie voor de Monumentenzorg*), which at the time included a number of influential Modernist architects among its members, was asked to approve a plan for rebuilding the tower in the same year. The plan by S. de Clercq to restore the state of the tower as it was prior to the fire was immediately denounced by famous architects such as H.P. Berlage, K.P.C. de Bazel, J. Stuyt and J.A.G. van der Steur. The sculptor A.W.M. Odé was also opposed to rebuilding the tower in the same form, as was the art historian A. Pit and the director of the Netherlands Department for Conservation, Jan Kalf. The members would have preferred a new tower in modern design. H.P. Berlage saw it as a matter of principle. He was able to imagine that 'people in Zutphen felt affection towards the old tower, but to decide all of a sudden to rebuild it in its original form after everything that has been said in recent times about this issue is asking quite a lot in the view of the speaker. The speaker can well imagine a modern design that would find favour with the people of Zutphen'.[4]

The discussions to which Berlage was referring had to do with the drafting of the policy document entitled *Principles and regulations for the preservation, restoration and enlargement of old buildings*, published in 1917 by the Netherlands Society of Antiquities. Article XVI of the *Principles* opens with this proposition: 'rebuilding vanished parts of a building is a lie against history'. The same article also states that, while there are possible exceptions to this rule, these are only those 'rare cases where it can be done with complete certainty and where it is totally possible to carry it out'. [5]

The architectural avant-garde had effectively placed a taboo on the imitation of art and architecture from the past. Berlage and his associates regarded imitation as anti-artistic. The imitation of historical styles, the Modernists declared, had been the downfall of nineteenth-century art. By this they meant Revival styles and the imitation of historical styles, which they regarded as a lie against one's own times. The imitation of historical styles indicated a lack of creativity.

This Modernist standpoint on nineteenth-century art has by now more or less totally run out of steam, but something of it apparently still remains in the collective cultural unconscious. Ideas can sometimes become detached from their context and start leading a life of their own. Something like this may also have happened with the taboo on reconstructions in architecture. This taboo is rooted in the idea that art is supposed to be something other than professional craftsmanship, a notion that was still fairly revolutionary in the nineteenth century and which originated in the artistic revolt against academic rules for art.

Romantic Ideas about Art

In his *Conjectures on Original Composition* of 1759, Edward Young wrote that something original is the product of genius and never comes from imitating other models: 'It rises spontaneously from the vital root of genius … imitations are often a sort of manufacture, wrought up by those mechanics, art and labour, out of pre-existent materials not their own.'[6] Since the Romantic Movement, artists have been expected to be guided by their artistic sense and not to slavishly copy other models. In 1801, therefore, Philipp Otto Runge experienced it as a problem to carry out the instructions of his client, because they were in sharp conflict with his artistic conscience.[7] The idea of artists having a mission is perhaps older than Romanticism, but that period elevated it to something sacrosanct. An essential element is the rejection of the academic rules of art in order to make room for authentic art – art, that is, that is no longer subordinate to the traditional canon. Stendhal, too, expressed his exasperation with second-generation imitations of the classical models on his visit to the 1824 Salon. He wrote that there were more than two thousand perfectly painted scenes from the school of Jacques-Louis David, but that these paintings had absolutely no soul: 'Was I moved by anything genuine, anything based on personal observation? Sadly I wasn't; everything I saw there was a copy of a copy.'[8]

Originality was more highly prized by Stendhal than any compliance with academic traditions. Artists, he thought, should keep up with their own times. 'Il faut être de son temps', Deschamps wrote in 1828, to which Ingres replied by asking why one should keep up with the times when the times themselves were out of kilter. Charles Baudelaire then joined the fray. In his *Le Peintre de la vie moderne* (1868) he wrote that 'le grand défaut de M. Ingres, en particulier, est de vouloir imposer à chaque type qui pose sous son oeil un perfectionnement plus ou moins complet, emprunté au répertoire des idées classiques'.[9] In 1866, the famous novelist Emile Zola declared, 'What I expect of an artist is not any sweet dreams or dreadful nightmares, but that he gives all of himself, heart and soul, that he displays a candid, clear and forceful individual character. I feel a hearty distaste for the little devices, the calculated pieces of flattery, everything that is affected … I feel a disgust for the word "art", as it implies all kinds of obligatory agreements and absolute ideals. What I look for in a painting is a person not a pretty picture.'[10]

Zola meant roughly the same as George Eliot, who wrote in *Adam Bede* (1859) that a painting of an angel might well be perfect, but the depiction of the unvarnished reality is much more moving: 'Paint us an angel, if you can, with a flowing violet robe, and a face paled by the celestial light … but do not impose on us any aesthetic rules which shall banish from the region of Art those old women scraping carrots with their work-worn hands, those heavy clowns taking holiday in a dingy pot-house … it is so needful to remember their existence …'[11] This social side of art, however, left Charles Baudelaire cold. In his definition of Romanticism from 1846, he stressed the aspects he saw as higher: 'Qui dit romantisme, dit art moderne, c'est-à-dire intimité, spiritualité, couleur, aspiration vers l'infini, exprimées par tous les moyens que contiènnent les arts.'[12]

The Modernists have taken over the Romantic idea of the artist as a seer and have then tried to introduce it into the world of conservation. The notion that art only exists due to the activities of inspired artists and not to the repetition of traditional formulae is only as old as Romanticism, at least as a collectively received opinion. Before that time, the imitation of generally acknowledged models was a duty and not a dastardly deed. In literature, the Romantic ideal of art was still defended fairly recently by Jan Greshoff, who argued that it was impossible for literature to be created without some 'irresistible inner urge'. 'Art', he wrote, 'needs to be born of an uncontrollable inner excitement. And this can never come about by orders from above. Never!' He was in turn severely reprimanded by Godfried Bomans, who thought it incredible that so widely read an individual as Greshoff did not realize how comparatively new this viewpoint was.[13]

Modernism and Conservation

In 1920, the members of the National Historic Monuments Commission were presumably not aware of the Romantic origins of their ideas, because they were not aware that there could be any other guidelines, either for the seventeenth-century city mason Edmond Hellenraet who had designed the tower or for the twentieth-century residents of Zutphen. The latter, however, had not heard of 'modern' ideas about art and, because they stuck to their guns, the tower was eventually rebuilt not in the modern manner, but as a reconstruction.

In general, the Commission did not find much support for modern ideas about art outside the progressive elite. Since, however, the opinion of this group was the only one to be taken seriously, the dislike for imitations continued to prevail and was taken over by a younger generation both in the Commission and in the Department for Conservation. In 1948, the Commission advised the Minister of Education, Art and Science 'in rebuilding the church towers that have been destroyed in war of some other disaster, to inform the owner that a competition for a modern design is desirable'.[14]

This advice was rarely heeded, however, because, as just stated, the general public showed little understanding for this viewpoint. Only the Eusebiuskerk in Arnhem, the Willibrorduskerk in Hulst and the Martinuskerk in Weert have been given new, modern towers.[15] Despite the indifference or downright hostility of the general public, however, the Modernist opposition to reconstructions continued to flourish in various government bodies. In 1980, the Commission declared that no support could be expected from the government for the reconstruction of buildings that had completely vanished, because this 'can have an artificial impact' on 'the living architec-

15   The tower of the church of Eusebius in Arnhem in 1935 with its seventeenth-century steeple

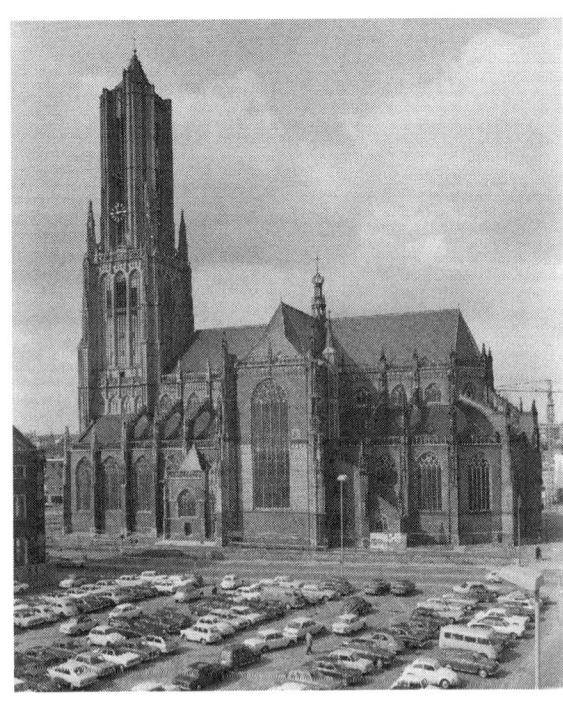

*16   The church of Eusebius with the new tower
designed by Theo Verlaan (1955)*

tural stock'.[16] It was supported in this by Article 15 of the *Charter of Venice* of the International Council of Monuments and Sites of 1964, in which one finds the following sentence: 'All reconstruction work should however be ruled out a priori'.[17] In a later publication, however, the Commission did register its approval for the following statement by C.A. van Swigchem: 'The reconstruction of a building or block of buildings that has been lost in a disastrous manner can be necessary if very great national and emotional interests adhere to it, and the identity and history of a community depend on it.'[18] It is a half-hearted formula, in which reconstruction is effectively rejected, being permitted only in exceptional cases. Replicas were rejected, while at the same time it was recognized that one sometimes had to yield to emotions, if they were held nationwide.

The opposition to the reconstruction of destroyed monuments relates not only to the legacy of Romanticism and its influence on the Modern Movement, but also to the fear of surrendering the work of conservation to nostalgic ideas. In enlightened circles nostalgia is held to be an emotional affliction of the ignorant. It is thought of as a symptom of degeneration, a sentimental and misguided form of homesickness for an idealized past, a flight from the present to a dreamland that has never existed. Viewed in this light, it is a sickly expression of the fear of reality. One should feel sorry for people who feel nostalgia and today few, even among the most ardent conservationists, will admit feeling such emotions. In the world of the preservation of historic buildings it was always a swear word and in that of nature conservation, the idyllic feeling for nature that prevailed in the period after the First World War has been seen as 'unnatural' and even decadent since the 1970s. The ideal of the harmonious landscape that one could still find in the Netherlands in 1900 and which the movement for natural conservation was concerned to preserve was driven out by the less romantic notions of the biologists.

In the historical conservation movement, too, hobbyist antiquarians have been replaced by university-trained architects and art historians. This group of academics has also endeavoured to purge their profession of nostalgia. The marginalization of the nostalgic adoration of nature has meanwhile led to biodiversity being seen as more important in nature conservancy than the restoration of the farmlands in the second half of the nineteenth century. This theoretical shift is the result of the professionalization and increasing 'scientization' of government policy. The reconstruction of landscapes in their primal form was the result of these processes. In historical conservation, the reconstruction of the original architectural state was, however, opposed by arguments from modern artistic theory. In terms of content, the management of nature and the preservation of historical buildings are diametrically opposed to each other, but they both have this in common – that specialists have impressed their scientific stamp on policy in both fields – the biologists in the field of nature conservancy and the architects in historical preservation.

There has been plenty of criticism of ecological nature conservancy

17   Frauenkirche in Dresden in 1930

ROMANTIC MODERNISM

from both farmers and philosophers. They have argued that ecologists have erroneously claimed a monopoly on notions concerning the appreciation of nature. Is there also a similar danger of a monopoly in historical conservation? Isn't the hostility towards nostalgia just as great in this movement as it is in nature conservancy? It is hard to say for certain, but in their dislike of nostalgia, the two movements have presumably grown towards each other. The question remains, however, of whether nostalgia is always such a bad thing.

The Frauenkirche in Dresden

What is wrong with wanting to reconstruct vanished monuments? In conservation circles in Germany after the fall of the Berlin Wall in 1989, this question provoked uproar. With the downfall of the Communist regime there was a desire to erase all memories of the Stalinist past of East Germany, and so to make way for the emergence of old, repressed memories. People tried to overcome the trauma of their recent past by once again picking up the thread of the history prior to that period. In an atmosphere like this, support was sought from generally familiar historical symbols, such as monuments that function as reminders of the national or local past. Berlin, for example, was urged to rebuild its castle, while in Dresden a similar campaign was waged for the rebuilding of the Frauenkirche (designed by Georg Bähr in 1726), to the great displeasure of the art historians and architects in the conservation movement. In an editorial in the journal *Kunstchronik* in October 1993, we read the following: 'Sehnsüchte nach Identifikations-Bauwerken, die, wie immer man sie deutet und wertet, das nationale Selbstwertgefühl möblieren, sind unterschwellig und dadurch gefährlich wirksam' (the wish for recognizable buildings, familiar beacons in the residential environment, can be dangerous, because it can potentially mobilize a sense of national pride). The attitude of the editors of the *Kunstchronik* was understandable in view of the German past, but in another light it could be regarded as a rather overheated response to see a link between people's attachment to an environment they felt familiar with and the murderous nationalism of the Nazi era. The reconstruction of an historical architecture that had been destroyed was labelled by the editors as 'Symptom einer unnatürlichen Identitätssuche' (a symptom of an unnatural obsession with one's identity). Not only was it dangerous, it was also unnatural.

Another German professional journal, *Deutsche Kunst und Denkmalpflege*, took a less pedantic approach. While admitting in 1991 that they did not agree about the reconstruction of the Frauenkirche, the editors invited two specialists, Heinrich Magirius and Ulrich Böhme, to discuss the issue.[19] Magirius, an art historian employed by the Saxony branch of the *Landesamt für Denkmalpflege* (Conservation Department), recalls that immediately after the war the Evangelical Lutheran church council voted to rebuild the church, but that this had been prevented by the Stalinist city council. With the rise of the East German peace movement in the 1980s, the ruin became a war memorial. Today of course, Magirius wrote, one can hide behind the notions of people like Georg Dehio who had always fiercely opposed the imitation of vanished monuments, but around 1900, artists still believed in the creativity of the Modernists. They believed in the art of the future, more than that of the past. Our generation no longer shares this belief and, furthermore, it has to be understood that after the *Wende* of 1989 people in Dresden began to feel a need for their own great historical artworks to give them faith in the future.

Ulrich Böhme, the director of the site office of the Evangelical Lutheran church in Saxony, argued for the ruin to be preserved. There were indeed plans for reconstruction afoot but, according to Böhme, these were not realistic. The ruin later became a monument to the collective guilt of the nation. It was the city's last remaining war ruin and should be preserved as a monument with the cautionary theme of 'Never Again'. Furthermore, Böhme went on, the situation in the city has changed so enormously that a copy of the former church – that would be a fake anyway – would end up being built in a totally different context. On top of that, the congregation really does not need this particular church – there are enough churches in the neighbourhood. The enormous sum required for reconstruction could better be spent on some good cause. Böhme assessed the cost of a total reconstruction at half a billion marks.

In 1991, the National Society of Conservationists (*Landesdenkmalpfleger*) in Germany hoped that the differences could be bridged by adopting a resolution at their annual general meeting in Potsdam. The delegates, who came from every part of Germany, then solemnly declared that since history was irreversible, one could not possibly reconstruct a monument that had been destroyed. The value of a historical monument lies essentially in its material age, including the traces that time has left in its structure, none of which can be repeated or imitated. The society stated that while it could well understand the desire of the public to rebuild the historic buildings destroyed during the Second World War, no reconstruction could ever be anything other than an 'expression of the present day'.[20]

Dresden took little notice of the *Denkmalpfleger*, however, and in the same year the decision was taken to rebuild the church. The conservationists' resolution was powerless to influence policy. All it did was give a picture of the *communis opinio* of one professional group about what it described as 'Grundfragen des Denkmalverständnisses in der Öffentlichkeit' – basic questions about conservation in practice. But given that Dresden had rejected the Potsdam resolution, one might wonder why it was passed at all, let alone with such a display of authority.

Shortly before his death in 1993, the German architectural historian Hanno-Walter Kruft wrote an article in the *Neue Zürcher Zeitung* about the shockingly low level of the discussions on the subject – by which he meant the Potsdam resolution. Of course he agreed with its tenor, but in his view it didn't go nearly far enough. The core of the matter, namely the ethical question, had been overlooked in Potsdam.[21] According to Kruft it was delusional to think that a monument can be rescued from ruin by conservationist measures, let alone by reconstructions: 'Die Festschreibung auf einen zeitlosen Zustand des Nichtalterns ist ebensowenig wünschbar wie die Herstellung eines ursprünglichen Erscheinungsbildes durch Rekonstruktion, in der der Faktor Zeit geleugnet wird' (the creation of a timeless state is as undesirable as the reconstruction of the original appearance, because in both cases the progress of time is denied). It was his conclusion that it would be an anachronism to wish that monuments could in fact be conserved: 'Es wäre eine anachronistische Forderung zu verlangen, dass Monumente grundsätzlich zu pflegen seien'.

After stating his position, which implied the redundancy of the entire field of conservation activities, Kruft recalled that the demolition of a monument can even have some historical value. It can be a *damnatio memoriae*, an expression of revenge or a political protest. A good example here might be the Protestant iconoclastic fury of the sixteenth century. A similar fury in the former Democratic Republic of East Germany had had a political content. When a monument is deliberately destroyed, its reconstruction would mean a revision of history, something that was morally unacceptable and a form of improper manipulation. Reconstructions, according to Kruft, originate in the nostalgic feelings of people who haven't faced up to the past and who want to present us with an image of history other than the real one. When all is said and done, reconstructions are forgeries. The authorities responsible should realize that their decision was improper, even if it was politically inevitable. The reconstruction is an 'Ausdruck der Restauration' and reflects a disoriented retrogressive social situation. What Kruft found particularly infuriating was the support that reconstructions like this got from historians, art historians and professional conservationists. The result was to give such reconstructions legitimacy in the eyes of the general public. The fact that the public wanted to suppress certain aspects of the past was deplorable enough, but that its attitude was also validated by supposedly scientific arguments was nothing short of a scandal. Anyone who supported such reconstructions had sunk to the same level as those barbarians who destroyed monuments.

Kruft's readers might well find his arguments a little overwhelming. Hadn't he perhaps overreacted a little to an issue that, given the amount of new development taking place all over East Germany in the 1990s, can only be thought of as unimportant? All that was involved was a few exceptional initiatives, not for instance the reconstruction of the entire inner city of Dresden. For Kruft, the retreat into pre-war nostalgia meant a denial of the Second World War; he backed his argument by quoting Alexander and Margarete Mitscherlich, who saw this phenomenon as indicating an 'Unfähigkeit zu trauern' – an incapacity for mourning. Reconstructions are a symptom of this phenomenon, in his view. It is a harsh judgement that is undoubtedly based on guilt feelings and in that regard it is understandable.

It may, however, be the case that so severe a verdict has the opposite effect from that intended. A past that is so tainted may leave one feeling inconsolable, so that the desire to remember untarnished chapters in one's national history can be seen as merely human.

Who was Kruft actually thinking of when he spoke of reprehensible people who betrayed authentic scholarship? He certainly had Jörg Traeger of the University of Regensburg in mind. In 1992, Traeger had supplied the advocates of the rebuilding of the Frauenkirche in Dresden with theoretical arguments.[22]

Was Jörg Traeger's attitude criminal? Whatever the case, he didn't indulge in emotional explosions, though he may have had more reason to do so than Hanno-Walter Kruft. The protests against the rebuilding of the Frauenkirche originated in the former Federal Republic of West Germany and, according to Traeger, one had to be aware that conservation had followed a totally different path there than it had in the Democratic Republic of East Germany. West Germans shouldn't think that the residents of Dresden needed them to tell them how they should remember the Second World War. On top of the war, the former Democratic Republic had also had forty years of State Communist repression to cope with. The eighteenth-century Frauenkirche has nothing to do with either Nazism or Communism. Under the Communist regime the residents of Dresden had to put up with the ruin of the church being treated as a monument of the Second World War. With the fall of Communism, however, it had taken on a new meaning. They had waited for forty years for an opportunity to restore the building and now that this was finally possible, Western Germans had the nerve to inform them of new theories that prohibited them from doing so. The people of Dresden regarded the famous Baroque church as a symbol of European culture that could not be destroyed either by the Third Reich or by the forty-year 'socialist perspective' and they saw its rebuilding as a moral duty. Traeger's argument was that the Potsdam resolution was based on an over-simplistic hypothesis; this was particularly evident in the closing sentence that aimed to limit the task of conservation to the authentic structural material ('Denkmalpfleger sind einzig den nicht reproduzierbaren Geschichtszeugnissen verpflichtet'). It is clear that the first task of conservation was to protect the historical material; in everyday restoration practice, however, it is of course impossible not to make reproductions. Conservationists, Traeger concluded, would be at odds with themselves if there were no longer any possibility of making copies of dilapidated parts: 'Maybe it sounds provocative and I know that this is something that dogmatic people refuse to listen to, but one can't avoid the conclusion that in cases of need architecture can be copied'. As an example he cited the Unter den Linden opera house of Georg Wenzeslaus Knobelsdorff of 1741 that had been destroyed and rebuilt three times. Nothing authentic remains of this building and yet is considered a historical monument. With this sort of reproduction the aim is to ensure the continuance of a historical phenomenon – 'Es geht um Überlieferung' (it has to do with tradition).

Hanno-Walter Kruft was not the only one among Jörg Traeger's colleagues to effectively excommunicate him. A year earlier Georg Mörsch, a highly respected theoretician in the field of conservation, had stated his anger with him. He confined himself however to a few marginal comments 'in the hope that others would take up their pens'.[23] One of them who did not hesitate to do just that was Manfred F. Fischer – on the invitation, what is more, of the editors of *Kunstchronik*.[24] Fischer, too, thought of himself as superior to ordinary laymen who were incapable of understanding that architecture that has vanished has gone for good. He saw it as thoroughly alarming that academically trained art historians should rush to the aid of architectural reconstructions with theoretical arguments. According to Fischer, Traeger had concocted a theory of profound superficiality ('tiefgründige Oberflächlichkeit') based on the 'fatal mistake' that the design of a building can be repeated in the same way as musical compositions are played over and again with the help of a score. Fischer denounced this notion, because a design is never the same as the completed building. Furthermore, later alterations and the historical traces of the actual use of the building are absent from the copy and these form an essential part of the value of historical architecture. There is yet another factor, that of time: an artwork can only be created once. A copy is a forgery of the authentic work by definition. Fritz Schumacher had said the same thing back in 1906 about the rebuilding of the Michaeliskirche in Hamburg. Imitation cannot claim our respect, he declared, because it lacks 'der echte Hauch aus einer Zeitepoche' (the genuine atmosphere of its own age). Even a musical composition is never performed twice in exactly the same way because musicians' interpretations are always different. That art cannot be repeated, according to Fischer, is also an idea one finds in Walter Benjamin's work and in that of Georg Simmel.

Manfred F. Fischer hadn't a good word to say for anyone who doesn't agree with him. This sometimes meant that he overreached himself, because his scorn for his opponents led him to underestimate them. Jörg Traeger would certainly have read Walter Benjamin and would know as well as Fischer that the past can't be repeated. 'Selbstverständlich kann eine Rekonstruktion das Original nicht voll ersetzen, vor allem nicht die Schicksalspuren' (it is obvious that a reconstruction can never replace the original, least of all the traces left by the passage of time), Traeger wrote, thus letting people know that he was no greenhorn. 'Architektur ist notfalls ersetzbar' (when necessary, architecture is replaceable) – that was his thesis. Conservation should not exclude reconstructions, because to a degree they are also accepted in the restoration of the cathedrals; historical architecture, however, is inseparable from the time and place of its original construction, so that reconstruction can never be anything more than a visual memorial.

Manfred F. Fischer thought he could undermine Jörg Traeger's thesis by citing former architectural reconstructions that were not viewed as copies in the eyes of patrons and critical contemporaries, but as new creations. In the mid-nineteenth century, he argued, people were well aware that the rebuilding of the basilica of San Paolo in Rome was not a proper reconstruction, but an idealized copy of an early Christian church. In the rebuilding of the Campanile in Venice it was also understood that the new tower was only an 'Abbild' (image) of the old one. With the Michaeliskirche in Hamburg, what was involved was not so much a case of reconstructing the church itself as of a building that symbolized the city of Hamburg.

Fischer failed to notice that these examples actually support Traeger's thesis rather than the opposite. Traeger also said that reconstructions could never be anything more than an image. It is also astonishing that Fischer presented an example of an architectural reconstruction from his own practice in the Hamburg Department for Conservation to back his case. What was involved was two houses that formed part of a row of classical houses on the Rathausmarkt. These two houses were burned down in 1990 and according to Fischer it would have been 'ein blutleeres Gedankenspiel' (a cold-blooded mental game) to do anything other than rebuild faithful copies of them. This is precisely what Traeger advocated. Nothing remains of their controversy then, save the fact that Fischer felt uncomfortable with the notion of reconstructing a building that was destroyed a long time ago. The rebuilding of Warsaw, in his view, should have been carried out immediately after the war, 'ohne grosse Zeitverzögerung' (without any major delay) and that was something different from a reconstruction fifty years later in an environment that had changed completely. This was why Fischer was so opposed to the plan to rebuild the *Stadtschloss* in Berlin, even though he still mourned its definitive demolition in 1950: 'Der Schmerz hierüber ist nicht mit der Zeit verheilt, und die heutige Ödnis an der Stelle des Geschehens hält diesen Schmerz, das Gefühl des Verlustes und den ohnmächtigen Zorn über diese Barbarei wach' (The sorrow about this loss has not been healed over the years, and the ugliness of the site keeps alive one's pain and impotent anger at the barbarous act). In his view, things had reached a point of no return and if the former castle were to be rebuilt this would be done in an environment that was totally different, so that the building would look 'like a dispossessed ancestor who no longer has any family or friends'.

In the catalogue of 1993 for the exhibition on proposals for rebuilding the *Stadtschloss* of Berlin, Wilhelm von Boddien compared the right to rebuild with one's right to receive treatment after an accident. Fischer rejected this comparison, because an accident was something quite different from an event in history. The latter may indeed be a tragic accident, but that was just the nature of history. Fischer spoke approvingly of an article by Tilmann Buddensieg in the *Süddeutsche Zeitung* of 30 December 1992, in which he wrote that reconstructions of vanished buildings really amounted to a criticism of contemporary architecture. This argument – namely that historical architecture is necessary as a compensation for the inhumanity of modern architecture – was also deployed by Wolfgang Thierse. Fischer agreed with this criticism, because in this way historical architecture was downgraded to a mere stage prop that you could resort to where necessary.

Manfred F. Fischer could only see architecture as an unrepeatable artistic creation. In this regard he concurred with the planner Fritz Schumacher, citing his phrase about 'echte Hauch aus einer Zeitepoche' (the real spirit of the period). This romantic view of the artist is difficult to combine with Jörg Traeger's ideas about conservation. Fischer did not see any contradiction here and this explains why he sometimes came up with misleading examples. When he raised the question of the reconstruction of Hamburg after the Second World War, he declared that time never stood still and that it was wrong to stop the clock of the 'Prozesshaftigkeit' of urban development at an arbitrary moment of history. To illustrate this, he wrote that the new city centre might well be viewed as a monument in fifty years' time. What the generation of the Second World War could only view as a tragic loss, was for 'unsere prozesshaft denkende Generation' – our process-oriented generation – worthy of protection. The new buildings of the 1950s might be seen as the new monuments of Hamburg. Fischer's viewpoint is erroneous, however, because an assessment after fifty years is quite another thing than solving a problem fifty years ago.

That the debate could be conducted in a less aggressive manner was demonstrated by Achim Hubel in his detailed contribution from 1993. Apart from a couple of reservations, Hubel was fundamentally in agreement with Traeger. According to him, a public discussion should be fostered about the basic principles of restoration, similar to that which took place at the beginning of the twentieth century.[25]

The way that a number of leading scholars responded to Jörg Traeger's ideas suggests that the spokespeople of the conservation movement in Germany were moved by emotion rather than argument. Jörg Traeger opened his reply by saying that 'the barrage of abuse', was to be expected, but that he remained astonished by the fact that his opponents couldn't care less about the human side of the question. One critic even argued that the damage done by war should be retained as a historical document. Traeger replied by alluding to an article in a paper about Kabul, the capital of Afghanistan, which had been reduced to rubble by lengthy bombardments at the beginning of 1994.[26] Jörg Traeger's critics overlooked the general human need to restore what has been damaged in wars and natural disasters. Adducing ethical arguments against reconstructions in Kabul would seem not merely arrogant, but lacking in humanity.

Art and Imitation

The notion that art is solely the product of inspiration and creativity rather than of the correct application of artistic rules was one that gained almost universal acceptance during the Romantic era. Classicism with its notions of order, symmetry, disposition, distribution, eurhythmy, decorum and its principles of the harmonious orders of columns was an inassailable ideal of civilized architecture until Romanticism. In the nineteenth century, this ideal was overthrown both by the rise of Romanticism and by rationalist criticism of architecture. This criticism had already emerged in the eighteenth century, with for instance the *Essai sur l'Architecture* by Marc-Antoine Laugier of 1755. His thesis of 'les parties essentielles' containing every form of beauty is the direct antecedent of the principles Eugène Viollet-le-Duc derived a century later from the Gothic architectural system. In it, the form was subordinate to the function (la construction commande la forme).[27] Louis Sullivan's famous formula of 1896, 'form follows function', that became the battle cry of twentieth-century architectural Functionalism, has therefore a long ancestry.[28]

The criticism of Romanticism was levelled particularly at the Baroque and Rococo periods. These styles were suddenly seen as expressions of a degenerate and rigidified courtly art form in which ostentation prevailed at the expense of all else. The arts had to be liberated from this pretence and a new look needed to be taken both at nature and at the art of the Greeks. This was the subject of Johann Joachim Winckelmann's book, *Gedanken über die Nachahmung der Griechischen Werke in der Mahlerey und Bildhauerkunst* of 1755.[29]

While Winckelmann inaugurated an enquiry into the art of the Greeks, John Ruskin turned his mind to nature. He felt an excessive hatred of Classicism which he described in *The Stones of Venice* of 1851 as 'base, unnatural, unfruitful, unenjoyable, and impious' (III, 192). Ruskin propagated a new, modern art that drew its inspiration from nature and which he summed up in the aphorism, 'Nature is the art of God'.[30] His mission has to be viewed against the background of the nineteenth-century battle of styles. Architecture appeared to have become bogged down in a fruitless struggle between historical styles (Classicism versus Gothic) and Ruskin saw it as his mission to rescue it from this quagmire. The conflict led eventually to architectural anarchism, an eclecticism that progressive architectural critics ridiculed as a veritable tower of Babel and an architectural carnival.[31]

In this view, the nineteenth century has gone down in history as the most inartistic century of all, except for a few rationalists and a few romantics who paved the way for modern art, such as John Ruskin or William Morris of the Arts and Crafts Movement. They were among the 'pioneers of modern design', to refer to the title of Nikolaus Pevsner's influential book.

In his survey of the architecture of the previous century, the German Chief Government Architect, Paul Mebes, wrote in 1908 that the eighteenth century was the last period in history with a distinct style. After that, architecture fell into a deep decline, becoming bogged down in a restless and dead-end quest in a labyrinth of styles 'without there being any understanding for the artistic spirit of separate styles'. All that remained after around 1800 was 'Schwäche und Armut' (feebleness and poverty).[32]

Paul Mebes did not foresee any advent of a modern architecture, because the entire nineteenth century had already searched for that unsuccessfully. He regarded it as more sensible to return to the period when the quest for a new architectural style had not become an end in itself. His conclusion then was that the only thing that could rescue architecture was a return to the period before Romanticism, namely to Classicism. The Modernists, while sharing his negative verdict on the nineteenth century, rejected his conclusion. In 1908, the Modernist Adolf Loos wrote his famous essay 'Ornament und Verbrechen', in which he depicted the architects of the nineteenth-century decorative styles as criminals and imbeciles. This hatred of Revival architecture was shared by most of the adherents of the Modern Movement, the gist of their criticism being that the nineteenth century had displayed a total lack of creativity: 'There are whole decades in the second half of the nineteenth century in which no architectural work of any significance is encountered. Eclecticism smothered all creative energy', wrote the first historian of the Modern Movement, Sigfried Giedion, in 1941.[33]

John Ruskin's romantic thesis, that imitation is not art, underlies Giedion's later accusations. This was why Ruskin had anathematized restoration in architecture back in 1849: 'it is impossible, as impossible as to raise the dead, to restore anything that has ever been great or beautiful in architecture ... the spirit of the dead workman cannot be summoned up, and commanded to direct other hands, and other thoughts. And as for direct and simple copying, it is palpably impossible'.[34] This idea was adopted later by the conservationists, in response to the Modern Movement's excommunication of Revival architecture as a despicable form of imitation. From that time on, people also felt free to condemn the restorations of the school of Eugène Viollet-le-Duc as uninspired imitations of medieval work.

These ideas found their most fertile soil in Germany around 1900. The curator of monuments and antiquities in Bavaria, Georg Hager, declared in a lecture in 1905 that conservation had reached a new stage of development now that the imitation of historical styles was understood as having damaged the artistic quality of the monuments restored: 'nicht um Stil, sondern um Kunst dreht sich die Frage' (it is a question not of style, but of art). Monuments should be restored then by artists and not by copyists. For this reason, Hager was also opposed to the rebuilding of the Campanile on the Piazza San Marco in Venice that had collapsed in 1902. The art-historical value of the tower had been destroyed and could never be brought back to life by a reconstruction. A 'slavish copy' is not art. His lecture was received with great acclaim, amongst others by Georg Dehio, professor of art history at the University of Strasbourg and Paul Clemen, curator of monuments in the Rhineland, both of them founders of the conservation movement in Germany. On this occasion, Dehio said 'Scheinaltertümer hinstellen ist weder wahre Kunst noch wahre Denkmalpflege' (imitations of historical monuments are neither true art nor true conservation). Among the specialists in art of his acquaintance, he said, there was just as much interest in old masters as in modern art.

In his response, Clemen referred to what John Ruskin and William Morris had written about faking art, and he quoted Anatole France who had described nineteenth-century neo-Gothic as 'faux' and 'haïssable'. Clemen also thought there should be no conflict between old and new art: 'es gibt nur gute Kunst und schlechte Kunst' (there is only good art and bad). By bad art, Clemen meant copies, the borrowing of the exterior features of old artworks, clichés, in other words. Good art results from following the 'Gesetze des Schaffens' with 'Schöpferkraft' – the creation of something original and real.[35]

Around 1900, the Romantic notion of real art as opposed to stereotypes was taken up by architects and art historians, at least those who felt an affinity with Modernism. This could be seen for example in 1909 at the Tenth Conservation Day in Trier when a passionate plea was launched against the total reconstruction of the Michaeliskirche in Hamburg (1751-1762) that had been destroyed in a fire in 1906. Even though the decision to rebuild the church in its identical eighteenth-century shape had already been taken – a decision that had the support of a great number of the residents – the architect E. Högg of Bremen pointed out it had been taken on improper grounds. Due to the essential alterations imposed by fire precautions, the introduction of modern construction techniques and electrical installations, an exact copy was in any case impossible. But apart from this, different building materials had also been chosen, such as concrete for the ridge beams instead of wood (with a deviating profile). The use of new techniques and materials would violate the logical harmony of structure and outward form, so that the rebuilt church would give an incorrect impression of the eighteenth-century monument. Most of his conservationist colleagues, he said, agreed that no artist is capable of copying the craftsmanship of eighteenth-century sculptors and plasterers. The new church would therefore be a 'vollständige Neuschöpfung', a completely new work, and one without any artistic appeal, because one cannot expect anything of artistic value when the artist is bound by stylistic requirements ('wenn man dem Künstler die Krücke der Stilvorschrift mitgibt'). What is preferable – an inauthentic copy or an original artwork by a young artist? Högg thought that the immature work of a young artist was a thousand times preferable to the 'nichtssagende Phrasengeklingel verbrauchter Formen' (the meaningless noise of second-hand forms).

E. Högg's speech was greeted with 'lengthy applause'. The next to speak was Anton Hagedorn as the representative of the city of Hamburg. Professor Högg had conveyed his view of the matter with passion, Hagedorn said. As an outsider, however, he didn't understand what was involved. First of all, the large sum of money that had been collected for the conversion, including a considerable contribution from a former resident of Hamburg who now lived in America, could never have been raised for building a new church. The residents wanted their beloved building back, especially the tower, which was a 'Wahrzeichen', or landmark, of Hamburg. We had to take account of the feelings of the residents and given this background of imponderabilia it was 'völlig unerheblich und ganz gleichgültig' (completely insignificant and altogether irrelevant) of Mr Högg to complain that the ridge-beam did not have exactly the same form as the original. After all, what was at stake was the overall picture. That was what the Hamburgers wanted and one had to take account of their wishes.

The next speaker was the well-known art scholar and Privy Councillor Cornelius Gurlitt of Dresden. The church, he declared, had already been burned down three times and on each occasion it was rebuilt according to the prevailing taste of the time. Now that the Hamburgers have opted for a copy, they have for the first time in their history lost this 'kräftige Selbstgefühl' (powerful sense of themselves). Once again, there was tumultuous applause.

The architect of the reconstruction, the *Geheimer Oberbaurat* Professor Hofmann of Darmstadt had some difficulties with the speeches by Högg and Gurlitt. While in general architects carry out the wishes of their clients, he said, in this case when it was the people of Hamburg who commissioned a rebuilding of the church along its broad lines they opposed this approach, and recommended treating the commission as an experiment with modern forms. Hofmann thought this was an odd attitude to adopt and one that he expected would be quite unpopular in Hamburg. Quite apart from that, he added, Högg's verdict on the plans was mistaken. The small deviations in the design of the new parts, such as the ridge beam that he mentioned, were the logical result of employing new construction materials. The eighteenth-century architect of the church, Ernst Georg Sonnin, would have done the same if reinforced concrete and cast stone had been available to him. The chairman of the meeting asked Högg if he wanted to reply to this; but the latter didn't and so the debate was closed.[36]

We do not know what Högg was thinking at that moment, and perhaps it doesn't really matter, because the people of Hamburg were perfectly entitled to rebuild their church in its old form if that was what they wanted. The argument of the opponents of this plan was that in the restoration of monuments it was better to have the lost parts of the building done by a contemporary artist rather than replace them with imprecise copies. Why was that better? Because real art cannot be copied. Its distinguishing feature is its originality and it does not lend itself to templates. But the opponents of the project took little account of the fact that the people of Hamburg did not want 'real art' – they just wanted their church back. They did not have any objection to replacing an original with a copy and would probably have agreed that a copy is less valuable than an original work. The only question was whether the city government were to deprive the residents of their copy on the ground that it had no art-historical value, at least according to the new meaning that Romanticism had given to the notion of *art*.

According to the influential German art theoretician Hermann Muthesius, modern art could not be viewed separately from the way that older art was restored. Between 1896 and 1903, he was living in London with a state commission to carry out research into the applied arts and domestic architecture in Great Britain. There he was converted to modern functional design as propagated by the Arts and Crafts Movement. Muthesius became the apostle of 'Sachlichkeit' or Functionalism that aimed to replace the stylistic imitations of nineteenth-century architecture. Efficiency and functionalism would also be the founding principles of the Deutsche Werkbund founded in 1907 by Muthesius and others. In his view, the nineteenth-century architectural masquerade was no longer to be taken seriously and his conclusion was that architecture was expelled from the ranks of the living arts – 'aus der Reihe der lebendigen Künste verschwunden sei'. The copying of historical styles, he continued, was reprehensible not just in architecture but also in monument restoration. The big mistake was that the nineteenth century built new buildings in old forms and restored old buildings as though they were new. It was an illusion to think one could put oneself in the shoes of the master builders of the twelfth or thirteenth centuries: 'It is no exaggeration to say that none of the past centuries with their wars, fires and revolutions have been as harmful for historical architecture than what has been done to it by architects it in the nineteenth century in the name of conservation.'[37]

This criticism is understandable but what is harder to comprehend some hundred years later is the deep contempt that the Modernists of 1900 felt for nineteenth-century stylistic imitations. Muthesius could not stand the sight of a 'plebejisches Surrogat' next to the 'altes nobles Original', because 'Echtheit und Nachahmung stehen zueinander wie Öl und Wasser' (authenticity and imitation are as oil is to water). The corollary of this contempt was an unbridled admiration for everything that was new and original. In Muthesius's view the emergence of a new art would inevitably lead to a different method of restoration.

Jan Kalf had drawn the same conclusion back in 1899 when he said that there was but one principle in architecture, namely 'that the sole logical appearance (form) of the exterior of a building was determined by the function it has to fulfil in each specific case. This means that a large part of post-medieval architecture is effectively condemned.'[38] Jan Kalf was well informed about recent developments in modern art. He was a member of the Catholic art society in the Netherlands, De Violier, and he regularly published essays on the art of his day and on art-historical subjects. In 1918 he was appointed director of the State Department for Conservation and this function gave him the chance to put his artistic ideas into practice in conservation projects. He wrote the introduction to the above-mentioned *Principles* (Grondbeginselen) of 1917 in which he distanced himself from the imitation of historical styles and declared himself an adherent of John Ruskin. Quoting Ruskin's *Seven Lamps of Architecture*, he wrote that restoration means 'the most total destruction which a building can suffer: a destruction out of which no remnants can be gathered: a destruction accompanied with false description of the thing destroyed'. He went on to discuss the ideas of Alois Riegl, Cornelius Gurlitt, Paul Clemen and others with whom he had become acquainted during the *Denkmalpflegetage*. The modern notion of the artist had thus been granted an important place in the *Principles* of 1917. Sculpture or carving that needed replacing, for instance, was not to be copied: Article XIX states that, 'It should not show the forms of an earlier period and it should be the work of an artist.' These modern ideas about the role of the creative artist in conservation were shared by most of the members of the National Historic Monuments Commission, as reorganized in 1918, figures such as K.P.C. de Bazel, H.P. Berlage, J.T.J. Cuypers, A.J. Der Kinderen and the sculptor A.W.M. Odé.

A leading representative of the modern trend in architecture, J.J.P. Oud, who was appointed a member of the Commission in 1935, defended these ideas on a number of occasions. For instance, after the bombing of Rotterdam in 1940, when the Commission issued its recommendations about the rebuilding of the Laurenskerk, Oud was diametrically opposed to E.H. Ter Kuile. The latter was an advocate of reconstruction, arguing in the Commission meeting of 8 May 1950 that, 'The restored church as seen from the outside will be no less authentic than a series of other restored monuments, such as the Dom in Utrecht, and it will even be more authentic than the cathedral of 's-Hertogenbosch. Restoration as I understand it will mean the restoring of the church to the form it had before May 1940, in purely historical forms, that is, and these are sufficiently known and documented. I see no value in employing "contemporary forms", and regard them as reprehensible in this case.'

Not only did Oud combat reconstruction; he also designed an alternative: a modern church structure with a public square behind the tower. Explaining his plan, he wrote that it 'should be appreciated with the creative energy that has created the values of former times that are so precious to us from the past.' Copying Gothic shapes was in his view an unworthy activity and he saw it as his task to purge it from conservation activities. His conflict with the traditionalists in the conservation movement was described by Ed Taverne at some length in 1983. One striking fact is that Taverne assessed Oud's plan as 'an attempt to safeguard the purity of the architectural assignment, thus deliberately excluding every false concept of history'.[39] His suggestion that Oud's new development plan was better in an architectural sense than Ter Kuile's reconstruction plan can perhaps be explained, if we assume that his verdict was to a degree based on the artistic principles of the Modern Movement. If this assumption is correct, it is proof that the Romantic ideas about art, that saw imitation as taboo and honesty as a basic prerequisite, were still alive and kicking as late as 1983.

The Modern Movement and the Postwar Reconstruction Period

Unlike the city around it, the Laurenskerk was eventually rebuilt in its old form. The modernization of Rotterdam had Jan Kalf's full support. In a report dated 21 May 1940, he had even urged further demolition of the monuments, because this would ensure that nothing would get in the way of designing an entirely new master plan for the city.[40]

This was what was done almost everywhere in the bombed cities of Eu-

18 The Lakenhal (Clothmakers' Hall), Ypres in 1919

19 The Lakenhal in Ypres after reconstruction

ROMANTIC MODERNISM

rope, with the devastation generally being treated as a chance to modernize the city centres. Where it was decided to carry out an integral reconstruction of the old city, as happened in Warsaw, some scrupulous followers of Georg Dehio's 1905 principle, 'Konservieren, nicht restaurieren', declared themselves ambivalent with regard to reconstructions. Looking back in 1974 on the reconstruction of Warsaw, Jan Zachwatowicz stated, 'I must admit that at the time I was torn by conflicting feelings, when – as an architect and conservator, who had always had nothing but respect for the worth of the authentic monuments of our culture and their building materials – I drafted a plan to copy the monuments and moreover on such a gigantic scale! ... By reconstructing the ruined objects we were acting in conflict with every principle of restoration that had prevailed so far; and yet we were complying with the will of the community by at least restoring the image of that which had been forcibly removed from the map and the history of our people through the schemes of others. We regard what we have done as a dramatic exception to the basic principles of restoration that we continue to respect.' [41]

How was it possible for someone, standing in the rubble of Warsaw, a city that like none other was destroyed by the Germans in such a terrifyingly systematic way, to still concern himself with principles of restoration drawn up around 1900 to call a halt to the historicizing restorations of the nineteenth century? No one, not even the people drafting these restoration principles, could have taken into account the possibility of a disaster on this scale; the conservationists simply did not have such a thing as a contingency plan. The artistic notions of the Modernists could not possibly have prevented the literal rebuilding of the city of Warsaw, but Jan Zachwatowicz's memoirs do show how powerful an influence they had on the practice of conservation.

Due to a remarkable find in the library of the Catholic University of Louvain, we now know how widespread Modernist notions of art already were after the First World War. The find comprised the correspondence of the Belgian architect Huib Hoste with a number of prominent Dutch architects. Hoste had fled to Holland during the war and in 1918 he posed the question of what his colleagues in general thought about the rebuilding of the cities destroyed by the war and in particular about the reconstruction of the Lakenhal and the Belfort of Ypres. Hoste's questionnaire showed that a small minority favoured a total reconstruction – Jan Stuyt, P.J.H. Cuypers and H. Brugmans, the Chairman of the Heemschut League. Opposed to reconstruction were the sculptors J. Mendes da Costa and H.L. Krop, the architects G.F. La Croix, M. de Klerk, W.M. Dudok, T. van Doesburg, H.P. Berlage, J.A.G. van der Steur, J.J. Weve, G. Versteeg and J.B. van Loghem. There were also some artists who argued for the preservation of the ruins, while some had no definite standpoint. A.J. Der Kinderen thought it a difficult question, and proposed that the general populace should be invited to participate in any decision-making process.

Most of the Modernists among the artists and architects firmly rejected on artistic grounds a reconstruction that the local council had already decided to carry out. They argued that rebuilding in the old form would only result in a 'lifeless copy' or 'stage set'. W.M. Dudok thought there was absolutely no point in reconstruction, because no art results from just copying something: 'All rebuilding (and for that matter all stylistic imitations) are not only essentially without any artistic value, but their aims are also completely one-sided and hopelessly superficial.' Dudok also thought that Belgium should take account of the requirements of the modern age and that it now 'had a chance like none other to bring about something great and good'. T. van Doesburg thought that a reconstruction could be 'only a dead copy' because 'style is the product of a certain awareness of an age and that this product is the result of the level of aptitude the culture has attained both materially and spiritually'. M. de Klerk argued the following: 'The greatest danger that I see in the rebuilding or even the restoration of historical buildings of previous ages is the fact that the idea and energy invested in an old building stands in the way of the responsiveness and openness to new architecture. The atmosphere in which strong new art thrives has no memories in common with the old; this knowledge of the old should be seen as nothing but so much dead weight.' J.B. van Loghem hoped that modern artists would get commissions for reconstruction and that, 'supported by the will of the people', they would ensure that 'no copy of the old hall will rise but an entirely new artwork emerging from a modern spirit according to currently prevailing norms'.[42]

In Belgium, too, there was a great deal of opposition to reconstruction. The architect E. Dhuicque, for instance, who had done an internship with Paul Léon in Paris, was a fierce opponent of such developments. He was a corresponding member of the Royal Commission for Monuments and Landscapes and in 1915 he was put in charge of the protection of artworks in the combat zones (the Mission Dhuicque, as it was known). He carried out a veritable crusade against the reconstruction of the Lakenhal that he thought should be preserved as a ruin. He was supported in this by the progressive elite and also by commonsensical local government officials who saw no point in rebuilding something that no longer had any useful function and which would cost a great deal of money at a time when there were plenty of better uses for it that would cost little in comparison. These administrators and Modernist architects, however, were no match for the local population who were moved mainly by nostalgia.

In 1918, the influence of the Modernists was still too tenuous to prevent the reconstruction of the fourteenth-century Lakenhal from going ahead. As early as 1917, J. Coomans, the city architect of Ypres, made the case for reconstruction: 'Notre beffroi qui est le monument de la cité par excellence doit revivre; sa résurrection est un besoin pour nous: parce que ce sera une protestation éclatante contre la sauvagerie de l'ennemi.' Work on the reconstruction began immediately after the war ended but was only completed in 1955. This historically faithful reconstruction was anything but typical of the rebuilding of the Belgian cities, because with the exception of the most important historical monuments the cities were not reconstructed but rebuilt in traditionalist styles. Just as the Modernists wanted to take advantage of the devastation of war to give the cities a new, contemporary appearance, the traditionalists wanted to purge architecture of everything that didn't belong to the region. Even before the First World War, traditionally minded architects were up in arms against everything that didn't tally with their picture of local architecture. In Flanders, for instance, they argued, the old Flemish style with stepped and pointed gables should be reinstated. The trade journal *De Bouwgids* had propagated it as long ago as 1911: 'The *Bouwgids* aims to be the organ of everyone among the younger generation of architects who, averse to all forms of academic dallying with Grecian and Roman Revival styles, have come to realize that it is the indigenous national style that best approximates the true aspirations of our Flemish people.' The traditionalists despised the Revival styles of the nineteenth century just as much as the Modernists did. In 1917 Jules Coomans declared that the traditional crafts in regional architecture had become extinct during the nineteenth century 'when our art was overwhelmed by the chaos and anarchy of an impotent eclecticism'.[43]

The architecture of the post-war reconstruction period in Belgium acquired a much more distinctly regional character than it had had hitherto. In Dinant for instance a 'Meuse Renaissance' style was prevalent everywhere, while in Louvain 'Brabant Baroque' was all the rage and Ypres opted for 'Bruges Gothic'. The damage of war was seen in a sense as an opportunity to reinvigorate the allegedly regional style. For many people, this did not mean wanting to regain what had been there before, so much as building what they thought *should* have been there. What they meant by this was an architecture that was supposedly typical of the local, traditional style of construction. Coupled with this was a rejection of any outside influences.

In the exhibition catalogue of *Resurgam* (1985), Marcel Smets wrote, 'In the absence of any certainty about a reality destroyed by the war, this memory of an idealized formal language offers something palpable to hold on to. It is cherished as a nostalgic souvenir that, in spite of the traditional power of the cultural heritage that has been destroyed, rarely refers to a concrete reality. The images shown remain abstractions that convert history into a model. They provide a sort of stage set with the aim of commemorating the remnants of a lost homeliness, and that therefore only includes those elements that reinforce this statement about security.' Smets's conclusion was that 'this idyllic conception' got bogged down 'in its fundamental denial of the social reality'. There was a grave housing need and yet only purely formal questions were discussed. According to Smets that had a 'rather sour, elitist flavour' and he called the Belgian reconstruction period 'an incident' in a development that was already under way before the outbreak of war. What did Smets think was behind this development? That the housing department wanted to draw up 'rules and regulations' to ensure 'minimum housing conditions for the voters'. Unfortunately he did not give any examples of these living conditions.

There were also historically faithful reconstructions, for instance in Arras, where the Gothic town hall with Renaissance extensions and the seventeenth-century buildings around the great square in front of it were rebuilt in the same forms. In general it was felt that important historical architecture should be reconstructed with archaeological care. J. Coomans was of the same opinion but he added that a different rule applied to domestic architecture, which was less important. This rule, as said above, was that these houses should be designed making use of local and regional features of style and construction.

In Germany, the First World War had consequences beyond the fact that the country had to confront the ignominy of its defeat. The scale in which entire cities and important cultural treasures had been destroyed was unprecedented and the German people were blamed for all of this. The image of being a population of barbarians provoked a huge upsurge of nationalist feelings. One of the forms this took was an emphasis on the cultural importance of German architecture.[44]

The war had stirred up feelings that were already present in the population. Around 1908, part of the medieval centre of Stuttgart was demolished and replaced by new developments in a style propagated at the time by the *Heimatschutzbewegung*. In charge of the artistic side of this development was Theodor Fischer, while Karl Hengerer, Paul Bonatz, Richard Dollinger and others were responsible its implementation. The aim of this style was to generate a 'Vorstoss gegen des Volkes verdorbenen Geschmack, gegen dessen Vorliebe für eitlen Putz und fremden Schein' (an assault on the decadent taste of the populace, and on their liking for pompous stucco and alien appearances). After the National Socialists took power in 1933, the notion of conservation was deployed to bolster the German character of the architecture. The *Reichsbund Volkstum und Heimat* was founded for this purpose. From then on, the theme of all the redevelopments that took place was to advocate a regional character and demolish anything that displayed foreign influences.[45]

After the Second World War, the reconstruction of German cities was defined by another tradition, that of the planology of the Third Reich. In this respect, Germany in the 1930s was a modern state that was obsessed with the notion of a 'totale Planung', the fundamental reorganization of the entire German state, including the cities. Almost all the big cities were expected to be adapted to facilitate economic expansion and meet the needs of modern motorized traffic. This meant large-scale breakthrough streets and a new architecture to the greater glory of the new Reich. Immediately after the surrender of France in 1940, Adolf Hitler ordered Berlin to be rebuilt as the new capital of the new German Empire, to give outward form to the 'die Grösse des Sieges' (the glory of the victory). Well before the Allied bombings began, the German *Raumplanung* had begun its work on the modernization of the whole empire and the reorganization of the historic cities on behalf of the 'neuzeitliche Bedürfnisse' – to meet the needs of the new age.

In their classic work, *Kriegsschicksale Deutscher Architektur*, Hartwig Beseler and Niels Gutschow show clearly how the futuristic visions of the National Socialist planners of the 1930s to a great degree determined the rebuilding of Germany even, sporadically, up to the 1970s.[46] When Berlin was devastated by carpet bombing in 1943, city planners saw it above all as offering new possibilities – at least this was the cynical opinion of Dieter Hoffmann-Axthelm: 'Der Krieg hatte endlich alles das, was ihnen ein Greuel war, diese wilhelminische Stadt mit ihren Stuckfassaden, einfach abgeräumt. Jetzt konnte neu begonnen werden.' [47] Contempt for the built 'Ungeist' (stupidity) of the nineteenth-century Revival styles was often accompanied by a desire for a more healthy living environment. After the bombing of Lübeck in 1942, the authorities felt that a reconstruction in the old forms was not desirable because the streets were too narrow for modern traffic and because the old, historic houses did not meet modern social needs and hygienic requirements. When the mayor, Hans Pieper, went to the government with traditionalist proposals he was put in his place with the remark that: 'die heutigen Menschen sich in die Seele des Mittelalters nicht hineindenken können. Deshalb werde es komisch wirken, wenn man die mittelalterliche Bauweise wieder nachmachen wolle' (contemporary man cannot place himself in the soul of the Middle Ages. The effect is merely comic when people try to copy medieval architectural styles).[48]

In general, modern planners had little respect for old city centres when they were not easily accessible, whether they had National Socialist leanings or were influenced by the Modernist dreams of Le Corbusier. As is well known, the famous architect had designed a plan in the 1920s for a high-rise neighbourhood in the centre of Paris. This contempt shown by urbanists and planners for the historical and non-logically determined structure of the human habitat could count on the approval of those who no longer wanted to be reminded of their warlike past. This was particularly the case in post-war Germany, where they gave their blessing to modern architecture and rejected any notion of the restoration of what had been there before. There were exceptions, such as Freudenstadt, that was rebuilt in the traditionalist style of the Stuttgart School.[49]

Apart from a few exceptions, however, there was a taboo on such developments among progressive architects during the post-war period. The professional press did not want to be reminded of the National Socialist past of this trend in architecture, nor did it want to know about the *Heimatschutz* that had waged a campaign of slander in the journal *Heimatleben* against everything of non-German origin.

As for the reconstruction, the conservationists in general adopted the government's position: rebuilding was to take place according to modern ideas, and modern notions of art were to be the guiding principle. According to Hartwig Beseler and Niels Gutschow, the conservationist movement ended up as a footnote in the reconstruction of Germany. It had resigned itself in advance to the demolition of what had survived of the historical 'Bausubstanz', or architectural substance. In the postwar period, the con-

20 *The market square in Freudenstadt*

servationists also wanted to distance themselves from the besmirched *Hei-matschutz* movement and this made it impossible for anyone to advocate rebuilding according to traditional principles. They ended up entrenched in the limited area where the 'Entnazifizierung' of the 'Arbeitsintentionen' (the denazification of the aims of work) did not apply, as, for instance, in the field of restoring major monuments, such as medieval churches and castles.

In the restoration of buildings of this sort, ideas about conservation were admittedly less obstructed by modern planning theorists, but even here the nonchalant rebuilding of the old historic forms was not always permitted. Modern notions of art have played an important role in the frustrations in this field, too. Unlike the Belgian situation after 1918, modern notions had enormous influence on conservation practice in Germany after 1945.

In 1948 the modern design for the rebuilding of the Paulskirche in Frankfurt by Rudolf Schwarz and Hermann Krahn was given preference over proposals for reconstruction. The view of the jury was that the rebuilding should be carried out 'in the spirit of our age', because 'we have no reason for casting doubt on our own ability and thus copying something from a distant past or resurrecting it with false pathos'. Similar language was also used to criticize the plan to reconstruct Goethe's house in Frankfurt. The influential cultural administrator Hans Schmitt wrote that he rejected the reconstruction on the basis of modern ethical theories of art: 'im Sinne des ganzen ethischen Gehaltes der modernen Gestaltungsbewegung kann ich nur sagen, dass der beabsichtigte Wiederaufbau des Goethehauses kategorisch abzulehnen ist.' In referring to the ethical implications of modern design, Schmitt was presumably thinking of the honest use of materials preached by the Deutsche Werkbund and which the Bauhaus called 'Materialgerechtigkeit'– an aesthetic principle by which natural materials, such as unpainted wood and untreated stone where considered 'more noble' than painted or finished materials. In his 1907 book, *Wesen der Kunst*, Konrad Lange declared that the use of *stucco lustro* in imitation of marble was a lie against the 'Holy Ghost of Art'. In his 1898 work, *Das Schöne und die Kunst*, the famous art theorist Friedrich Theodor Vischer condemned sculptors who finished their stone statues with paint.[50] This aesthetic principle has the same Romantic roots as the Modernist dislike of copying monuments and in combination these two notions have influenced virtually all postwar restorations. It was apparently impossible then for the conservation movement to avoid being influenced by Modernist aesthetics. A few decades later, the aesthetics of materials was overtaken by new historical ideas; what remained, however, was the conviction that imitating vanished buildings was morally reprehensible.

With regard to the battle, which was waged for many years, about the rebuilding of the Knochenhaueramtshaus in Hildesheim that had been destroyed in the war, Jürgen Paul concluded in 1979 that the conservationists had improperly given their backing to the opinion of a number of famous architects who had spoken out against the reconstruction. Richard Riemerschmid spoke of a 'grosse Verlegenheit mit einer kleinen Verlogenheit' (a huge embarrassment about a trifling dishonesty). The former director of the Bauhaus, Walter Gropius, said that a reconstruction would be nothing but a 'con trick'; Friedrich Tamms talked of 'Tote erwecken' (raising the dead); in the view of Otto Völckers, it was 'sentimental-kleinbürgerliche Entgleisung' (a sentimental petty bourgeois derailment), Paul Schmitthenner used the word 'Respektlosigkeit' (disrespect) and terms such as 'neuer Wein in alter Schläuchen' (new wine in old bottles) and 'schlechte Theaterdekoration' (mediocre stage sets) were bandied around. The conservation movement, rallied round opinions like this, while at the same time fully supporting the complete reconstruction of the Romanesque churches in Hildesheim with the argument that remnants of these churches had been spared, whereas nothing remained of the old establishment of the butchers. Jürgen Paul accused the conservationists of 'intellectual arrogance', because they clung to Modernist doctrines about the one-off character of artworks and to their faith in the creative abilities of modern artists. They had overlooked the fact that the famous building of 1525 was a symbol of the city and that the citizens of Hildesheim who had suffered the shock of the bombardment needed a symbol to preserve the continuity of their city's identity. The contempt displayed for this basic human need testified to their arrogance. The people of Hildesheim didn't want an 'original artwork', or an 'authentic historical document', or even some 'daring creation in the spirit of our age'. All they wanted was to have their city's beloved symbol

21 *The Altstadtmarkt in Hildesheim with Dieter Oesterlen's new building of 1964 on the site of the former Knochenhaueramtshaus*

back once more.[51] Since 1964, a Modernist hotel and an office block have stood on the site of the building. But the memory of it has remained, and in 1984 the Council came up with a plan to demolish the modern complex and build a copy of the old monument there instead. The same thing has also happened in other places: in Mainz, where in 1978 the old façades on the market place were reconstructed; in Frankfurt, where the old houses on the east side of the Römerberg recieved a similar treatment in 1980; in Hanover, also in 1980, where the façade of the Leibniz House was reconstructed, albeit on another spot; and in Braunschweig, where in 1985 the City Council finally decided to rebuild the weighhouse that had been razed to the ground in the war.

The conservationists' criticism of this sort of reconstruction is partly based on the principles of the beginning of the twentieth century, but it would seem that these principles are beginning to lose their credibility. The question, then, is which arguments, if any, the conservationists can still deploy in their struggle against the reconstruction of vanished historical buildings.

22 *The Knochenhaueramtshaus in Hildesheim as reconstructed in 1989*

Self-seeking Romantics

Authenticity

Authenticity is quite a different thing from originality. It denotes a histori-cal object, whether or not damaged or altered, whereas the term 'originality' refers to its first state. The copy of the Villa dei Papiri in Malibu, commis-sioned by J. Paul Getty in 1974, can thus be described as the original version of the authentic first-century villa in Herculaneum. The villa in California is an attempt to give the original building a new lease on life, because the real villa in Italy is no longer original, but 'merely' authentic. In our modern parlance, only the material substance is accepted as authentic; the word can never be applied to a replica. There is no need to make things more compli-cated than they already are, and Nicole Ex was perhaps a little rash in her book, *Zo goed als oud. De achterkant van het restaureren* (1993), to introduce other forms of authenticity besides that of materials. She introduced notions such as 'conceptual authenticity' (the artist's intention), 'functional authentic-ity' (the original function of the object), 'ahistorical authenticity' (the original situation) and 'historical authenticity' (historical development). In my view, this makes matters unnecessarily complicated, because she goes on to argue that in restoring an artwork from the past one has to make a choice between these different forms of authenticity: 'One thing is at any rate certain and that is that every intervention implies a choice, which usually prioritizes one form of authenticity over another to a greater or lesser extent.' What is confusing here is that it attributes different meanings to the notion of 'authenticity'. It is assimilated by other meanings, so that virtually anything becomes permis-sible in practice. If priority is given to the aims of the artist, the restorer has no choice but to alter the existing state of the work. It is no longer authentic in the normal sense of the word but, according to Nicole Ex's definitions, the new situation, by which she means the restored intentions of the artist, can be called authentic. This is more than confusing; it is downright misleading because, taken to its logical conclusions, it would mean that a copy of the original state of the work would have the same historical value as the historical substance itself. For this reason it seems better to reserve the notion of authen-ticity for the materiality of the artwork itself.

The recent attempts to broaden the notion of authenticity out of a desire to do justice to certain cultural traditions outside Europe is another matter entirely. This subject was discussed at length in 1994 at a conference in Nara organized by the International Council on Monuments and Sites.[1] The need to encourage greater respect for local definitions of the cultural heritage and of the continuity of local restoration methods does not mean that the historic substance can no longer be called authentic. The European definition of authenticity was not called into question by the conference in Japan, but it did recommend that other matters besides the historical substance were entitled to be called authentic.

The notion of authenticity is presumably as old as the hills; it is certainly as ancient as recorded history. The belief that a historian has to base his work on authentic and thus faithful sources was already subscribed to by the Greek historian Thucydides, the author of the *History of the Peloponnesian War* (written between 431 and 410 BC), as can be seen in his statement in the twenty-second chapter of the first book: 'As for my account of the war, I have followed the principle of not adopting everything I was told, nor did I let myself be guided by my own impressions. I was either a party to the events I have described or else I wrote down what eye-witnesses told me, after checking their accounts as thoroughly as possible. Even so it was by no means easy to discover the full facts, because different eye-witnesses give different accounts of the same events.'

This passage discusses the reliability of sources and the authenticity of eye-witness reports, but the Greeks also had an idea about authentic monuments. In his text *Against Leocrates* from the fourth century BC, the Athenian statesman and writer Lycurgus wrote that in 479, just before the Battle of Plataeae in which the Persians were decisively defeated, the Greeks swore an oath that 'no single shrine that had been burned and destroyed by the barbarians would be rebuilt; instead they would be preserved as monuments of sacrilege (ὑπομνημα της των βαρβαρων ασεβειας) for future generations.' The Greek idea, then, was to leave their ruins in their authentic state for posterity. In Pausanias, too, there is a question of protecting monuments inasmuch as they are historical documents. In his *Description of Greece* of the mid-second century BC, Pausanias tells the same story as Lycurgus – that the Greeks refused to rebuild some of the temples that had been destroyed by Xerxes's army, deciding instead to preserve them for ever as 'monuments of hatred' (του εχθους υπομνηματα). 'This is why', Pausanias wrote, 'the shrines in Haliartos, and that of Hera in Athens on the road to Phaleron, and that of Demeter in Phaleron have remained until this day in their half burned-down state' (book 10, chapter 35).

Special protection being given to a building because as an authentic object it preserves something memorable from the past is therefore as old as Western civilization. Since Romanticism, however, the term 'authenticity' is also used in an entirely different way. From this period onwards it no longer relates just to the unadulterated object itself, but also to the genuine character of the expression. The new meaning of the concept originates in a different idea about the artist's work. All at once, artists who copied the work of other artists were called inauthentic. The first sense of authenticity (historical substance) is sometimes equated with the second (the artist's sincerity) although in fact they have nothing to do with each other. A recent example can be found in Geert Bekaert's critical essay on the 'maintenance of our heritage' in the twenty-first century.[2] In it he speaks of his concern about all the historical imitations that are tolerated in the world of conservationists. According to him, the cultural heritage should not be just a 'cultural make-believe world', but should remain a living thing and that can only occur if it is incorporated in present-day culture in an 'authentic, creative and critical way'. In this sentence, 'authentic' means something like 'genuine' or 'honest'.

The way in which the two meanings were combined in Romanticism can be seen for instance in the work of Stendhal. In his 'Salon de 1824', published in the *Mélanges d'Art*, he complained about the lack of sincerity in painting. What he expected from a painting was that his heart should be touched by 'quelque chose *de vrai*', by something true. In the Salon of 1824 he did not see a single painting that stood the test. He regarded the academic painting of the school of Jacques-Louis David as downright boring; all he saw in it was a copy of an imitation – 'je ne vois que la copie d'une imitation'. Stendhal called for a similar sort of sincerity in restorations of monuments. An example of this is his criticism of the restoration of the Triumphal Arch of Titus in Rome. This arch, erected in honour of this Roman emperor to celebrate his conquest of Jerusalem in 71 AD, had been reduced to a mere vestige of the ancient structure by the beginning of the nineteenth century, being incorporated into the medieval city walls as a entrance gate. The restoration, which in fact was a total reconstruction, was carried out shortly after 1810 by Giuseppe Valadier on the orders of Napoleon who had occupied the Papal State since 1809.[3] In his *Promenades dans Rome* (1828), Stendhal denounced this restoration by pointing out that it was a copy: '... il ne nous reste donc qu' une *copie* de l'arch de Titus'. According to Stendhal, an artist was required to be sincere even when he was restoring something.

John Ruskin was of the same opinion and he described in passionate terms how deep his contempt was for all forms of copying, especially imitations of classical architecture. In *The Stones of Venice* of 1851, he declared that all architecture that harked back to Roman or Greek examples was to be rejected as the expression of a false mentality. The absolute nadir in his view was the Basilica of San Giorgio Maggiore in Venice by Andrea Palladio of 1565, mainly because of the illogical and forced introduction of two tympanums (on top of each other) in the front façade. Eighteenth-century Classicism was also insufferable in his eyes, as he explained in his *Edinburgh Lectures* of 1853, using the New Town in Edinburgh as his example. He thought that Queen Street in particular was unspeakably boring, because the same elements were repeated ad infinitum. Architecture should never be monotonous: 'All things that are worth doing in art are interesting and attractive when they are done. There is no law of right which consecrates dullness.'

Imitation for Ruskin in the restoration of monuments was just as reprehensible as it was in architecture and he therefore condemned every intervention beyond simple conservation as a historical lie. Old architecture must not be encroached upon, because every intervention leads to a falsification and it is thus better to let it crumble into dust – 'its evil day must come at last; but let it come declaredly and openly, and let no dishonouring and false substitute deprive it of the funeral offices of memory', Ruskin wrote in his *Seven Lamps of Architecture* (1849).

The logic of his argument sounds implacable and almost no one took it upon himself to refute it; there were, however, practitioners who pointed out that one should respect restoration operations as a necessary evil, as it was desirable for a much-loved historical building to be preserved for the next generation. In other words, a minimal degree of deception is necessary if one is to escape the deadly clutches of time. John Ruskin refused to have anything to do with calculating compromises like this and his lack of flexibility was incomprehensible to architects commissioned to restore old buildings. On the other hand, the way that restorations were carried out around 1850 was itself so relentlessly destructive of everything that was not seen as original, that, in retrospect, Ruskin's indictment sounds much more reasonable than the arguments of the advocates of restorations. It is difficult to understand therefore why Ruskin's simple thesis did not get a broader welcome from those who led the great restoration campaigns of the nineteenth century. If an old building is seen as a historical document, as an expression of the artistry of architects from a distant past, then it would certainly seem misguided to want to correct a document like that. Why was this self-evident fact so often denied? Perhaps it was because a principle that in itself is logical easily falls prey to the hard reality of the everyday. In the eyes of the average nineteenth-century art connoisseur, a Gothic chapel that had been deformed by eroded carving or by bricked-up windows was a sorry victim of centuries of neglect and contempt. In Ruskin's day, the outward form of most medieval buildings was hardly fit to be seen any more. And it was in precisely this period that this art and architecture had become hugely popular. It is understandable, then, that lovers of this form of art saw all these dilapidated, incomplete and maltreated monuments as a public disgrace. It was only logical that they felt it necessary to spruce the Gothic architecture up here and there and make it presentable once again. On the other hand, as just said, Ruskin's reaction to the production of historical lies that were the result of the whole gamut of restorations and reconstructions is equally understandable.

What is harder to understand is that Ruskin refused to countenance any form of restoration or repair work; nor is it understandable that some architects dared to claim that they could step into the shoes of their medieval predecessors, 'de se mettre à la place de l'architecte primitif', as Eugène Viollet-le-Duc put it.[4]

In the world of conservationists as it is today, there is, I think, more understanding for Ruskin's viewpoint than for that of Viollet-le-Duc, because the latter's approach has led to authentic medieval buildings being replaced with reinterpretations. If Ruskin's advice had been followed, hardly any restoration work would have been done at all and we would still see our cathedrals in all their authenticity, complete with Baroque interiors, crumbling stone carving and half-finished towers. The charge levelled at architects like Viollet-le-Duc may then no longer be in vogue, since their work is now prized as examples of nineteenth-century architecture, but their historical lies and criminal treatment of the Baroque and of Classicism cannot of course be undone. In his *Histoire du Vandalisme* of 1958, Louis Réau complained that the choir of Notre Dame in Paris had been converted by Viollet-le-Duc into a completely empty space (nudité désolante), when he ordered the demolition in 1857 of Jules-Hardouin Mansart's choir of 1700. Viollet-le-Duc did this, moreover, out of pure contempt for the Baroque – in his report of 1843 he wrote that the Baroque interior had 'aucun intérêt sous le rapport de l'art'.

The widespread destruction of art that accompanied the restoration of medieval architecture is a grisly chapter in the history of conservation. That does not mean that reconstructions have always been conducted at the expense of the historical fabric. The completion of Cologne Cathedral may well have meant the demise of a superbly picturesque whole, but the rebuilding was carried out without any of the art being destroyed. The church was completed as a symbol of a nationalist political idea, as a sign of hope that the German nation would once again be 'one', as it had been in the Middle Ages.[5]

The 'restoration fever' the German art historian Wilhelm Lübke complained of in 1860 was in the first place a form of rehabilitation related to the need for a national identity in the new, modern Europe. It was a matter of recovering prestige and respect after the Napoleonic wars. The idea behind the repair of medieval architecture was also to restore the sanctity of historical monuments, to render justice to previous generations and settle scores after centuries of neglect. Anyone who complained about a mistaken interpretation of a Gothic profile or mentioned the decline of authentic building materials, or who called reproduction a form of rewriting history, was simply ostracized.

Today architectural reconstructions are often opposed by referring to Ruskin. There are few people today prepared defend the approach to restorations used by Viollet-le-Duc and his followers. The consensus is so general that it sometimes feels as though we have forgotten how different the situation was at that time. It is hard for us to imagine how the conservation movement could for so long have encouraged a practice of restoring buildings to their original state. It is also hard to understand what could have possessed Gilbert Scott to reconstruct the façade of the north transept of Westminster Abbey down to the minutest details rather than respecting the eighteenth-century restoration and carrying out repairs where needed. 'Of the original details ... it is nearly impossible to form anything like a correct idea', Scott wrote in 1861 about the restoration of this façade. As a result,

23 *The Drakenburg House on the Oudegracht in Utrecht (1958)*

24 *Drakenburg after 1969*

virtually everything in it is based on the learned guesses of the nineteenth-century master builder.[6]

The failure of present-day conservationists to understand anything of why architects like Viollet-le-Duc or Scott felt compelled to restore buildings to their original form, is possibly due to the long-running campaign against all the architects who wanted to make the past more beautiful than it had ever been. This battle made Ruskin's adherents deaf and blind to the motives of the 'reconstructionists' who, as just said, had until recently the total support of conservationist organizations. It is, for example, by no means easy to comprehend why in 1969 Theunes Haakma Wagenaar gave the Drakenburg House on the Oudegracht in Utrecht a medieval stepped gable once again. The nineteenth-century façade fitted into the cityscape as it had developed historically and its archaeological reconstruction now looks curiously unfashionable. What can he have intended with this reconstruction? Did he want to display the medieval origins of this city castle as a tourist attraction and to add to the glory of the city? I suspect that this and similar reconstructions were the result of a piece of successful historical research that he couldn't resist putting into practice straight away. The discovery of some medieval remains in a city is a festive event that contributes to one's understanding of local history and should therefore remain visible, no matter how badly it fits into the city image as it has developed. Presumably architects like Scott were so under the spell of the image they had formed of Gothic architecture that they felt the need to foreground their archaeological discoveries in practice. Was it not their duty to resurrect the Gothic style in a situation where it was in a state of ruin everywhere? The urge to revive this almost-forgotten beauty was much more important than the documentary value of what still remained of Gothic architecture. Was it wrong to correct the eighteenth century's distorted image of the Gothic style, because that would mean failing to do justice to archaeology as a science, or because the Romantic wanderer would then be deprived of his 'master's signature'?

In the modern age, Eugène Viollet-le-Duc might have replied, one works in a much more motivated way; one's personal style is guided by the objective results of scientific analyses. He claimed to understand the Gothic style better than the architects of the medieval period themselves. Modern science, precisely because it was so far removed from the Gothic in time, could make stylistic analyses of the different schools of architecture and so accumulate all the knowledge needed for a faithful restoration – to restore to life, that is, the deformed architecture according to the prescripts of the Gothic master builders. Nobody said it in so many words, but the restorers may well have seen Ruskin as someone who had become stuck in the past, who had turned his back on the modern age, even rejecting the achievements of modern historical studies.

Extremists

How could Viollet-le-Duc not have understood Ruskin's ideas about restoration? Maybe part of the explanation lies in his faith in historical scholarship. Artistic principles, as he saw it, remained applicable for ever – 'leurs principes restent vrais à travers les siècles, l'homme est toujours le même', he wrote on page six of his *Entretiens sur l'Architecture* of 1863. It does not matter, then, when something was built as long as it was done in accordance with the right principles.

Ruskin and Viollet-le-Duc had in common that they both advocated extreme positions and it was probably due to their enormous influence on ideas about restoration that their views attracted more attention that the much more reasonable viewpoint of someone like Edward A. Freeman of 1851, or that which the French governmental advisory body, the *Comité des Arts et Monuments*, proposed in 1839. Freeman, who was a historian, was impressed to a degree by Ruskin's rhetorical passion, but he straight away distanced himself from Ruskin by arguing that the replacement of dilapidated parts was a necessary evil ('if any portion of the fabric is dangerous, it must be rebuilt'). Earlier than Freeman, the *Comité* had explained that while it was better to preserve than to replace, there was nothing wrong with normal maintenance.[7] Should the replacement of damaged parts all at once have to be condemned, just because Romanticism had discovered the medieval stone carver? Should an ancient monument be left to fall into rubble out of respect for the inimitable signature of the master? For many people, this sacrifice on the altar of Romanticism was too much to stomach.

John Ruskin, of course, did not see it as his business to take a closer look at the problems that arose with the restoration of deformed monuments and he had no interest in putting Edward Freeman in his place. This makes his argument less relevant to the question of how far the notion of 'authenticity' is useful in conservation. Ruskin said nothing about later alterations to monuments. Are these also authentic? Is the signature of the great-grandson of the master also sacrosanct? He preferred to leave problems like that to others.

Later Changes

How could Ruskin's ideas and those of Freeman be reconciled? How could justice be done to authenticity while still insisting on the need to restore historical buildings? According to William Morris, this was achieved by having a restoration carried out 'in the spirit of one's age'. The basis for this solution lay in the foundation charter of the *Society for the Protection of Ancient Buildings*, published in 1877 in the magazine *Builder*. It included the statement that restoration was a nineteenth-century invention and that in previous ages there was no such thing as 'forgery', because additions were always 'wrought in the unmistakable fashion of the time'. In this way, William Morris hoped to be able to get around the inevitable downfall of historical monuments by carrying out repairs in contemporary forms.

But this was maybe a pseudo-solution that was worse than the evil it was intended to cure, because the old form was no longer preserved even as a copy. At least with a reproduction, one can see the historical form; when a new-fangled form is put in its place, the very memory of the old one is erased. Despite this disadvantage, this creative form of restoration maintained its appeal in conservation circles. It was however a plausible solution for a dilemma, because on the one hand, lip service was paid to Ruskin's prohibition and on the other, the monument was saved from ruin.

The thesis in the manifesto of 1877 that 'forgery' did not occur in earlier ages because everyone then worked in the spirit of his own age was not entirely true, but it did sound convincing. In Holland, Jan Kalf, who was appointed director of the Netherlands Department for Conservation in 1918, believed in it unreservedly. In his introduction to the *Principles* (Grondbeginselen) published in 1917, he wrote that in previous ages restoration had been carried out 'in all frankness', by which was meant that 'we do it in the fashion of our own times'. The Modernists' solution also caught on in Germany, especially with art historians such as Georg Dehio and Cornelius Gurlitt. In 1905, the *Konservator* Georg Hager of Munich made the case for creative restoration in a lecture, 'Über Denkmalpflege und moderne Kunst' ('On Conservation and Modern Art'). According to Hager, it was 'nicht um Stil, sondern um Kunst dreht sich die Frage' (the issue was one of art not of style). In the same year, the German art historian Georg Dehio proclaimed the same notion.[8]

The suggestion that restorations in the past were always carried out in the style of one's own time was misleading; there are enough examples of the opposite being achieved, despite the great difference in architectural periods, as, for instance, the historicizing completion of the west tower of the Dom in Xanten in Germany, the stylistic unity in Cologne Cathedral and Westminister Abbey. After the Middle Ages, the classicist rule of *conformità* provided a solid basis for stylistic adaptations. There are enough examples of historicism in pre-nineteenth-century architecture to show that William Morris, Georg Dehio, Jan Kalf and their numerous adherents were in this instance only telling half of the truth.[9]

One of the few dissidents was Paul Clemen of the *Rheinische Denkmalpflege*. In his forthright dissertation of 1933, he distanced himself in no uncertain terms from Dehio's position of 'konservieren, nicht restaurieren' – even calling it 'eine schönklingende innerlich schiefe und unwahre Phrase' (a sentence that sounded impressive, but was inwardly misguided and untrue). According to Clemen, Dehio was wrong because one cannot draw any clear distinction between conservation and restoration. What is one supposed to do when part of an old building had fallen into ruin and has to be replaced? Are you supposed to say 'fiat justitia, pereat monumentum'? Again, according to him, it is a Romantic error to proclaim that monuments should be left to 'die in beauty', because far too many things have perished and it is specifically the duty of conservationists to preserve monuments for as long as possible.[10]

What Clemen wrote in 1933 doesn't sound particularly shocking, but the fact that he felt obliged to ram home such an obvious idea speaks volumes. It is, however, rather strange that he made no attempt to put Dehio's 'error' in a historical light and expose the pedigree of these notions. Perhaps he did not realize that the notion of 'authenticity' had acquired a dual meaning in the course of the nineteenth century. It no longer related simply to the object itself, to the historical structural material, but also to its artistic quality, to the genuine character of the expression.

Even if it is an unwritten law in present-day conservation that later changes are also authentic and deserve to be protected, in practice it is not always easy to implement this law. Take, for instance, Jan Duiker's Zonnestraal Sanatorium in Hilversum, built in 1928. With a masterpiece like this, who would want to retain the unforgivably crude later changes? The wide aluminium window sections have destroyed the beauty of the design. The original slender lightness of the small iron sections summons up an entirely new world, one of modern means of transport, such as airplanes and ocean liners. The unrestored building remains the authentic monument, but apparently no one wants to keep it that way. Let us go back to 1928 then and get rid of all the later additions, because these have, to use Viollet-le-Duc's words, 'aucun intérêt sous le rapport de l'art'.

Even if one treats the concept of 'authenticity' as having only one meaning, namely that which refers to the historical substance itself, this does not help us solve the question of how to restore historic buildings. The question remains how far completions or additions are worth preserving. It

25 The Zonnestraal Sanatorium by Jan Duiker in Hilversum in 1928

26 Zonnestraal in 1986

is arguable that conservation should in the first instance retain the ancient monuments in the state they have been handed down to us – the authentic state that is; it is by no means obvious however that conservation should not be permitted to remove later additions and to reconstruct elements.

Pinnacles and Coach Doors

The imitation Gothic pinnacles installed over the choir of the Domkerk in Utrecht in 1982 are presumably not yet treated as part of the authentic architectural stock of the church. To be honest they should never have been added to the church, because it isn't even known if these pinnacles ever existed, but they do not deform the church. They are an expression of concern, even if a mistaken, exaggerated, and above all, unhistorical form of concern.

This cannot be said of the coach doors installed about a century ago in the seventeenth-century lower front of the house at Noard 5 in Workum. These doors were certainly authentic, but were also an anomaly, not to mention a crude encroachment. The idea of the pinnacles was to give additional ornament to the outward architectural form of the church, whereas the doors were a functional alteration introduced without any eye for the integrity of the front of this dwelling. It might make sense then to disqualify doors like this from being covered by building regulations, even if they do date from as long ago as the end of the nineteenth century. That wasn't what happened however in 1979, when the Department for Conservation had to take a decision about the reconstruction of the front in Workum. The owner, the Hendrick de Keyser Society, wanted the doors to be replaced by a reconstruction of the former front, but the Department prohibited this, arguing that the doors had to be preserved as part of the architectural history of the premises. The society appealed against this prohibition. In the appeal, the society's lawyer stated that the Historic Buildings Act of 1988 was passed with the aim of 'preventing monuments from being destroyed or damaged, not to give the minister and his advisors the last word about how the restoration was to be carried out, rather that entrusting matters to the good judgement of the rightful owners, especially when the latter were only concerned to ensure a good restoration of monuments and when they have proved able to carry out such an end with the advice of experts'. After this worthy if wordy period, it is not surprising that the official concerned beat a hasty retreat and withdrew his objections to the reconstruction. The viewpoint of the Department for Conservation was admittedly not entirely unfounded, because it was based on the belief that the entire architectural history of a building was of interest, including the alteration to the front. But it had to make way for that of a society which was confident of acting in the spirit of conservation, namely by restoring a monument that had been violated. In Workum it was regarded as improper to preserve the authentic. The doors were removed, because their historic and artistic value was also not that great. 'Coach doors' were really a polite name for what were in fact not much more than barn doors.

27 Noard 5 in Workum with the coach doors (1964)   *28 Noard 5 after the restoration (1986)*

Seen in this way, the Department might have done better to oppose the addition of the fantasy pinnacles in Utrecht rather than granting them a subsidy, because the choir of the Domkerk would then have remained authentic. It would perhaps also have been well advised not to force the issue in Workum even though the principles it was defending were correct. No one could have objected if the authorities had rejected the pinnacles as redundant prettifications. All they would have needed to do would be to point to the lack of sufficient historical evidence. Why didn't they do so? In retrospect, I think that at that time the Department had no problem with an approach that had a pedigree going back to Viollet-le-Duc, the aim of which was to create an ideal architectural image. In Workum the position adopted was from the start impossible to maintain. It was in a tradition that went back to John Ruskin and was thus an extreme one. From these two examples, it can be seen that conservationists are still torn between two extremes. In this grey area of doubt about what can and what cannot be deemed acceptable, there are plenty of possibilities.

Modern Archaeology

In Japan, authenticity, according to Nobuo Ito, means something like originality or trustworthiness, a notion that is somewhat divergent from the

Western sense.[11] In the West, only the object itself can be called authentic – nothing else, not even a perfect copy. In Japan this distinction hardly exists. What people are concerned with there is mainly whether the reconstruction is trustworthy in a scholarly sense. This is a big issue currently in Japan, because the building of copies of lost architecture seems to have become a national sport which, according to Adolf W. Ehrentraut, has mainly to do with nostalgia for the powerful empire that Japan once was.[12] These reproductions are often based on little more than scanty finds. This was the case with the reconstruction of the Yakushiji monastery buildings in Nara. The monastery comprised a number of buildings surrounding the Golden Hall, founded in 710. This hall was later destroyed on various occasions, but was rebuilt each time, most recently in 1852. For a long while there was no trace of the remaining buildings. Nonetheless, some years ago the National Research Institute for the Cultural Heritage of Japan decided to restore this entire complex to its eighth-century state. In 1997, a journalist of the Japanese daily *Yomiuri*, Asami Nagai, asked the director of this institute, Migaku Tanaka, how he could defend a reconstruction based on so little material evidence. The director replied by saying that the reconstruction really had an educational goal, that of illustrating the history of Japan. The journalist's question was about historical trustworthiness whereas the director's reply referred to national history.[13]

Just as Eugène Viollet-le-Duc transformed the ruins of Carcassonne between 1852 and 1879 into a complete medieval fortified city, a few years ago Saddam Hussein ordered the ruins of the palace of King Nebuchadnezzar in Babylon to be converted into a scale model. The Dutch journalist Joris Luyendijk visited the palace in 1999 and, after some initial scepticism, he had to admit that this Iraqi version of Disneyland appealed more to one's imagination than did a field strewn with rubble.[14] Giving a vanished building a new lease of life is done at the expense of archaeology as science, because the authentic remains are incorporated into the new development and this hampers any future research. But what applied to the archaeologists of Saddam Hussein was also true of the reconstruction of the Stoa of Attalos in Athens of 150 BC that was reconstructed in 1956 by the American School of Classical Studies.[15] Seen this way, there appears to be little difference here between West and East.

Archaeologists, too, can get carried away by scholarly fantasies. According to a recent study by John K. Papadopoulos, the reconstructions that Arthur Evans carried out in concrete in Knossos between 1920 and 1930 were, to an important extent, the product of the lurid imagination of the great British archaeologist. For instance, there is no evidence whatsoever for his thesis that there was once a royal palace in Knossos and there has also never been any such thing as a 'Minoan culture'. The entire project was Evans's invention, including all the names he gave to the different rooms.[16]

The reconstructions in Athens, Babylon and Nara are three-dimensional historical pictures with educational and tourist purposes. Reconstructions like these have to be able to withstand the charge of archaeological

29 *The Stoa of Attalos in Athens (reconstruction of 1965)*

trustworthiness. In this regard, they diverge somewhat from the definition Viollet-le-Duc gave of the concept of 'restauration' in his *Dictionnaire Raisonnée* of 1866. According to him, restoration was an activity that has the goal of restoring an old building to its perfect state – a state that possibly never existed in the past ('rétablir dans un état complet qui peut n'avoir jamais existé à un moment donné').[17] Viollet-le-Duc wanted to idealize the past on the basis of the picture he had gained of it during his studies. But for his Japanese, Iraqi and American colleagues, being true to history was the priority. Viollet-le-Duc's 'modern' definition would seem to have ended up in the dustbin of history, since even tourists want to be confronted with the real, unvarnished past and not some ideal image. For a Romantic rationalist like Viollet-le-Duc, architecture was a method, an ensemble of artistic and technical conventions and techniques that can be learned and applied, so that a project designed in 1250 can still be implemented in 1850 in the same way as a musical score can always be played. If this description of his ideas is correct, then one can perhaps also appreciate that he attached less importance to any so-called later alterations. All that mattered for him was the essence of the work of art. With regard to the later alterations or traces of decay, these have come about more or less haphazardly over time, and cannot be treated as in any way countervailing the original concept.

Bad-mannered Buildings

Artistic Insults

There are people who think that art is supposed to subvert existing conventions and that artists, if they feel it is necessary, may be permitted the freedom to insult others. The odour of artistic sanctity that artists sometimes claim for themselves has resulted in the making of scribbles on reproductions of old art something that can be presented to the general public in the context of exhibitions in museums. I am referring to the *Übermahlungen*, or Over-paintings, by Arnulf Rainer. Not long ago, this artist's scrawls were exhibited in the Lenbachhaus in Munich. The art critic Sacha Bronwasser wrote in *de Volkskrant* (2 October 2001) that the series of scrawled-on artworks was 'brilliant', and, she added: 'On each occasion Rainer attempts to convert the essence of an image into colour and line.' These lines are full of emotions, she explains, and 'at times they seem uncontrolled'. Sometimes they are so uncontrolled that the original scene, one by Giotto or Botticelli, for example, is hardly visible. Rainer's scrawls are a contemporary form of commentary on old artworks. It is not a coincidence that they look as though they were made by a four-year-old child, because it is precisely the obsessive ferocity and cruelty of an infant that these scrawls convey that make Rainer's images so unpleasant. It is as if the artist wants to subject the unsuspecting museum visitor to a mental shock. His aim, maybe, is to unmask a certain sort of art appreciation as a lazy and self-indulgent form of enjoyment. The predictable respect that the average museum visitor feels for the art of the old masters has to be undermined and the behaviour of a child that spares nothing and no one is a useful means to this end.

It is possible that the way that Arnulf Rainer and his sympathizers deploy their work to launch an assault on the museums with the aim of both insulting and educating has an influence on contemporary architectural codes of practice. There are good manners and bad in architecture. Jacob van Campen's town hall building on Dam Square in Amsterdam is rude in the sense that the enormous block does not fit in the intricate structure of the medieval city. Suddenly it rose there in 1665 like a massive, unmanageable and arrogant castle in the midst of the tiny wooden houses of ordinary citizens. Its disproportionate size strikes one immediately; one only needs

30 *Les deux plateaux by Daniel Buren in the Cour d' Honneur of the Palais Royal in Paris (1986)*

to picture how Amsterdam would have looked in the mid-seventeenth century. Today we see it with different eyes – eyes that have learned that such disparities can disrupt an urban body. In the seventeenth century the town hall was considered one of the wonders of the world and one assumes that most of the city's residents took pride in it. They probably viewed the scale of this building as an architectural achievement. But later, especially at the turn of the twentieth century, when increasing numbers of similar large blocks began to appear, residents began to realize that this increase in scale formed a danger to the familiar urban image. After foreign tourists and famous architects had compared the seventeenth-century canal city, with the beauty of Venice, the time had come to devise ways of protecting the historic city.

Some people, including many artists and connoisseurs, behave as though the development sketched here never took place. They think that what was possible in the seventeenth century should also be possible now. Their preferred model is the vainglorious town hall with its uninhibited allusions to the masters of the Renaissance, rather than the civilized and restrained architecture of someone like Adriaan Dortsman in the same century or the work of the Van Gendt brothers in the nineteenth century. Still less do they recall the academic traditions of the eighteenth and nineteenth centuries; all that interests them is the architecture that broke with these traditions.

That is why in his article in the Dutch newspaper, *NRC Handelsblad*, (13 September 1991) the expert on modern art Rudi Fuchs got so angry with people who, when offered commissions, cannot make up their minds straightway, but first have to wonder whether their design will fit in properly with its surroundings, after which they 'want to weigh the pros and cons all over again'. Fuchs was referring to Ger Lataster's ceiling painting in the Mauritshuis in The Hague, an abstract composition that, according to these musty 'calculators', doesn't fit into the seventeenth-century palace, but that to Fuchs's great glee was still carried out. Now you can see, he wrote, 'that even after Cornelis Troost people have still produced paintings. This feels like a good lesson for many museum visitors.'

The lesson, then, is that history doesn't stand still and that museum visitors should not only come and look at the paintings of Cornelis Troost, but also at modern art. What Fuchs presumably found galling is that the average visitor would still rather look at a work by Troost than one by Lataster. Fuchs feels very let down by this and wants to teach the visitor a lesson because, in his view, the average visitor is stupid. This lesson would also have to be an 'in-your-face' one, with the great entrance hall of this seventeenth-century palace as the proper place to teach it. Fuchs also seems to think that Ger Lataster's modern painting can claim a place there, confident that in a hundred years time it will still be prized as a twentieth-century contribution to the history of the Mauritshuis. After all, the objects that we protect today as historical monuments were also new once – the first Baroque building was also viewed as a curiosity in a society used to a more balanced Renaissance style. Baroque was an innovative trend in the arts and the label 'innovative' is enough to confer a sacrosanct status on an artwork. Why did Rudi Fuchs pick on Troost and not someone else? I think it is because Troost is still seen as the representative of boring eighteenth-century bourgeois art – exactly the opposite of what is thought of as art since the rise of Modernism in the last century.

A comparable example of the promotion of modern art in an historic building is *Les deux plateaux*, an artwork installed in the Cour d'Honneur of the Palais Royal in Paris. It consists of 260 striped segments of columns that Daniel Buren designed in 1986, commissioned by the Minister of Culture, Jack Lang, for the courtyard of Cardinal Richelieu's townhouse built in 1629 after a design by Jacques Le Mercier. Anne of Austria lived there later, and in 1672 it was taken over by Philippe d'Orleans. According to Janneke Wesseling, this is a case of an extremely successful work of art: 'it is definitely not an ugly artwork as its opponents have averred. It is in fact a huge success.' Its superiority, according to her, is above all due to the fact that Buren, as a Marxist, was in full revolt against the establishment.[1] In France there was a great deal of criticism of the idea of adding anything to the courtyard of one of the major monuments of the seventeenth century – a design that was already quite outstanding with its beautiful colonnades. The greatest complaint was that this was already a perfect space and that Daniel Buren's columns destroy that perfection. Wasn't it a little bit childish to make a rebellious gesture in 1986 against an establishment of 1629?

It is curious that designers are still interested in rebelling against the

31 Office blocks by F.J. van Gool on the Weteringschans, Amsterdam (1979)

establishment, as though nothing has changed since the Romantic Movement first emerged. 'We are tired of seeing Palladio and other historical masks', Coop Himmelblau said in 1980, 'because we don't want architecture to exclude everything that is disquieting. We want architecture to have more; we want architecture that bleeds, that exhausts, that revolves, and even breaks; architecture that burns, that stings, that rips, that tears under stress. Architecture should be cavernous, fiery, smooth, hard, angular, alluring, repelling, wet, dry, throbbing.'[2]

'Fuck the Context'

If he hadn't told me himself, I would never have known that the two office towers from 1979 opposite the Rijksmuseum in Amsterdam are actually supposed to express scorn. Some years ago I was informed by the man responsible for these buildings, the former chief government architect F.J. van Gool, that he believed that the man who built the Rijksmuseum, P.J.H. Cuypers, had made a hopeless mess of it. This was why Van Gool had installed those pinched little windows on the front looking out on the museum. He wanted his towers to make an ugly face at a building that he saw as ugly. In order to avoid engaging in any dialogue with his despised neighbour across the street, he designed two recalcitrant, severe-looking blocks. That is why their little windows stare so scornfully and standoffishly at the water. They are blocks that utter imprecations and for this reason they don't suit this civilized canal where its neighbours always display so much nineteenth-century courtesy. Shortly after they were built on the Weteringschans, the poet Gerrit Komrij cursed back at them in his column 'Het Boze Oog' ('The Angry Eye') in the weekly *Vrij Nederland* (3 November 1979). He said that F.J. van Gool was a misanthropist who deliberately made ugly buildings because he thinks that something beautiful is worthless. Pleasure is a sin. Komrij quoted an interview with the architect, in which he said that 'what I made there is a solo of 312 windows' with the result that, 'a slight confusion is created and the surroundings are put in perspective, things that I needed to do justice to both the building and its surroundings. I have provided the building with sufficient ego but not so much as to deflate its surroundings.' Komrij called this 'twaddle'. The Rijksmuseum was also mentioned in this interview and Van Gool's comment was that his 'project did not engage in any discussion with the Rijksmuseum; after all there was nothing to discuss with it, don't you see?'

Is it not strange that the hatred of nineteenth-century Revival styles has lasted a whole century? What were the motives for this hatred? What is so ugly about all the patriotic carving on the façades of the Rijksmuseum? Moreover, the layout of the museum is in fact very traditional – at least its ground plan is. Unfortunately I was born too late to understand what it was that architects like Van Gool found so infuriating about the nineteenth century. And maybe I was born too early to be able to understand why the response to nineteenth-century ugliness needed to be ugly itself. Why didn't Van Gool design a beautiful eye-pleasing building to show that he was a much better architect than Pierre Cuypers? It must have been because he didn't give a damn about beautiful architecture and because he also couldn't care less that his towers made the Weteringschans a bit more ugly. The Modernists never thought twice about whether architecture fitted into its surroundings. Rem Koolhaas's recent motto, 'fuck the context', made its first appearance in European culture a long time ago, albeit in different phrasing, with the birth of Functionalism and all that that implied.

Compared with the tyranny of the modern concrete giants in the centre of Brussels and London, the situation in Amsterdam is still perhaps fairly favourable, but for local residents, each new project means a new threat. Take, for instance, the letter by H.M. van Emden, a member of the staff of the Royal Academy of Sciences in Amsterdam in the *NRC Handelsblad* (9 January 1990) about the new head office building of the Bank of Pierson, Heldring and Pierson on the Rokin which he called a 'terrifying example' of the city council's attitude towards the historic city. He described this building as a 'red monster, huge, massive, pompous, monotonous and clashing with its surroundings.' It was indeed only the last of a line of colossi lacking in all style to be built on the Rokin. Some years previously, the grey hulk of the Rokin Plaza had been erected opposite the bank on the site of the Polen Hotel that had been burned down, while next to the bank was a large boring edifice, Cees Dam's Options Exchange. These are all build-

32 Office building in Prague by Frank Gehry (1996)

ROMANTIC MODERNISM

ings that behave like thugs, impudently occupying a spot where they don't belong and where they don't fit in literally or figuratively. Sometimes they are so exceptionally ugly and the hatred felt for them is so great that the city curses them collectively. That is what occurred with the Burgemeester Tellegenhuis, better known locally as the 'Maupoleum', after the property developer, Maup Caransa. This building, built in 1972, has been awarded an honourable place in Jaap Huisman's survey of the fifty ugliest buildings in the Netherlands. He thought that the Maupoleum was 'presumably the most hated building in the centre of Amsterdam'. [3] The prize for the second place should perhaps go to the Nederlandse Bank building on the Frederiksplein, built in 1968 by M.F. Duintjer. A circular tower was added to it in 1990 – something that the architecture critic Max van Rooy felt obliged to deal with at great length. He wrote about the top of this 'garish, fat, round tower', a design of J. Abma, that it 'had been sawn off at a bit of an angle … giving it a low forehead and we all know what a low forehead means.' The feet of the building are not even visible so that we don't know if it can stay up on its own legs, so that 'it stands there, a little nonplussed at its own sudden appearance, reflecting the light like a cheap gob-stopper dreaming it is a crystal ball.' The bank building, Max van Rooy concluded, was a weird-looking camel with two misshapen humps, 'a giant invalid animal, but one that still looks as though it has plenty of mileage.' [4] This remains to be seen however, because in June 2002, the Dutch TV impresario Wim T. Schippers floated a proposal in his programme to have the bank demolished and to rebuild on its site the highly popular music hall palace, the Paleis van Volksvlijt that burned down in 1929. This plan was applauded not only by the essayist Rudy Kousbroek, as was to be expected, but also by the celebrated urban planner Riek Bakker, who was the last person one would have expected, and by the architect Moshe Schwartz.

Apparently the current vogue among artists, architects and contractors is not to give a damn about the urban surroundings of their buildings. The authorities and organizations responsible for the fate of historical areas sing a completely different tune, but their story is hardly heard. Their formal statements remain virtually unread, as one can see from the fact that they have provoked no discussion. In 1975, for instance. the *Declaratie van Amsterdam* was published. It states that, while one cannot totally exclude new developments in historical city centres, they should only be allowed on condition that 'the new building is designed to fit in with its surroundings with regard to proportions, design, size and scale, and that traditional materials must be used'. [5]

This recommendation roughly amounts to encouraging historicizing new developments. In the *Washington Charter*, a declaration about the protection of historical cities of 1987 by the ICOMOS (the International Council on Monuments and Sites) a degree of artistic self-restraint is also recommended: 'When it is necessary to construct new buildings or adapt existing ones, the existing spatial layout should be respected, especially in terms of scale and lot size.'

33 Haas Haus in Vienna by Hans Hollein (1990)

Pious statements like this are in strident contrast with the reality. This is not due to the powerlessness of the responsible authorities, but rather to the circumstance that many of their own architects and advisors totally disagree with such declarations. This in turn is due to the conservation movement having become fixated since the 1970s on the idea that a historical city only has a future when its architecture follows the trends.

Architects are sometimes like top fashion designers and when they become world-famous they behave like superstars. The American architect Frank Gehry is a case in point. Mildred Friedman, the author of the foreword to his book, *Architecture + process. gehry talks* (1999), writes, presumably with his approval, 'More than any other architect of his generation, Frank Gehry is an innovator whose vision reaches beyond the accepted aesthetic and technical constraints of twentieth-century architecture.' His vision, it would seem, is much greater than that of other architects, who are unfortunately still bogged down in Modernist traditions. Gehry is thus not exactly blessed with modesty and perhaps that is only right and proper with a famous artist. Nonetheless when he is building in a historical city, he would only be showing normal respect if he were to take account of the surroundings. Gehry's book also discusses the office building of the Nationale Nederlanden insurance company from 1996 that he built in the historic part of Prague on the banks of the Moldau. The design is explained by the architect himself, 'My effort is to work contextually, but not to pander to tradition.' He says that he is guided by other principles, 'living in my time instead of in the past.' He describes at length how difficult it was to design something on this nineteenth-century quayside that he could feel satisfied with. He eventually succeeded, he writes, but unfortunately people like Vaclav Havel didn't understand him. These people regarded themselves as European intellectuals, he argued, and felt an intense dislike for postmodernism. When they got a chance to see his design, they thought that what they were looking at was indeed a case of postmodernism and started lecturing him: 'They didn't understand where I was going.' If you design an ordinary building, then you comply with people's expectations, but 'as soon as somebody does something unexpected everybody gets angry. Nevertheless, we won – fifty-eight to forty-two.' Frank Gehry sees his contribution to the architectural culture of Prague as a sort of football match and it has to be said that this office building with its agile curves does have something of a sports mentality. What of course wasn't mentioned in this gifted artist's book was the angry letters in newspapers and the negative criticisms in the professional journals, for instance, by Zdenek Jiran in *Architekt*.

Not far from Prague is Vienna and in that city another modern building has occupied a prominent position in the historical centre. I am referring to the Haas Haus, built in 1990 opposite the cathedral of St. Stephen and designed by Hans Hollein. In the 1998 *Michelin Guide* one reads, 'People who object to it fail to understand that by his bold treatment of volume, Hollein has restored vastness to the junction between Stephansplatz and Stock-im Eisen-Platz. By following the old curving lines of the area, he has opened up the view of the Gothic church visible on arrival from Graben.' The pedantic remark in the guide is maybe not quite accurate. It is not true to say that the view of the cathedral from the Graben has been improved by Hollein, because the 'old curving lines' were there already and didn't need designing all over again. That is the first point; the second is that most of the criticism pointed out that the design of the new Haas Haus, this 'Glass monster surrounded by historical buildings' as it has often been called, has pretensions that are all its own, so that does not fit well in a sensitive spot like this. Hollein's design may well be a work of genius, but it was not spared by the Viennese public whose taste tends to be somewhat conservative. The buildings directly opposite the cathedral are probably more acceptable to the general public, although they are examples of a totally unimaginative architecture of the 1950s reconstruction period. These boring façades are admittedly not worth a second glance and hence they are in a certain sense invisible. There is nothing here to catch the eye and that is perhaps their only merit. The Haas Haus is an artistic scream violating the silence of this historic square. It is hardly surprising that the Viennese find it upsetting.

There is a 'machine à habiter' on the Rietveld, a street in Delft, that was built in 1996 and designed by the architectural firm of Cepezed. This house is not an assault on its surroundings; instead, it is both dignified and distinguished-looking. The design displays a restrained modernism that is averse to

34 Rietveld 58, Delft by Cepezed architects (1996)

any bragging; the simplicity of its design makes it beautiful. Some people were admittedly unhappy with its presence here, but there were also some positive responses, including one from the *Heemschut* journal (October 1996) that is reputed to be notoriously conservative. According to a former member of the Historic Monuments Commission, Wiek Röling, this house is an instructive example for conservationists. He felt that it fitted well into the historic city and called it 'peaceful' and 'pleasant and with good scale and proportions'. Moreover, he said, 'it belongs simply to our times, but without any of those funny roofs that only serve to disguise the date when it was built.' Wiek Röling's opinion was welcomed by the conservation department in Delft, but that enthusiasm was not echoed by C.J. Bardet, who was employed at the time as an architect by the Department for Conservation. He confessed to being taken aback by the positive responses in *Heemschut*. According to him, this Modernist house was an encroachment on the beauty of the city and he didn't understand how the local conservation department could possibly have approved of it. He saw his world collapsing around him. The whole essence of conservation was turned upside-down by this development and, worse still, this dastardly blow had come from a former member of the Historic Monuments Commission, Wiek Röling.

The house to the left of the Modernist house is an imitation historical monument. The original house had listed status, but at a certain point it caved in and was then removed from the list of historic monuments. It was then rebuilt entirely in the old style. The official from the Department for Conservation who had dealt with both requests – Cepezed's Modernist

35 Office building by Ben van Berkel, Nieuwezijds Kolk, Amsterdam (1996)

house and the imitation old adjacent house – did not see any problem in
the confrontation between the Modernist design and the historical buildings fronting on the canal. After all, there was a gap that needed filling and,
in his view, it was not the task of the department to judge the artistic aspect
of the design. He said that the modern house was a thing of its time and
that he did not feel uncomfortable with it. He was, however, bothered by
the adjoining property on the left, because it was only a poor copy of the
monument that had been lost. The owner had also asked for a grant but of
course he didn't get one. This official is a member of the modern generation, brought up with the Modernist movement in the 1970s, while Bardet
still adhered to the notions he had held before the Second World War.
Their ideas were diametrically opposed, as developments in Delft showed.
Just because someone upholds notions that do not tally with the Modernist
legacy, however, one cannot assume that they are incorrect. In defence of
Bardet, one could argue that it was more the Department for Conservation's task to preserve historical urban situations than to build new, modern
architecture in historic cities, no matter how appealing that modern architecture may be. And the Cepezed house is undoubtedly beautiful.

A much less innocent instance was the state of affairs around the building in 1996 of the glass 'ship' on the Nieuwezijds Kolk in Amsterdam by
Ben van Berkel. Later on, this architect explained that his aim was 'to respond in a contemporary way' to the existing surroundings and that his
building 'cuts across the historic situation in a virtually organic fashion so
that the existing developments now stand in a new context'. The client, the

ABN-AMRO Bank, had requested a building that would fit in with the 'swinging' character of Amsterdam and the bank was presumably pleased with the result. The city authorities certainly were enthusiastic, with the exception of the municipal conservation department. In 1994 the Provincial Authority of North Holland described the plan as 'unique' and praised the way that it was 'adapted to the existing historical built environment'.[6] In *de Volkskrant* (24 August 1996) Hilde de Haan and Ids Haagsma wrote about the building as follows, 'Both in terms of proportions and details, and varying use of materials, Van Berkel makes the most of the environment, ensuring that the building is anchored in the historical city. But viewed as a whole, it looks somewhat lachrymose and garish like a belated outburst of the Amsterdam School. It's something we will have to get used to … but that shouldn't take long and over a couple of years we'll hardly notice it. This isn't any sample of new architecture; it's just good old Amsterdam in a new guise.' The architecture critic Bernhard Hulsman wrote in the *NRC Handelsblad* (15 October 1998) that the new building had been reviewed in euphoric terms by virtually all the critics, except for Max van Rooy. In retrospect, Hulsman wrote that Van Rooy was admittedly right: 'Van Berkel's design suffers from the fatal mistake that a building entirely composed of higgledy-piggledy shapes is appropriate in between the numerous small old Amsterdam premises with all their different gables … Van Berkel's compulsive liking for crookedness had taken on such absurd proportions here that even junkies only enter this shopping centre when they are desperate.' In order to make this huge edifice possible, four listed houses had to be pulled down and the zoning plan had to be altered. The bodies concerned did their utmost to ensure that everything had a smooth passage, as Geurt Brinkgreve tells us in his book, *Amsterdam verdient beter (Amsterdam deserves better)*, of 1997. The objections of the conservation department and the city building inspectorate were overruled on this occasion with methods that had the odour of an abuse of power.

In 1999, shortly after the Dutch capital had been graced with this architectural disaster, the calm and extremely beautiful provincial city of Zutphen was terrorized by the sudden appearance on the scene of a green erection, resembling a dragon, on the otherwise tranquil 's-Gravenhof. Its construction was a commission by the city Council and the design was by the firm of Rau & Partners and its aim was to provide premises for various municipal departments. It was favourably reviewed in *de Volkskrant* (19 March 1999) by Ids Haagsma and Hilde de Haan. They wrote that, in a city that hung timorously onto its past, this building was 'fearlessly modern'. 'However', they concluded, 'it is a Modernism that emanates respect for its surroundings, and relates to it in exemplary fashion in its measurements and proportions.' Thomas Rau's design was inspired by anthroposophy – by organic forms, that is. He had previously worked with Ton Alberts and Max van Huut on the ING Bank building in South-East Amsterdam. The alderman responsible, Gosse Noordewier, was also pleased with the result. Later he declared that Zutphen's residents would have preferred nothing better than to keep everything as it was, but he felt that the city 'had to catch up with the twenty-first century'. Nelly Wieringa of the Department for Conservation was of the same opinion. She admitted that the first task of conservation was to protect the old, but that preserving the historic function in the same place in the city was also an important consideration. Moreover, she thought the building extremely beautiful. In order to carry out 'the total concept of unifying monuments and new developments', she even agreed to the demolition of a 'building that was a protected monument' (Lange Hofstraat 5). 'Later', she concluded, 'when a good place was sought for the main entrance, it was also decided to demolish the old telephone company building'. Nelly Wieringa is proud of the result. She told Caroline Kruit: 'The last time I was there, they were putting up the green cladding. "Yes", I thought, "I did a good job there".'[7]

The new development was also highly praised by Tom Maas in the building trade journal, *Cobouw* (22 March 1999). He spoke of 'organic-style urban renewal' and said that the result was 'exemplary'. He also complimented the Department for Conservation for consenting to the demolition of four listed buildings in order to make room for the development, even though they contained remains from the thirteenth and fourteenth centuries. In Maas's view, the opponents of the development were wrong. There then follows an interesting passage. He thinks that a city's heart has to stay alive, because this is essential for its survival. 'A historic heart can only continue to beat when vital public functions like town halls are preserved. From the point of view both of planning and architecture moreover it would be strange if it was suddenly no longer possible to undertake anything after a thousand years of building operations. A generation that no longer dared to leave any trace of itself would be lacking in self-esteem.'

What Tom Maas fails to notice is that the Department for Conservation was set up to preserve where possible the elements of our rapidly vanishing heritage. He behaves as though certain functions are essential in a city from which most of the functions have already disappeared. The largest building in the neighbourhood, the Walburgiskerk, has long since ceased to be a church and has been turned into a museum. Even back in 1900, the centre was too small for virtually every activity that required more space than the average nineteenth-century warehouse building had to offer. All that remains today is domestic premises, small shops, a few cafés and a cinema. This is the fate of virtually all our historical cities, enlarged over the years as they have been with interminable suburbs. Virtually no historical city centre is capable of providing room for modern, large-scale amenities such as hospitals, schools, banks and supermarkets. Most municipal departments have also become far too large to retain their premises in the centre. Tom Maas's argument is erroneous, therefore, because the only way for a historic city to survive is by banishing the largest consumers of space.

The idea that this green-coloured town hall fits well in the urban scene of Zutphen appears with hindsight to be quite presumptuous. In any case, one would be hard put to it to maintain that the department acted with respect

36 The 's Gravenhof in Zutphen in 1950 with the medieval Revival-style post office

37 The new town hall, Zutphen by Thomas Rau (1999)

ROMANTIC MODERNISM

for the historic built environment and urban panorama of Zutphen. The demolition of four listed buildings and the neo-Gothic post office building cannot be labelled an act of conservation.

The Nijenhuis in Heino

The Nijenhuis is a country house in Heino, in the rural district of Wijhe. It consists of a house built in 1687 on the site of a fifteenth-century manor house. On both sides of the forecourt are seventeenth-century farm buildings. The two towers to the rear date from 1894-1896. The park layout dates from the last quarter of the seventeenth century and consists of a Classicist formal composition with vistas. The stretch of water to the rear of the building, known as the 'Grand Canal', is also part of this formal layout. Around 1800, part of the park was laid out again in the landscape style; the banks of the ponds were given curves and a winding, undulating wood was planted.

In 1957, D. Hannema, the former director of the Boymans-van Beuningen museum in Rotterdam, moved into the house and laid the foundations for the Hannema-De Stuers art collection. Both house and collection were bought in 1967 by the provincial authority of Overijssel, which decided to expand the museum in 1995. It was then that a battle broke out that sheds an interesting light on everyday legal and administrative practices.

Problems started when architect Gunnar Daan's designs for the extension of the country house were made public. The Department for Conservation was unpleasantly surprised by the plans and it tried early on to persuade the provincial authority to build the extension behind one of the farm buildings so that it would not impinge too much on the historical character of this monument.[8] This proposal was rejected by the provincial authority with the argument that the extension should have a certain splendour and charm. They then proposed that it should partly be built *underneath* the park, in an underground space with a glass pavilion on top and a bridge over the moat. This plan was approved in 1997 by the Department for Conservation. The following considerations were taken into account in the decision: 'The siting south of the *château* on the spot in front of the Grand Canal that is presently open is acceptable. Through continuing the construction underground, the visible part of the volume of the new development is reduced to a pavilion of glass, steel and a copper cupola, with a diameter of 7.5 metres and a height of 10 metres. As a result, there will be no negative competition between the new development and the *château* with its two late nineteenth-century towers. The architect has placed the pavilion on the axes of the main building and the Grand Canal so as to reinforce the impact of this essential axis.'

The extension was also positively reviewed by the building inspectorate of *Het Oversticht*, (a regional advisory body concerned with issues of conservation and the environment), the similar body for the local authority of Wijhe and the Libau consultancy bureau for conservation and building codes in Groningen. Won over by these favourable verdicts, the mayor and aldermen of Wijhe approved the plans on 16 April 1997. An appeal was at once lodged against their decision by the Heemschut League, the Foundation for Country Estates in Overijssel, the Netherlands Castles Foundation, the Baron van Ittersum Fund, the Cuypers Society, the Wijhe Historical Society and an inhabitant of Wijhe. The appeal was heard in the district court in Zwolle and on 16 September 1999 it declared the objections to Gunnar Daan's plan to be unfounded. The court based its verdict mainly on the positive recommendations of the bodies mentioned above. The magistrates of Zwolle thought that 'a sound and – within certain limits – objective opinion' had been given. That the plan was finally quashed in 2001 in the Raad van State (the court of highest appeal in Holland) was due to a trivial technicality in assessing the number of square metres the zoning scheme consisted of. A background role was also played by the fact that the historic Courthouse in Zwolle had become available for accommodating the Nijenhuis collection.

Were the judges right in allowing the favourable views of bodies of experts to prevail over those of other individuals and bodies? A group of landscape designers from the Technical University of Delft wrote a report on 12 November 1999 stating that Gunnar Daan's pavilion would be situated 'in the most sensitive spot in the heart of the composition of the ensemble' and that the cupola structure 'interrupts the spatial axis' and that it 'violates the relation between this axis and the house.' The authors of this report, C.M. Steenbergen, S.I. de Wit and B.B. Kwast concluded that the historical ensemble would be 'essentially harmed' if the extension was carried out. The landscape designers were admittedly commissioned to write their report by the Foundation for the Country Houses of Overijssel (*Stichting Buitengoed Overijssel*), but there is no evidence that these professors from Delft were any more corrupt than the civil servants of the Ministry of Culture or the staff of *Het Oversticht*. The writers of an extremely critical report of 1996, Ben Olde Meierink and Eric Blok were also anything but corrupt. Their verdict on Gunnar Daan's plan was also extremely negative: 'Due to the total concept of which the central symmetrical axis and the system of vistas are a part, this new development in the heart of the layout will damage the protected valuable assets in an extremely serious fashion.'[9]

Why did the judges take the side of the official, legally established bodies and not that of the protesters? Perhaps they were merely being sensitive to their task of defending the existing organization of society and thus attached greater weight to the correct functioning of the bodies concerned than to the question of what the Historic Buildings Act was originally set up to deal with. While one should no doubt pay the court the respect it is due, in such cases, a historian's verdict has more authority than that of a judge. A historian does not have any obligation to be guided by the social relations of the period he is describing. In his function as a historian he is superior to the judge, who has to take account of the institutions that legislators have set up and which, it hardly needs to be said, form the foundation for the democratic state. That does not, however, mean that the historian writing these words has reached a more considered verdict beyond any shadow of doubt. That is for history itself to decide, and the opinion of this historian may be totally quashed later by that of another much more sensible colleague.

It may be, however, that the judges dismissed the content of the objections too easily. They accepted the pronouncements of the official experts that the large glass garden cupola was placed in the centre of the layout 'in order to reinforce the effects of the axis'. Other specialists, who did not dispose of the extra authority of representing official bodies, argued the opposite. According to them the axis would be broken and violated by the cupola. What was a judge supposed to make of such a dispute between experts? He will go home in the evening and open his paper and read that the famous architecture critic Max van Rooy feels a great admiration for Gunnar Daan's design. 'Because the pavilion', he wrote in *NRC Handelsblad* on 13 February 1998, 'is meticulously placed on the central axis of the estate, so that the classical geometry that governs the estate is reinforced.' What member of the legal profession could be expected to think otherwise when what he hears in court is later confirmed in his evening paper? He goes for the safe option and he can hardly be blamed for that, except by a historian who doesn't understand how one could possibly confuse a visual axis with the notion of a *central axis*. A visual axis is an unimpeded vista in the middle of a layout such as one often comes across in Baroque gardens, for instance those of Versailles. An axis like this can be reinforced if something is placed at the end of the visual field, such as an obelisk, so that the gaze is drawn to a central point in the composition. It should, however, be obvious that no building can be placed athwart a visual axis like this, because then one can no longer see the whole axis. A structure on a visual axis disrupts the intended perspective. The experts who claimed that a visual axis can be reinforced by building something on it were confusing the notion of a visual axis with the central axis of an architectural composition. In this, the built structures are situated in a symmetrical relation with each other and the centre of a composition like this is usually emphasized by having a structure that is more striking, due to its height for instance. In a case like that it is conceivable that one could reinforce the central axis in this way, but this was not the issue at Nijenhuis. Neither the official experts nor Max van Rooy understood this distinction and the judge unfortunately went along with them. The other experts knew perfectly well what a visual axis was but – mistakenly as it proved – the judge lent more credence to the officials.

Postmodernism on a Historic Canal

When the residents of Groningen protested *en masse* against the building of a new museum in the Zwaaikom, a wide stretch of water belonging to the Verbindingskanaal, to their astonishment they got no support from the Department for Conservation. They had assumed that this department

38 The Zwaaikom, Groningen, 1990

39 The Groninger Museum by Alessandro Mendini (1994) (photo, John Stoel)

ROMANTIC MODERNISM

had been set up in the first place to put brakes on large new developments threatening the historical character of their cities. They thought that the legal instrument of the listed site in town or countryside was also intended for this end. The individuals and bodies that advise the Department for Conservation had very different ideas on the subject, however. They felt that the residents had not or were unwilling to understand that the beauty of Groningen was the result of centuries of development, and that it wouldn't have existed if previous generations had stopped the clock of history. The Department of Conservation's conclusion was that the museum as designed by the famous Italian architect Alessandro Mendini should be considered a new and artistic contribution to the protected townscape of Groningen.

This argument is hard to understand, because the Historic Buildings Act had been passed by the Dutch parliament precisely to protect historical values against new developments. What other purpose was this law supposed to serve? Was it to make historical cities even more beautiful by providing them with extra attractions in the form of avant-garde architecture? However that may be, in 1990, the City Council of Groningen decided to build the new museum in the Zwaaikom with the idea that, with its proximity to both the station and the city centre, the museum would function to 'reinforce the image and appeal of the city', with visitors being 'invited to spend money in the city', as Judith Beumer put it in the journal *Contour* of 1991. The mayor and aldermen of Groningen acknowledged in a letter to the city council on 20 August 1990 that the 'the area of the Zwaaikom was a valuable element in the city', but that in their view this did not mean that 'valuable elements are by definition inviolable. A city after all is a reflection of dynamic developments and not an unalterable entity. That implies that even valuable elements may be subjected to changes as long as these values are acknowledged. New, additional elements in the cityscape should then at least be equal in quality to what is already there. In this regard we have no problem at all with the response of the Department for Conservation. It regards the development that we have in mind as fitting into the context of a protected cityscape.'[10]

The plans for the new museum in the Zwaaikom were met with a storm of criticism. According to a questionnaire in the Groningen regional paper, the *Nieuwsblad van het Noorden*, 54.6 per cent of the residents interviewed were opposed to the proposed site. The city authorities therefore had little support locally for the plan. The council, however, must have thought that it could override these objections, given that internationally renowned architects such as Joseph Kleihues and Rem Koolhaas had recommended this site in the Zwaaikom. A number of organizations had filed appeals, for instance the Vereniging tot Behoud van een Waardevol Stadsgezicht, in het Bijzonder tussen de Emmabrug en de Herebrug te Groningen (The Society for the preservation of the protected townscape, in particular between the Emmabrug and the Herebrug in Groningen) and the Heemschut League. The journalist Ella Reitsma saw narrow-minded individuals and groups such as these quite insufferable. In her article on various new museum designs in *Vrij Nederland*, 16 March 1991 she called them 'querulous people', frightened that 'the new museum would spoil their view'. She must have thought that the residents of the posh Ubbo Emmiussingel were very bourgeois not to welcome the fact that their boring view across the water of the Verbindingskanaal, dug in 1877, was to be replaced by a genuine artwork of our own postmodern days.

This canal forms part of a belt that was laid out here in the same way as happened in many other nineteenth-century Dutch cities, after the old fortifications with their bulwarks, walls and gates had become redundant. Fortifications were turned into parks on the water of a canal, laid out in the English landscape style with monumental trees, lawns and winding paths. Military bastions were transformed into friendly parks, surrounded by superb villas in a variety of extravagant Revival styles. The unique feature of these nineteenth-century belts is that for the first time in history, parts of the city were laid out as public gardens; until then the ownership of a garden was confined to rich private houses, monasteries and the courtyards of almshouses. These belts are an outstanding type of public garden and in a large number of cities they are also legally listed sites. The Ubbo Emmiussingel is a tranquil, broad, slightly curving avenue, closed to through traffic, with rows of trees in the central plot and houses on both sides. Roughly half way along it the series of villas is interrupted on the south side by the Zwaaikom with the boathouses of the De Hunze rowing club.

Has Alexander Mendini's museum that was opened in 1994 actually harmed the historical value of this area of the city? Let us say that its character has been distinctly altered. Some people are enthusiastic about the changes, while others see them in a negative light. The only thing we can be sure of is that if nothing had been done there, there wouldn't have been any problem either. With the question of whether new developments are permissible in a valuable historical area, social considerations often play a key role – housing or job opportunities, for instance. Furthermore cultural interests, including historical beauty, usually have to make way for serious social or economic interests. One may deplore this, but society has little choice but to make the most of its limited space. In the matter of the new site for the Groningen museum, there was no conflict between serious social and economic interests and cultural concerns; what was involved rather was a battle between the arts. This is one of the curious features of this question. It was a battle between modern art and art of former times, between an exhibition space for modern work and a nineteenth-century monument of urban planning. According to the city council's brochure about the new development, the exhibitions building was intended to give extra dynamism to the city's image, to have international appeal and thus have a favourable influence on the 'consumerist spending patterns of visitors'. Indeed the museum is a major public attraction. The key question remains however of whether the layout of a public attraction on the southern city canal is of such great social interest, that other concerns such as the historical value of the site should be subordinated to it. The calm of this belt is now broken with more traffic and the inevitable swarms of visitors. A city centre with cafés and café terraces can cope with this extra business, but this is hardly the case with a green belt round a city. This belt remains a barrier between the historical city and the busy station area. The creation of an island in the Zwaaikom linked by a bridge to the station area has caused a partial breach in this historically evolved barrier, with the station area activity spilling over in the direction of the belt. The Raad van State thought otherwise, declaring in its order on 5 February 1992 that 'between the north and south banks there is no existing urban relation that might persuade one to preserve the present situation. Furthermore the Zwaaikom is not such a valuable historical element that altering its function is unacceptable. While one can grant the appellants the fact that developing the Zwaaikom results in a basic alteration in the urban image, this does not in our view mean that the character of the canal belt as seen from the Ubbo Emmiussingel is damaged.' The Raad van State did not say what the basis was for this verdict, but it was presumably prompted by the reports from central and local government departments. If this assumption is correct, then the Raad van State takes it for granted that what it calls 'Our Minister of Culture' and his civil servants have a monopoly on the truth. That this is not always the case is something the Raad van State knows full well and it is not impossible that in this particular case it came to a mistaken conclusion. It should have decided whose interests would be harmed if the museum had not been built here and it should have accepted the historic importance of the spot as a fact. The Raad van State did neither of these things. The conflict, as said above, was one between two notions of protection of the arts. They exceeded their brief in choosing sides here – art is not something for judges to decide. The museum was a present from its sponsors, the *Gasunie,* and that was that. For the sake of a gift a historical townscape was ruined.

The project received a great deal of backing from architects and planners. They advocated the urbanization of open suburban areas because, as they saw it, urban developments outside the old canals had reduced the nineteenth-century belts to a sort of green belt. The southern canal in Groningen, according to the architect Giorgio Grassi and the architectural historian Ed Taverne 'have largely lost their architectural value in the sense of serving as urban borders, as elements of colour and transparency' (*De Architect,* May 1988). They advocated that an island be created in the water to improve the isolated position of the station with regard to the city, by building a new route between station and city centre. As a new urban square, the island would be able to combine the now scattered elements of the city in a single composition.

Green belts with wide canals are part of the landscape of Dutch cities. You come to expect them girdling old city centres just as you do a medieval church, a market square and a town hall. Elements like this have lodged themselves in our minds as symbols. Old trees lining these canals mean more than what is meant today by 'green belts'. The canals round these belts are not empty stretches of water; in their proportions and in the course they take they remind us of their former defensive function. Open spaces like these, moreover, are still valuable as green buffer zones between the densely populated city centre and the nineteenth-century urban expansion areas or, as in Groningen, modern housing estates. It would perhaps have been more sensible in embarking on this 'intensification' policy to have made an exception for these silent canals. Why do all urban areas have to be 'intensified'? Are planners afraid of the void?

An American Waterfront in Amsterdam

To begin with, it was a first-class planning blunder to build the Central Station on Amsterdam's waterfront. Not that Pierre Cuypers's building itself was a mistake, but this marvellous railway palace ought to have been built elsewhere. The only reason offered in defence of the site is that it allowed the Damrak to preserve its function as an approach road to the city – a pretty feeble defence because it is obvious that the Damrak could have kept its original beauty even if the open waterfront had been saved. In the commemorative volume (1940) of the *Genootschap Amstelodamum*, an Amsterdam historical society, D. Kouwenaar wrote: 'The cruellest blow that could have been delivered to Amsterdam's own special beauty was the building of the Central Station that was opened in 1889, by which the former port city is no longer, in Vondel's famous phrase, "superbly open both on the Amstel and the IJ". Like a boom, like a barrier, Dr. Cuypers's edifice that in itself is impressive enough with its 300 metres long roof and its railway embankment at both ends lies athwart the old waterfront. Now, half a century later, it seems almost incomprehensible how it could have possessed people, how they could have been so blind to the dreadful consequences for the beauty of the city. It was an error, a crime in an aesthetic sense, no less dreadful for instance than if one were to do something similar in the Lagoon that Venice fronts on, the city that in so many respects reminds one of Amsterdam....' Kouwenaar added that it was the national government in The Hague that had imposed this solution on Amsterdam. What he failed to mention, but that we know now due to a study of the station square by Lydia Lansink, is that the original intention was to build a wide Parisian boulevard in front of the station. Various impressive designs were made, but none were carried out.[11] After Berlage's Stock Exchange building was put up in 1903, these plans vanished into thin air. If the boulevard had been built, the Damrak would perhaps not be the sorry sight it is today.

If Amsterdam hadn't had a lucky escape, the first mistake would have been followed about a century later by a second – the development of an American-style waterfront along the IJ. This project was developed in the decade between 1980 and 1990, but failed eventually because, after a while, investors ceased to believe in its financial viability. It was not because it wasn't up to scratch in terms of city planning that the project failed; on the contrary, it had enthusiastic support from leading architects and administrators. Here and there doubts were voiced about the feasibility of a construction project comparable in scope with the digging of the seventeenth-century ring of canals. One of those sceptics was Herman Selier, who raised the question in the professional journal *De Architect* of 1991 of whether the whole project wasn't a mirage. In this connection, the sociologist A.C. Zijderveld even spoke of 'megalomania' (*Het Parool*, 16 May 1990).

But everyone is agreed that the area fronting on the IJ is seriously neglected and must be refurbished. It consists of some windswept landing stages, ill-defined business terrains with plenty of scrap metal, empty sunless quaysides that no respectable person has any business visiting. The planning area is a run-down, messy piece of city periphery. To the east of the station a concrete traffic artery soars upwards past the nineteenth-century houses on the Ruyterkade. If you imagine the waterfront without this busy artery, you can easily think up all kinds of brilliant possibilities for laying out a very wide tree-lined promenade with views of the IJ. You could even dream that the little beach, known as *Klein Zantvoort* which stood here until the 1950s might be restored. Even with a policymaker who had an eye for the future and some sense of what people want in terms of modern entertainment, a proposal like this still wouldn't stand a ghost of a chance. What is more, he wouldn't even dare propose a similar land usage to any investor. So instead all that was proposed for the waterfront was expensive high-rise developments and, according to the *Nota van uitgangspunten voor de IJ-oevers* (the IJ bank memorandum) of January 1990, the chaotic network of roads was to remain intact, 'in broad lines in keeping with the present situation'. The larger part of this planning area extends west of the station, where the railway curves off in another direction. What we see here is a peculiarly chaotic landscape, with a solitary building of historic interest here and there, such as the gigantic grain warehouse on the Houthaven, a design of J.F. Klinkhamer of 1898, a maritime cathedral of brick with clerestories and a tower over the crossing. Just in front of the warehouse to the right is the Stenenhoofd, a wide roughly two-hundred metre long grass-covered pier that sticks out at an angle into the IJ. This breakwater gives one a splendid view across the IJ and, behind one, towards the city, over the Westerdok and towards the historic houses on the Zandhoek.

In the surroundings of the Barentszplein the historical city is still close at hand. There on the water, you feel the city centre at your back. That changes, however, as you go further west. That's where the biggest surprises await you, because more or less no one bothers to visit the terrain between the Tasmanstraat and the IJ today. It is a neglected corner, a maze of dead-end streets squeezed between the Nieuwe Houthaven and the Minervahaven. There are a few business offices and sheds. Then you suddenly emerge in a wilderness of scrub and muddy paths with old caravans and disused buses that have been converted into primitive homes. But however primitive this neighbourhood may be, the spot is truly beautiful. It lies on the water and you have a superb view of the shipyards on the far side of the IJ. The city is far off now and a rural tranquillity prevails. The last quayside, the Danzigerkade, branches out from this terrain; at its far end a derelict Russian ship was gleaming in the sun when I was there. Due to its unique situation, this forgotten area forms the ultimate planner's dream, especially when it gets better connections with the city centre. According to the council memorandum, the terrain will be 'restructured and through the functions to be developed there it will, in combination with the inner city, form a centre of great value for housing and shopping for all the residents of Amsterdam and visitors from outside'. The planners wanted to integrate the banks of the IJ with the main body of the city by improving connections with the historical centre. In this way the populace will be able to profit from the 'open expanses of the IJ, with its low horizon and sweeping panoramas'.

The memorandum began promisingly but the design drawings immediately put an end to any optimism; all you saw was a series of towers varying from fifty-five to a hundred metres high with a twenty-five-metre-high long wall of low-rise buildings between them. To the east of the station a tower was to be built while on the west side there would be two more towers (with a maximum height of seventy-five metres), while on the Barentszplein a hundred-metre-high tower was to be erected. In the direction of the city, two more fifty-five-metre-high towers were planned on both sides of the station. The actual front would consist of the twenty-five metre high strip of new development of which one got a foretaste in the Chamber of Commerce building with its reflecting façade that was delivered in 1990.

Why did the project fail? Apparently investors backed out. More importantly one should ask why Amsterdam's planners were so enthusiastic about it in the first place. They were probably obsessed with the spectacular explosions of high-rise developments in the old dockland areas of Hong Kong or in American ports. Those cities had selected the model preferred in Amsterdam, namely that of an impressive waterfront with a big-city appeal. In this connection the City Council came up with expressions like 'top locations', 'international appeal' and 'high-quality surroundings'. In its broad lines the plan for the IJ waterfront seems to be based on American or Asian examples. Why didn't the people concerned take a long look at the history of the area itself before focusing on all kinds of waterfronts from different continents? There is no indication in the memorandum of the history of the Amsterdam docks having played any role in this master plan. Weren't there enough clues in this history for new designs? One gets the impression that Amsterdam planners were only interested in money, and given investors' lack of interest, they were clearly mistaken even in that. The plan was apparently meant to give the city a financial injection, based on the assumption that you can't do that with modest small-scale volumes, a few cycle paths and plenty of green areas.

Similar projects in other cities have been commercially successful – one example is the Inner Harbor in Baltimore that has attractions such as a yachting marina, a maritime museum, a science museum, an aquarium, a historical ship, an exhibition building, a party centre, an amusement arcade and various hotels. In 1986, 7.5 million tourists visited the Inner Harbor; between them they spent 650 million dollars. Money! Isn't that what Amsterdam was looking for? Would the city centre residents have welcomed all that excitement? While the question seems to me a perfectly reasonable one, the memorandum did not discuss it at all. For children and businessmen the plans appear to have been very attractive, given the prospect of new attractions and the investments in prime sites; the residents of the city centre thought differently. They would not have gained any additional ordinary urban space; all they would have got from it would be a range of aquatic activities, mainly interesting for day trippers.

The historical city of Amsterdam is an artwork in itself and in 1989 it was declared a listed urban area. For this reason, the Amsterdam advisory conservation body, the *Raad voor de Monumentenzorg*, was consulted about the proposed development. With regard to the planned high-rise activities on the banks of the IJ, it declared that, 'a scaled-up perspective in front of the old urban silhouette in the form of a series of higher buildings (low in the centre and increasing in height towards the outer suburbs) fits in with the evolution of scale that the urban image has undergone over the centuries.' In its report dated October 1989, it behaved as though the city has become higher with each new historical development. This is a serious exaggeration, not to say misleading. Apart from the Central Station, a few churches, some warehouse buildings and the Port Authority building, the urban silhouette on the sides of the IJ has hardly changed until now. This is a very exceptional circumstance for a city of this size and one should treat it with great respect. But the *Raad* is also keen to show that it is willing to go with the times and its members were of course afraid of being thought of as nostalgic heritage campaigners. That is why they exaggerated so grossly and behaved as though it was a logical conclusion that a decision, once taken, was unalterable. Did its members think that their only task was to identify developments, no matter what their nature and then lend them their support? In 1990, the supervisor of the IJ bank project, Tjeerd Dijkstra, stated that 'increased scale and high-rise developments in the vicinity of historical city centres' ought not to be rejected because 'new developments and new cultural impulses cannot automatically be excluded'.[12]

But why do new developments and cultural incentives have to take the form of high-rise tower blocks? Why not put up low-rise buildings or something else altogether? Maybe because large-scale buildings and tower blocks are symbols of modern power, signs that are recognized by everyone because they refer to huge metropolises like New York and Hong Kong. Furthermore, tower blocks are very suitable for creating an urban axis. With these huge volumes, a strip of some kilometres can be combined in a single composition. The principal planner of the project, Gert Urhahn, attached great importance to this 'total composition' which, he wrote, 'is very carefully calibrated …from the city, to provide the sightlines from the historical centre with the spatial excitement that is inherent in our experience of

Amsterdam'.[13] A composition like this seen from the IJ can of course have a certain big-city atmosphere, but seen from the city centre the new, high-rise flats would dwarf the existing historical towers. The spire of the Oude Kerk, for instance, would no longer look tall then and would therefore become a bit ridiculous, like a toy-sized tower in the model city Madurodam in The Hague. Urhahn's composition may well have its own value as a stage set symbolizing a metropolis, but it conflicts both with the old city's scale and the character of the docklands area. This area is a typical rough-and-ready urban peripheral area. From the city, one can sometimes see the open water, but above all, you *feel* its presence. The transition from the city to the water is intriguing – the formal layout of canals changes here into long open quays and, instead of canal houses, one comes across randomly placed dockland buildings, so that the city seems to dissolve into more chaotic structures. It is this scene that Jacob Olie photographed in 1861 – the transition from the Korte Prinsengracht to the Westerdok, laid out in 1834. In the photo, one sees that the brick houses are replaced by lower wooden dwellings and sheds with their fronts reflected in the calm inland waterway. The photographer's viewpoint is outside the city, on a stretch of meadow, and he is looking back towards an urban phenomenon of deeply moving beauty – a city that for a moment reverts to its village origins as though it wishes to secure this image in its memory, before dissolving into the landscape.

A city is incapable of thinking, the modern planner replies as he turns the city back to front, converting the informal rear into a monumental front – a waterfront of international status. In Urhahn's words, 'a confrontation is thus sought between the forms of the new and contemporary and those of the timeless and historical'. It all sounds very daring and combative, as though the historical city is a ruthless enemy determined to resist the gigantic optimism of metropolitan builders. The battle they wage with the historical city is not entirely fair. Notwithstanding their lack of interest in the historic background of the planning area that verges on contempt (as said above, it was not once mentioned in the memorandum), their new developments do, in fact, benefit from the cultural and historic importance of the old city, because it was no coincidence that their prime location was situated not far from the centre of one of the most beautiful cities in the world and not in the satellite area of South-East Amsterdam. As far as I know, the planners haven't yet succeeded in erecting a city in that area that can hold a candle to any medieval town one cares to name.

Packaged Modernism

Saving energy is good environmental practice, and the Dutch Ministry of Finance provides grants for the insulation of new homes. According to Dyon Noy, however, writing in the house journal of the Nederlandse Maatschappij voor Energie en Milieu (Netherlands Society for Energy and the Environment), the *Novem*, there are some snags with this policy. Apparently once every chink and crack has been filled in, 'one is faced in the long or short term with unexpected surprises, both practical and financial'. Previously, Noy tells us, people's homes were ventilated in an 'unasked-for' manner via cracks and joints; but 'in recent years a shift has occurred from unasked-for ventilation to a deliberate form'. Most people's 'ventilation behaviour' leaves a lot to be desired. In practice it often happens that windows can no longer be opened and the mechanical air extraction system doesn't work properly or else it makes too much noise and so it is switched off, resulting in an unhealthy interior environment and a problem with damp.

Apart from a great deal of misery with building performance features indoors, the insulating system also causes a great deal of visual nuisance on the outside, as testified, for instance, since 1991 on the Pelkwijk estate in Winterswijk and on the Kleine Driene estate in Hengelo. According to Irma Thijssen of the *Novem*, the Pelkwijk estate, built in 1970, was composed of 'monotonous, grey building blocks', but it is now split up into five parts, 'each with its own identity' due to the use of a variety of different claddings for the façade – light yellow brick combined with Western red cedar, red brick with blue Resoplan plates and stucco work with different coloured areas. Seeing people were leaving the estate like a sinking ship in 1986, whereas there is now a waiting list for the homes, one might assume that the renovation has been a success. In the new design for the estate, implemented in consultation with the National Housing Council, one aspect should not perhaps be left unmentioned, even if it is possibly of subordinate importance in the eyes of the *Novem* and of the residents. It concerns the disappearance of the original design of the houses. The concrete houses of the Pelkwijk estate date from 1972, but were built according to Modernist principles – that is, they consisted of taut and functional simple forms in green surroundings. In the tradition of the Modern Movement that's all they were meant to be, and they were not made prettier than necessary. This severe purism has sometimes produced very acceptable homes, not particularly beautiful, but also not inappropriate, a neutral piece of equipment for living with large windows looking out on a green space. One can of course reject the compulsive sobriety of the Modernists as a backward-looking and unfriendly notion of design, but if you look at Pelkwijk today, you might think twice about jettisoning Modernist principles. How much more civilized and restrained were these houses built in 1972 compared with the childish sandpit-style architecture that has been put up in their place. The functionalist homes had no pretensions; all they consisted of was simple blocks with windows the width of the room. The cheerful shapes of the 'energy-saving' homes clash grossly with the surrounding green space; their tea cosies of American lumber crowning their façades make them look quite ridiculous. Less laughable but no less unpleasant was the result of the insulation programme on the Kleine Driene estate in Hengelo. The flats, designed in 1959 by the firm of Van den Broek and Bakema, may perhaps also not have been particularly beautiful, but at least they looked friendly with all that glass and those projecting balconies. Flats like this have been

40 Dwellings, Kleine Driene estate in Hengelo (1959)

41 Kleine Driene estate with insulation (1990)

built everywhere in the Netherlands and we've become a bit used to them. We have in a sense accepted and even learned to admire them perhaps. Now that Modernism has finally become a little bit assimilated, it has to be packaged and wrapped up, because we are expected to save energy. The flats that were so full of sunlight and air were converted in 1991 into thermal bunkers with narrow fenestration slits and small square windows. Why did this renovation have to be so extreme? Wouldn't it have been sufficient to install double-glazing? There is nothing the Department for Conservation can do about this, as it cannot intervene outside a statutory term of fifty years. Now that time seems to go faster than it did fifty years ago, perhaps this term ought also to be shortened. Today in 2009, the modernism of the 1960s belongs to antiquity.

Prestige and Power

It is not in the character of an organization to make public pronouncements about its own mistakes. This is why the policy memos of government departments are written in tones as cheerful as company publicity brochures. This is also true of the image the Department for Conservation has created for itself. The reality however is not always as rosy as it is depicted. Not so long ago, the department had a reputation for being a group of eccentric nerds who only needed to see a medieval brick to be over the moon. I remember that the gifted architect Mart van Schijndel, who died much too young, regularly referred to the officials of the Department for Conservation as the 'the medieval brick brigade'. Perhaps the exaggerated fixation on medieval walls was also a product of the social marginalizing of the sector. After the Second World War, during the Reconstruction period, the Department got all the money and room it needed to restore the national heritage – churches, castles, country houses and palaces. They were able to thrive in this socially forgotten corner that gave them the freedom to develop an exotic, somewhat unworldly sort of activity. This is how the image of conservation was able to take on the traits of a caricature, as though the profession was solely concerned with trivialities such as roof trusses, the history of the Dutch roof tile, Frisian red-fired tiles, Brabant farmhouses, Protestant church silver and Gothic tracery. The practitioners of this sort of specialization became hugely knowledgeable about materials and techniques, but hardly realized that they were seen as hopelessly stuffy by the outside world. The chasm between these specialists and the modern architects and planners was unbridgeable. Engineers are worldly people, who have to deal constantly with both clients and officialdom. As a group, civil engineers are mainly at the service of progress, but that doesn't make them philistines and, within reason, they support the aims of the Department for Conservation. What does 'within reason' mean, however?

In a speech at a meeting of the municipal Committee for Historic Buildings in Maastricht in 1968, J.N.G.M.A. Viegen said that 'in the present policy of conservation' more importance is attached to the city as a whole than to individual monuments, something that in his view must not be allowed to lead to an obsession with preserving the old, 'because a monument may be an old piece of our cultural legacy, but it is not always an element that can be effortlessly included in our present-day pattern of life and work. It is of the greatest concern that those people who feel called to be active in a cultural or aesthetic discipline in order to attain as widespread a preservation of historic buildings as possible should also reflect on the law of society, that where these buildings are incapable of coping with the current social and economic course of events, are no longer able, that is, to sustain any self-evident function, their preservation has become extremely questionable.'[14] In other words, something that no longer has any function should be pulled down. According to Viegen it is pointless and even antisocial to want to preserve something just because it is old or beautiful. Moreover there isn't any money to do so. Against the background of this completely rational and socially responsible viewpoint, it is easy to understand why for instance in the years that followed a large number of neo-Gothic churches that had suddenly become superfluous were demolished. Between 1967 and 1976, for instance, the urban silhouette of Breda was drastically altered by the demolition of three Gothic Revival churches – the church of the Ascension of the Virgin of 1890, the cathedral of Saint Barbara of 1869 and the church of Saint Joseph of 1897.[15] The financial argument, which Viegen incidentally did not mention, but which was frequently used by others, would seem at first sight to be a clinching one. On closer inspection, however, it isn't convincing at all, because if churches were protected by the Historic Buildings Act and demolition was outlawed, their market value on the property market would decline accordingly. What was involved then was anything but a sensible financial government policy, but something quite different – the sale of valuable ground by the owners of these buildings. The authorities adhered to the belief that it was antisocial to list buildings when they were no longer profitable, and so they had them pulled down. Where once our skyline was composed of Gothic Revival buildings with their high spires, what we have now is shoddy-looking old-people's dwellings finished in pale beige brick or something else equally unpleasant. One gets the impression that many nineteenth-century churches could have been rescued without any great financial sacrifices. With a modest transitional loan from the government they could have provided for their own maintenance after a while, for instance by being rented out as office space as has occurred in the Gothic Revival church of the Immaculate Conception, known as the Posthoorn church, on the Haarlemmerstraat in Amsterdam.

The destruction of a large number of neo-Gothic churches is probably not explained by the poverty of either Church or State; rather, it was due to a belief that the preservation of historic buildings is of secondary importance to the advancement of the economy, with the exception of the most important monuments. Nineteenth-century buildings were not held in such high esteem at that time. The economic argument also has no founda-

ROMANTIC MODERNISM

tion because it implies that the free development of the built environment could be impeded by the imposition of certain, not even particularly severe, restrictions concerning not much more than one per cent of the total building stock. Finally, the functional argument is also not very convincing, because a decade later when a large number of industrial monuments were made superfluous, the Department for Conservation, unwilling to be caught off guard yet again, conducted a fairly successful campaign to have these factory buildings given new allocations. The image of the Department improved as a result, as it showed itself willing to give a new function to premises that had been served notice. Extremely important too was the fact that it provided architects with a completely new field of activity. In this field, architects and conservationists have become allies. In June 2002, it was announced that the famous Swiss architect Peter Zumthor had been awarded the contract to convert the Flour Mill building on the Zijlsingel in Leiden. This immense group of industrial buildings from the last years of the nineteenth century was given a number of new functions and the contract fell to someone from the European architectural vanguard, indicating how the conversion of old factories has suddenly become a prestigious activity. In the reallocation of the nineteenth-century gasometers in Vienna that had become obsolete, the internationally renowned Parisian architect, Jean Nouvel, was even involved. He transformed one of them into a glass cathedral and shortly after it was opened in 2002, this project was celebrated worldwide.

Activities like this have given conservation a totally different reputation than it previously had in the days of Mr. Viegen. This change in image, however, was only noticed by those directly affected. Presumably, most contemporary architects still share Mr. Viegen's attitude – or, for that matter, that of J.J.J. van de Venne and L.J. Hartog. In 1969, during a workshop organized by the Royal Institute of Dutch Architects on the subject of 'the quality of life of the city centre', the latter argued that in 'a planning policy concerned with creating a synthesis between the old and the new, there cannot be any place for an over-anxious concern with our monumental heritage. The preservation of a monument can only therefore be justified, provided its individual value is indisputable, vital social and economic developments and traffic circulation form no obstacle and that it offers the possibility of a vital function in present conditions'.[16]

Most readers will have difficulty imagining what these gentlemen could possibly have meant by 'a vital function in present conditions'. I suppose myself that they must have meant that all the spatial requirements of the business and commercial world had first to be properly met and only then was it the turn of so incidental and bothersome a detail as the conservation of historical buildings. They of course avoided stating this philistine concept in so many words, resorting instead to learned terms such as 'synthesis' and 'evolution'. This, however, is more or less the gist of what they were saying.

This condescending notion of the role of conservation has left deep scars in the body of the historical city and there is no lack of examples to demonstrate it. I will confine myself here however to one typical case, the multiple commission for a new town hall in Deventer in 1966. The designs and the jury report were published in 1969 in the *Bouwkundig Weekblad*. The construction of this new town hall necessitated the demolition of many of the historical buildings on the Grote Kerkhof; what was truly striking was that this demolition was presented by the advisory committee consisting of H. Brouwer, A. van Kranendonk and C. Nap as something exemplary. They awarded the commission to the design of Aldo van Eyck. They particularly admired the way he 'succeeded in taking the principle of the structure of the historic city a step further', so that 'the new town hall would not conflict with the historic city, but rather complete it'. The panel concluded by saying, 'This is of great significance for Deventer, because its old city centre is still of such quality that it will be able to fulfil an important urban function for at least another hundred years, provided that this core is not encroached upon by new buildings with a totally different atmosphere, structure or scale.' It is clear from this report that Aldo van Eyck's design was seen as a welcome addition to the historic city. It would complete the city and putting up any other new buildings based on a different principle would only detract from the architectural quality of Aldo van Eyck's work. This statement must have sounded somewhat illogical in the ears of the Department for Conservation – how, after all, can the demolition of a part of the historical city ever be seen as not doing damage to the historically evolved urban structure, whether or not the new development had any quality? For that matter, to judge by the concept plan, it did not have much to recommend it, consisting as it did of long narrow building shapes with several series of small windows. The whole complex looks like a boring office monster, even though the volumes are staggered and are provided with continuous roof hips. In the press, Aldo van Eyck's design was lauded. In the weekly *De Tijd* (6 March 1968) Aldo van Eyck was quoted as having said that he thought that the Grote Kerkhof was 'a completely perfect structure' and that 'you shouldn't alter anything in it'. The reporter's comment was that, 'Aldo van Eyck has kept his word. On the side of the square where a block of houses largely had to make way for the new development, his plan consists of a simple, low front that is modestly recessed next to the massive monumental façade of the old town hall.' The reporter was thus of the opinion that the demolition of the old houses could not be called an essential alteration of this 'completely perfect structure' and that the word 'modest' could be applied in connection with the immense office block.

However that may be, the Department for Conservation was in fact consulted here; its offering consisted of a very brief text on the historical importance of the interior spaces of Jacob Roman's old town hall of 1695. It made no mention, however, of the demolition of the houses on the Grote Kerkhof, thus confirming the image people had of the department – that it consisted of a group of specialists solely interested in historic joisting and beautiful wood carving. To add insult to injury, moreover, the jury included in its report the fact that 'the suggestions' of the Department for Conservation were not binding and that 'they should not be seen as an obligatory part of the schedule of requirements.' If it still wasn't clear which way the wind was blowing, the little word 'not' was printed in bold. It was obvious where power lay at that time. The sole function of the Department for Conservation seemed to be to provide some information about a few beautiful rooms. Luckily, the plan wasn't carried out.

The Revival Styles and Time Regained

The Hatred of the Revival Styles

The unkindest cut that hatred can deliver is ridicule. Once a thing has been made laughable, it has little chance of reappraisal. Something that has only ever been hated does, in a sense, still enjoy a reputation. A baron's stronghold induces fear, but the fake castle of some nineteenth-century dandy makes one giggle. Even a dignified neo-Classical exterior can be made a laughing stock for good, with just a few well-chosen words. The historian Gerard Brom was a master in this art. Neo-Classicism, which he liked to label a 'public works style', was nothing more than 'a plaster-cast nincompoop ... a derivative, contrived, imitation beauty made up of hearsay, a corpse wrapped in the winding-sheet of a frigid doctrine ... a mannerism that had degenerated into a Punch-and-Judy show, determined at all cost to salvage some vestige of a Greek temple'. Brom was in no doubt that these empty forms of neo-Classicism were thoroughly ideological, because the façade of an antique temple was a symbol of Catholic emancipation. The dignity that the Catholics had entirely lost under the Republic could only be recovered during the monarchy by dressing up in the outward trappings of the prevailing power: 'where a wooden sham of three sorts of Greek column were tacked on top of each other, the despised Papist felt accepted by civilization at last'.

Brom hadn't a good word to say about the Gothic Revival either, except that the rediscovery of Gothic architecture was initially an inexhaustible source of inspiration and a new way of buttressing up Catholic identity. The pointed arch became a symbol of a mysterious sanctity and 'on purely incidental grounds' it acquired 'its inviolably sacred character, something that it never had in the Middle Ages; and so this arch became both badge and trophy, the pinnacle of Catholic emancipation quite by chance.' In the long run, however, the Gothic Revival rigidified and turned into a joyless piece of imitation. It became 'an obsolete language' that the Catholics clung to 'in order not to become carried away by dangerous novelties'. Brom devotes endless pages to the pettiness of the Gothic Revival; he tells how desperately dull it was, how formal and academic, how it lacked soul and character and was dead as a corpse, 'or perhaps a catafalque'.[1]

The contempt for the Revival styles didn't remain confined to the pages of history. In the twentieth century, action took over from words. An unbelievable amount of architecture was demolished and by no means always because the buildings concerned had deteriorated beyond repair. For instance, after 1945 entire districts in Berlin dating from the *Gründerzeit* period (the foundation period, just after German unification), were pulled down because nobody cared for this style any more. In Paris, too, entire nineteenth-century neighbourhoods continued to be demolished until well into the 1980s.[2]

The chorus of denunciation of the Revival styles reached a climax around 1900, but it had already had a long prehistory. There were people who complained at the outset of the nineteenth century that their age, in contrast with every other period, lacked its own architectural style. In 1837, the situation had become so hopeless that the editorial board of the *Allgemeine Bauzeitung* pleaded with its readers to put an end to the slavish imitation of former styles. 'We live', the same board declared some years later, 'in the present, not in the past, and architecture should observe this rule more than the other arts; it should show respect for works from the past, but it shouldn't try and breathe new life into them.' Similar thoughts were also proclaimed by the *Kunstblatt*. 'It is high time', the editors wrote in 1847, 'for the slavish craze for copying to be exposed for what it is.' A well-known architectural critic, R. Wiegmann, poked fun at the 'Masken- und Scheinarchitektur' in 1842, and in 1850 even a respectable professional journal like the *Allgemeine Bauzeitung* felt free enough to publish a tirade against the architects Charles Barry and A.W.N. Pugin, for making a 'Zuckerbackwerk' of their design for the new parliament building in London with a 'Überfluss von unbedeutenden kleinen Ornamenten' (an excess of irrelevant small ornaments).[3]

In France, too, the war of styles sometimes almost reached the proportions of a real war. Eugène Viollet-le-Duc's denunciation of the secretary of the Académie des Beaux-Arts, D. Raoul Rochette, in 1846 was indicative of the enormous gulf between the established order of the Académie and the recalcitrant innovators with their rationalist rhetoric. In 1846, Raoul Rochette replied on behalf of the Académie to the question of whether architectural training should also concern itself with the Gothic style. The question arose because a number of people had argued that Gothic was the proper style for building churches. Rochette argued that it was nonsensical to apply a style of architecture from the thirteenth century to an age that was in every sense different. 'Has any people', he asked, 'ever completely broken with its own age and with the future to return to its past?' The Académie, he went on, does not expect that humanity will rebel 'contre la nature des choses'. It (the Académie) should therefore comply with traditional Classicism and leave the Gothic style to rest in peace as a dead art form.

Viollet-le-Duc's response was scathing. Why, he argued, should France imitate the Italian Renaissance, when the Gothic style was the national artistic style? Why does the Académie reject an art that has achieved its highest degree of perfection in France? 'Is it perhaps that those people who have worked so hard to bring this art form to perfection were not members of the Académie des Beaux-Arts?' he asked. He kindly informed the gentlemen of the Académie about the principles of architecture. While tearing them to shreds, however, he ignored Rochette's question. Instead he issued a plea for the pure principles of the Gothic style.[4]

The issue of historicist imitations was initially only raised in progressive circles. It formed part of the modern revolt against 'bourgeois' art, the art of 'easy gratification and light entertainment'.[5] The criticism of everything the Romantics called 'disingenuous trappings' intensified as the Revival styles gained ground. These styles were rejected, however, not only because they were disingenuous, but because people associated them with industrially manufactured products, the outward form of which was geared to the taste of the newly wealthy bourgeoisie. And no social class has had as much abuse heaped on it as that of the *nouveaux riches*, because it tried to imitate the aristocracy with cheap factory-made imitations. It was this hatred of the superficial world of the middle class combined with the fear of the mass culture of the industrial cities that put weapons in the hands of critics like William Morris, Emile Zola and Gottfried Semper. Some Revival styles were also politically suspect, because they struck a chord with conservatives and all those who felt nostalgia for the hierarchical society of the Middle Ages. The conservatives claimed that the social order was being undermined by the movement for parliamentary democracy, with its demands for a constitution, universal suffrage and freedom of speech. The Gothic Revival was the symbolic backdrop for this nostalgia for a medieval epoch where harmony reigned and class struggle was unheard of. The designs of Gothic Revival architects such as A.W.N. Pugin, August Reichensperger and Jean-Baptiste Bethune kept people's hopes for a return of the *ancien régime* alive.[6]

Apart from the fear of social chaos and anarchy, people's dissatisfaction with the absence of an architectural style proper to their own age also played a role. Complaints on this subject recurred throughout the century and were probably to be accounted for by the breakdown in self-confidence that came in the wake of Romanticism with all its artistic liberties. It was one thing for an artist to defy academic traditions, but the world outside the academy lacked order and people felt correspondingly threatened. Furthermore, industry had taken over part of the market that was formerly the domain of the traditional arts and crafts. A spectre was abroad in society and this provoked jeremiads about the decay of culture.

This confusion of styles was also savaged by the historians of architecture. In his *Illustrated Handbook of Architecture* of 1855, the famous nineteenth-century architectural historian James Fergusson mercilessly condemned all Revival styles because art is the expression of a specific age and because the past could not be recalled.[7] Another even more celebrated authority in this field, Eugène Viollet-le-Duc, wrote in his tenth *Entretien* (1863) that the imitation historical buildings of his age 'look like bodies that have been robbed of their souls, remnants of a vanished civilization, a language that nobody understands anymore, not even the people who deploy it. ... The arts are sick, and architecture is dying in the heart of prosperity'. Viollet-le-Duc set his hopes on a new architecture in which *truth* was to be the basic principle. Aesthetic questions such as symmetry and outward forms were only 'conditions secondaires'.[8]

These ideas were to lay the foundations for the Modern Movement and faith in their universal validity would later lead to the moralistic rejection of the Revival styles by the Modernists. The Revival styles – with the exception, however, of the rationalist Gothic Revival – were in their view the expression of a degenerate century. The historians of the period adopted the Modernist viewpoint uncritically. A crude example is Klaus Döhmer's 1976 study of nineteenth-century architectural theory, in which he denounced the Revival styles, in keeping with the tradition of Romantic and Modernist artists before him. Even after 1848, Döhmer wrote, the art of the middle classes remained cut off from the 'fundamental terrain of social reality'. By this he meant that the *bourgeoisie*, in attaining economic welfare, had abandoned itself to empty pomp and had no time for the social conflicts resulting from the growth of the new industrial proletarian class. This is the same reality that William Morris had railed against a hundred years before. As late as 1976, Döhmer could still take offence at what he saw as a superficial historicizing aesthetic and blame the emerging bourgeoisie for the decay of art. With its 'Protestant work ethic and fetishizing of the profit motive', he wrote, it treated art as a 'luxury article'. The historicizing styles in his view were typical of the false consciousness of the nineteenth century.

Appearances Unmasked

The unmasking of the Revival styles, exposing them as the pseudo-architecture of a dishonest and decadent century, was an article of faith for traditionalists as well as Modernists. In combination, this contempt was so universal that in professional circles Revival styles were taken about as seriously as fairground attractions. It was only in the 1970s that art historians began to show an interest in them, but almost nobody yet dared claim that they might even be beautiful.[9]

Kenneth Clark thought that the neo-Gothic style was simply ghastly and wrote a book on the subject in 1928, *The Gothic Revival*. In his introduction he gave it short shrift. 'It produced so little on which our eyes can rest without pain.' Scholarly concern with the Revival styles was just about acceptable, but to praise them was beyond the pale. It was *bon ton* to condemn the nineteenth century, and that was that. Anyone writing about the origins of modern art usually began with a short description of the appalling taste of this period. Hans Curjel, the editor of a volume of articles by Henry van de Velde, started his introduction by saying that this artist was the first to raise his voice against the 'abuse of styles from the past'.[10] This was in 1955, when the contempt for the Revival styles was still universal.

With the Modernists the onslaught became positively bellicose. They based their art on the rejection of the nineteenth-century bourgeois mentality that they saw as leading to an absolute nadir in the history of the arts. In 1921, the architect J.J.P. Oud wrote that the history of architecture showed that the addition of decoration and ornament 'was an obstacle to achieving a pure form of architecture until our time'.[11] He went on to explain that it was only with the Modern Movement that architecture was able to attain the purity it had lacked, because until then, people had failed to understand that ornament was an expression of artistic impotence. What Oud meant to say was that the human species had walked in artistic darkness since primeval times and that only now with the arrival of Modernism had the light of truth finally prevailed. However nonsensical this train of thought may have been, it does display a refreshing self-confidence after an age of uncertainty about architecture's future. The Modernists looked back at the nineteenth century as an age that could not make up its mind which style to adopt – hence the decadent masquerade of Revival styles. In previous ages, too, people had sinned against purity, especially in the Baroque period and the age of Rococo that had degenerated into the voluptuous. In the Modernists' eyes, however, the prize for banality had to go to the Revival styles. According to Walter Gropius, the director of the Bauhaus in Weimar, the origin of all this aesthetic ghastliness lay in the training of architects, who were bombarded with notions about art history and aesthetics. This was nonsense in his view, because 'aesthetics has nothing to do with art'.[12]

C.N. van Goor, reviewing the seminal work *Um 1800* by Paul Mebes in the *Bouwkundig Weekblad* of 1908, blamed the ugliness he saw everywhere on the abolition of the guilds. 'The complete break', he wrote, 'with the traditional manner of building at the beginning of the nineteenth century has exacted a heavy toll. After a period of absolute impotence, an indecorous pursuit of every possible previous architectural style has begun and this has lasted until our own day.' According to him, the abolition of the guilds in 1795 left the field open to cheapjacks and shoddy workmen. Henceforth, clever manufacturers could fob off machine-made imitations of craftsmanship to the rising bourgeoisie, who thought they could get something beautiful for less money. According to Paul Mebes, the only remedy was a return to architectural traditions prior to 1800. Van Goor agreed, arguing that the old traditions were essential for cultural continuity. The Revival styles, by contrast, testified to 'a complete lack of a healthy artistic feeling in general and of any public art in particular'.[13]

The decline in architecture was denounced at the start of the twentieth century just as it had been in the nineteenth. In the early 1900s, modern art had yet to conquer the world, but it had, however, already begun to have an impact, with figures such as Bruno Taut. In the journal *Frühlicht* (1920) he declared war on the 'Wichtigtuerei', or self-importance, of the 'Grabstein- und Friedhofsfassaden' (gravestone and churchyard façades) of the Revival styles: 'zerschmeisst die Muschelkalksteinsäulen in Dorisch, Jonisch und Korinthisch, zertrümmert die Puppenwitze ! Runter mit der "Vornehmheit" der Sandsteine und Spiegelscheiben, in Scherben der Marmor- und Edelholzkram, auf der Müllhaufen mit den Plunder!' (destroy the limestone columns, Doric, Ionic and Corinthian, annihilate the foolery! Down with the 'pretensions' of the sandstone and window panes, break to pieces the marble and wooden lumber. To the dunghill with all this rubbish!). In sentences like these he vented his rage on the bourgeois Renaissance Revival productions of the *Gründerzeit*.[14]

The Dutch architect Jan Gratama was anything but a fanatical Modernist, but his scorn for the Revival styles was no less virulent for that. In 1916, he praised H.P. Berlage for having brought the curtains down on this lifeless masquerade with his introduction of a new realism. This meant that 'all pseudo-architecture, all pointless ornament, the whole mess of distorted, beautiful historical motifs, pointless turrets and balconies, surrogate materials, cement and zinc decorations, all those prettified but empty interiors in polished copper and plush were seen for what they were, a totally bourgeois degeneration of what architecture really is'.[15]

The civil engineer and Delft Technical University professor, J.G. Wattjes, didn't belong to the Modernist avant-garde either, but he too regarded it as beyond dispute that the 'nineteenth century, that has been so exceptionally fruitful in the sciences, had hardly done anything for architecture'. He argued that the blame lay mainly in the imitation of the outward features of historical architecture: 'the works carried out in a Revival style of this sort thus lack not only the charm of the style imitated, but also any artistic value of their own, due to the disparity between their essence and the randomly chosen outward form'.[16]

In the end, the wave of abhorrence carried all before it, so that finally even the man in the street knew that a nineteenth-century façade with Renaissance-style decorative work was ridiculous. That the Renaissance in its turn had imitated antiquity was apparently not a problem.

Cityscape and Tradition

H.P. Berlage much admired the writings of Gottfried Semper and he presumably applauded the scornful remarks this German architect and theoretician of architecture made about the Revival styles of his age. Semper thought it ridiculous to invent new styles of architecture, when a generally accepted style already existed, namely Classicism, that had been invented by the Greeks and Romans and rediscovered and elaborated on in the period after the Middle Ages. This development was in turn replaced by neo-Classicism with its archaeological sources of inspiration. In his view Revival styles were pointless experiments and doomed to failure. As a daunting case of a recent, extremely contrived piece of frippery, Semper pointed to Charles Garnier's opera house of 1870. He also lamented the building of the wide boulevards in Paris, because they disrupted the harmony of the old city. Tradition in architecture, Semper said, is a precious thing and it is as arrogant to try and invent a new style of architecture as it would be to invent a new language.[17]

The idea that historical cities are worth preserving and that the beauty of traditional architecture easily falls prey to new planning schemes and architectural experiments is also found in the work of some Modernists – Adolf Loos and Hendrik Berlage, for example. Nobody jeered at nineteenth-century sham architecture as ferociously as Loos did, especially with his proposition that the nineteenth-century obsession with ornament was a symptom of degeneracy. He had no problem, however, in casting aside his objections when the cityscape of his native Vienna was threatened. In 1914 he blamed the *Heimatkünstler* who wanted to turn a cosmopolitan city into a village with their 'picturesque' farmhouse-style architecture. The imitations of Italian palaces with which Vienna had been stuffed full from the 1870s onwards at any rate gave it a big-city feeling and eighteenth-century architects had also copied Italian models. 'Ich bin für die traditionelle bauweise', he wrote, by which he meant that architects had to take the character of their surroundings into account.[18]

In Berlage, too, one finds the idea that historic cities are artworks in themselves and that it is the task of modern architects to give new urban expansion areas a similar beauty. His article of 1883, 'Amsterdam and Venice', was a eulogy to the beauty of historic cities and a plea to protect Amsterdam against modern encroachments. 'The conservation of the beauties of an illustrious age is of national importance; they are recognized everywhere. Let Amsterdam do the same! The loss of the picturesque beauties of our capital will be mourned too late.'[19] It was in the same vein that he also began his more widely known article of 1894 on 'Architecture and Impressionism' in the journal *Architectura*.

According to Berlage, however, the nineteenth century had done violence to this beauty. He declared that the nineteenth century had been the age of ugliness. He wrote in 1904: 'Our grandfathers, our fathers and we ourselves have lived and continue to live in surroundings that are unprecedented in their ugliness.' He identified capitalism as the cause of this cultural poverty. Yet capitalism was a necessary stage in his view, because it would provoke a counter-movement, that of socialism. Something similar, he argued, had also occurred in the arts. The hegemony of the Revival styles was therefore necessary if architecture was to be rescued from the 'swamp of total degeneracy'.[20]

With these words, he must have had his own designs in the neo-Renaissance style in mind, such as that of his first design for a new Stock Exchange building in Amsterdam of 1885, the design for a new town hall in Zutphen in 1889 or the house at Herengracht 115, built in 1890. In these cases he probably chose the Renaissance Revival style so that the buildings fitted in with the architectural character of the city. This was hardly surprising, if one bears in mind the period when he was working. Indeed,

42 Design for a new town hall in Zutphen by H.P. Berlage (1889)

43 Oude Turfmarkt 147 (third from right) in Amsterdam by A.L. van Gendt (1884)

ROMANTIC MODERNISM

one can safely say that the image of Amsterdam was mainly determined by the vogue of Renaissance Revival façades designed in the second half of the nineteenth century by architects like A.L. van Gendt and his two sons, J.G. and A.D.N. van Gendt, by G. van Arkel, A. Salm, J.A. van Straten, Cornelis Outshoorn, A. N. Godefroy and others. The Dutch historian of the architecture Vincent van Rossem recently produced a survey of the neo-Renaissance buildings in Amsterdam and concluded that the architectural image of the city centre is to an important extent determined by 'the buildings of the period from 1875 to 1914'.[21]

The nineteenth century, then, had a better understanding than the twentieth of the need for urban harmony. If by way of a mental experiment one was to imagine Amsterdam without the Renaissance Revival, one's picture of the city would simply vanish into thin air.

Berlage discussed the phenomenon of the Revival styles on another occasion, in 1924. He wrote then that out of the 'complete breakdown' of nineteenth-century culture and the ensuing 'architectural chaos', two styles were created which 'could not be denied a certain logical raison d'être' – the neo-Renaissance and the neo-Gothic. The study of the Gothic style had restored the rational principles of building while the Dutch Renaissance formed the apex of the national architecture of the Netherlands. He added, however, that these styles did not reveal the character of their own age and were therefore unnatural and doomed to perish.[22]

For all their promise, then, the two Revival styles were conquered in their turn by another nineteenth-century myth, namely that an architectural style had to be an expression of its own age. Berlage had also read this in Semper, who said in 1853 that architecture is of necessity the expression of 'social, political and religious institutions'. [23] According to this train of thought, the Revival styles were an expression of the cultural poverty of the nineteenth century. Later on, the Modernists took over this viewpoint, while rehabilitating the 'hidden ingenuity' of the nineteenth century as revealed in the technological culture of engineers. This rehabilitation, as is well known, was then taken up by the historians. Henry-Russell Hitchcock wrote in 1929 that the peculiar tragedy of the 'Age of Romanticism' was that its most beautiful monuments cannot be called architecture at all. The most beautiful products of the nineteenth century, he said, belonged to the category of utility buildings – 'bridges, for example, and exposition halls … it is nearly true therefore that there was no altogether great Romantic architecture as such'.[24]

Architectural Time Regained

What in fact did Berlage mean in 1924 when he spoke of the 'logical raison d'être' of the Renaissance Revival style? His argument was that it was an attempt to make the Dutch Renaissance of the seventeenth century 'applicable to the new age'. Given his own former Revival designs, Berlage must once have attached some credence to a rebirth of the traditional architectural style of the Netherlands, but in 1924 for understandable reasons he didn't feel he had to excuse himself for youthful convictions that had since been exposed as false. His lecture of 1904, discussed above, perhaps gives some answer to what he actually meant by this 'logical raison d'être'. It seems that he saw the Renaissance Revival style as an instrument for restoring the harmony of the historical cityscape as it had been up till about 1850: 'The fact that there still existed a certain style', Berlage said, 'is the reason why the last offshoots of the Renaissance, the old houses of the beginning and middle of the previous century, still appear pleasing to us, notwithstanding the architects who made them. They only serve to testify to the power of a past stylistic period that was such that even its last, sober representatives had qualities that win our admiration.' Until about 1850, Berlage meant, there wasn't any break with the past; this only occurred with the emergence of a variety of styles, of eclecticism. This breach could perhaps have been healed by bringing back the style of the Dutch Renaissance. That is what Berlage probably meant in 1924.

Some years later, Hitchcock said something similar. He greatly admired the 'rationalist Classicism' of the beginning of the nineteenth century, but he felt that the buildings that were deliberately built in the medieval style were of a distinctly inferior quality and were in any case far less distinguished than the work produced 'within the bounds of the Classical Revival'.[25] The nineteenth-century architectural style, according to Berlage and Hitchcock, remained unspoiled until eclecticism reared its head. The architectural tragedy of the nineteenth century was the breach with the tradition of Classicism.

Berlage was not the first to acknowledge the importance for city planning of the picturesque architecture of the Dutch Renaissance. He was following here in the footsteps of Isaak Gosschalk. Gosschalk regarded Dutch architecture of the turn of the seventeenth century as the artistic highpoint of the national style. In the journal *Eigen haard* of 1875, he wrote that, 'all the buildings of this age have something individual, something with a zest for life … these good traditions survived for another hundred years, only gradually making way for the cold gentility that appears foreign to us because it is no indigenous style and doesn't fit in with our national character.'[26]

According to Auke van der Woud, the great flowering of the Renaissance Revival in the 1880s can be explained amongst other things by the 'discovery of the picturesque cityscape'.[27] In 1859 A.N. Godefroy concluded that 'the mixture of brick and stone of the early seventeenth century' is typical of our country and deserved imitation for this reason.[28] In a speech to the Society for the Advancement of Architecture in 1884, C. Muysken said that the Dutch Renaissance style was excellently suited to the Dutch cities, which 'are not particularly monumental but are certainly picturesque.'[29]

Auke van der Woud quoted a sentence from the journal *De Portefeuille* of 1886 that Berlage would certainly have agreed with – that in Amsterdam 'a multitude of beautiful façades have been built, inspired by seventeenth-century examples' which 'give the street [the Ruyterkade in this case] a lively picturesque appearance'. The beauty of a historical city was therefore served by continuing to work in the architectural style that defined its historical character. This must have been Berlage's 'logical raison d'être' of the Renaissance Revival. Since the other Revival styles were unable to meet this requirement, the Renaissance defeated them and enjoyed a short-lived place in the sun at the end of the nineteenth century.

It is curious that Marcel Proust never made the connection between his system for stopping time and the Revival styles of the nineteenth century. In *Le Temps Retrouvé* (1927), he explains how time can be halted by allowing the past to return in the present. Memories evoked, for instance, by a certain melody or sound can endow certain events with something of eternity. Due to the miraculous return of the past in the present, Proust became reconciled with transience and even with death. The act of remembering sometimes works as a remedy against one's fear of the future. In a sense, this resembles the attempts made in the nineteenth century to restore the past to life. It was in this century that more people than ever before became fascinated with history and thus also with historical architecture. It may probably be suggested that the Revival styles initially served to recapture the links with the past that had been broken by modern times; only in the second instance did they serve ideological ends.

Building an imitation Renaissance house may have been the snobbish bid of the *nouveau riche bourgeoisie* to appropriate the power that the nobility had lost, but in the first instance, it was presumably an attempt to preserve the past in the present and thus to cast out all notion of transience. This was of course an illusion, and the same goes for Proust's pages in 1927 about time regained. Nonetheless, the desire for continuity and the restoration of a world that was seen as threatened by Socialism and steam engines had almost the entire culture of nineteenth-century Europe in its thrall. This hankering after the past was, however, scoffed at in the twentieth century and the sight of these Revival style buildings still evokes feelings of condescending affection.

To our modern way of thinking it is impossible to resurrect the past in this way. The recreation of a historical style of architecture is an illusion and can never fool anyone. That at least was how the nineteenth-century rationalists saw it and the Modernists after them shared their views. In this, however, they were more radical than the Romantics, because the Modernists have turned their back on the past and discouraged its study in the hope that the future will be more beautiful than anything the past had to offer. The Romantics, on the other hand, have gone down in history as tragic antiheroes. The mistake the Modernists made lay in their failure to recognize that implacable hostility to the past was not essential to buttressing up their own *raison d'être*. Less short-sighted, Berlage understood this when he denounced the damage done to Amsterdam in his day.

The Renaissance Revival style is one reason why the cityscape of Amsterdam has remained intact. The illusion created by their architects was an admirable attempt to revive the past by means of an architectural decor, to exorcize people's fears and to reinstall the past in the present. In the end, all that excess began to cloy, but the illusion was beautiful and it has given rise to an architecture that has a melancholic splendour. It is maybe precisely this hankering after an idyllic past that explains why the Revival styles evoke something that has more to do with nostalgia than aesthetics. It is as if all they could achieve with their emphatic repetition of past architectural motifs was to convey their impotent longing for lost beauty. The beauty evoked in this way may be contrived, but in a certain sense it remains moving. In the last decade of the nineteenth century, imitation sometimes ended up as a parody of historical architecture. In the free, almost aimless and cheerful style that developed, for instance, in Parisian domestic architecture and which was raised to unprecedented heights in Amsterdam by Jan Springer, the neo-Renaissance changed its character. It became less commemorative and more like a piece of theatre, less sombre too, because the remaining elements of seriousness were laughed away in a carefree decor of drunken Palladian orders.[30] It goes without saying that the Gothic Revival, with its religious roots, was incapable of achieving such carefree abandon.

The purges of the Modernists put an end to this carefree spirit. Their victory, however, should not lead us to conclude that the Renaissance Revival style was an architectural dead end. Berlage came to that conclusion in order to secure his place in the history of architecture and the Modernists followed him in this, but was their contribution to architecture any better than that of the Revival styles? They wanted to break with history, but in the beginning of the twenty-first century, their project has come to seem just as heroic and tragic as the attempt of the nineteenth century to restore the past. In the final analysis, the Modernists were also pursuing an illusion, that of the 'First Machine Age' that, with its inhuman blocks of concrete, also proved a one-way street. Compared with these, the nineteenth-century illusion appears somewhat more humane. This is perhaps why we are becoming increasingly fond of the Revival styles.

Nostalgia and Imitation

Imitations and Emulations

The copy is an act of homage to its original and repeating it is an act of commemoration. It may not be possible to improve on the original artwork, but the copy does offer a pleasing experience, because it recalls the admiration of people of former times for the original. In his *Essay on Taste* written in 1759, the art theoretician Alexander Gerard wrote that 'similitude is a very powerful principle of association which augments our pleasure'. 'When excellent originals are imitated', he explained, 'the copies derive their charms, not merely from exactness of imitation, but also from the excellence which they represent.' In his eyes, imitations were 'agreeable', because they generate 'a strong tendency to comparison', thus fostering 'a gentle exertion of the mind'. The copy always enjoys something of the reflected glory of the original and this is what makes it valuable. This is true of copies but also of emulation, the free imitation that strives to equal the object imitated. The latter was one of the artistic conventions of Classicism. In the introduction to his *I Quattro Libri dell' Architettura* (1570), Andrea Palladio wrote that the architecture of 'gli Antichi Romani' and the classical treatise on the subject, *De Architectura Decem Libri*, by the Roman architect Vitruvius set the highest criteria. Later on, Vitruvianism lost something of its universal legitimacy as a result of the rationalist study of scholars such as Claude Perrault in 1673 and Edmund Burke in 1757, but it would be many years before the Classicist canon was finally dismantled; as late as 1846, the secretary of the Académie des Beaux-Arts, D. Raoul-Rochette, was persuaded that the ideal of beauty as upheld by the Greeks and the Romans was universal, by which he did not mean that their architecture had to be copied, but that it was worthy of imitation: 'non pas à copier les Grecs et les Romains, mais à les imiter, en prenant, comme eux, dans l'art et dans la nature, tout ce qui se prête aux convenances de toutes les sociétés et aux besoins de tous les temps.'[1]

Imitation in the sense of the copying of classical architecture is something quite different from the production of copies; there is nothing to indicate, however, that the latter phenomenon was regarded as unacceptable. Replicas have always had a right to exist. Most Greek sculptures of

44 The market square, Diksmuide, Belgium, before 1914

45 The market square, Diksmuide, after the post-war reconstruction

ROMANTIC MODERNISM

the fifth and fourth centuries BC are only known to us through Roman copies. According to Richard Krautheimer, most Carolingian bases, capitals and mouldings north of the Alps were copies of Roman originals from the Rhineland. Architectural imitations played an important role throughout the Middle Ages. 'A great number of edifices', he wrote, 'were erected throughout the Middle Ages with the intention of imitating a highly venerated prototype.' One such prototype was the Church of the Holy Sepulchre in Jerusalem, which was imitated on countless occasions between the fifth and seventeenth centuries. One of the most celebrated examples dates from the early eleventh century when Bishop Meinwerk of Paderborn sent Abbot Wino to Jerusalem to measure the church so as to build his own church 'ad similitudinem S. Jerosolimitane ecclesie'. One striking feature of these medieval imitations is that it was not so much the outward form that was copied as specific characteristics, but that doesn't alter the fact that the essential aim was to copy a revered edifice from the past.[2]

Every architectural style has been spread by means of imitations or free copies. The distinct unity of style in the great French cathedrals of the thirteenth century is a good case in point: 'A classic mode of thought in architecture', Henri Focillon wrote, 'is as stable as a beautiful language, which, once established, has no need of neologisms.'[3] However that may be, it remains a fact that this unity could only be achieved through imitations. In the end the Gothic style was replaced by Classicism, but imitation as such retained its prestige. Between 1660 and 1664 for instance Louis le Vau completed the largest part of the Cour Carrée in the Louvre in the style of the original elevation by Pierre Lescot of 1549. Throughout Europe, palaces were built after classical models and the parks surrounding them were adorned with imitations of classical statuary. Louis XIV had replicas of the most famous classical statues brought from Italy and installed in the gardens of Versailles and other monarchs followed his example.[4] In the art of landscape gardening too imitation prevailed, even during the Romantic period, or rather despite Romanticism, since a great number of Baroque gardens were altered at that time in more or less direct imitation of the English landscaped parks.

It is true that artistic imitation began to be seen in a bad light during the nineteenth century, but at the same time it gained ground due to historicism – the imitation of historic styles, preferably those that alluded to the national heritage. Historicism in its turn was driven out by the Modern Movement with the argument that architecture had above all to be functional and that stylistic imitations were a tragic mistake perpetrated by the nineteenth century. Nonetheless, despite its rational and humanitarian ideals, the Modern Movement never succeeded in totally eliminating imitation. Why was this so? Perhaps the explanation is that it is simply impossible to create an architectural design that is based a hundred per cent on functional requirements and which does not contain the slightest reference to other works of architecture. Presumably no architect is capable of completely ignoring his feeling for form and designing as a sort of automaton, without any memory of the architecture he or she had once been taught to admire. Pure functionalism is perhaps a fiction after all.

In the nineteenth century then, rationalists and Romantics began to undermine the foundations of Classicism, arguing that imitating the great models of the past was in fact the opposite of art, because art was supposed to originate in the imagination. But at the beginning of the nineteenth century this idea certainly had no universal acceptance and, according to the art critic Etienne Delécluze in the *Journal des Débats* of 1828, it was even dangerous. The notion of *originality*, he argued, could lead to mistaken ideas and exaggerated expectations, 'because it is an attribute of feeble minds eagerly to want to invent something new, even at the risk of being thought weird.'[5]

Delécluze remained an adherent of the Classical canon, even after this had entirely lost all authority. 'Nous sommes à la veille d'une révolution dans les beaux-arts', Stendhal wrote in 1824.[6] This revolution was directed against academism and against imitations of classical art. Stendhal accused the academic artists of his time of producing work that was totally lifeless. In architecture, too, people longed for something new; no new style, however, had been invented and from time to time voices were raised deploring this. In 1834, for instance, the German art historian Franz Kugler complaining that his own age had produced no distinctive style and that later generations would call us 'imitators' (Nachahmer).[7] The French architect, Eugène Viollet-le-Duc, said something similar in 1863. In his view, the nineteenth century that had been so fruitful in the field of the natural sciences was incapable of producing anything in the field of architecture other than 'pastiches'.[8]

Seeing that his own contribution to the architecture of the nineteenth century was mainly inspired by medieval models, he could just have well have accused himself. Even if he managed to forget his own 'pastiches', he might well have read what his colleague, Charles Garnier, the architect of the Opéra in Paris (1875), had said about them in 1869 – namely that, while Viollet-le-Duc's restorations were excellent, his architectural projects suffered from his excessive reverence for antiquity. 'We love antiquarianism', Garnier said, 'but we need it as an aid and not as a mistress; we want to learn from the past, but we also want to create something new (nous voulons créer).'[9]

The English historian of architecture, James Fergusson, also had objections to the imitation of historic styles. In his book, *A History of the Modern Styles in Architecture*, (1862) he said that 'imitative work can never appeal to our higher intellectual faculties'. Imitating something, according to him, was an ignorant activity and architects should therefore 'give up all imitation of past styles'. They had to try and develop a new style, he wrote, but he omitted to say how one was supposed to set about that.

The new style only emerged at the turn of the twentieth century and its arrival was a cause for universal celebration, coupled with frequent reminders about how, in the dark ages of architecture back in the nineteenth century, people like Kugler and Fergusson suffered under the ignorant hegemony of Revival styles. How they would rejoice if they could have seen their dream of a new and original architecture finally fulfilled! The true prophets of the nineteenth century were men like Kugler, not those who had advocated historicism all their lives. Against this background, it is understandable that the concept of originality began to gain in prestige while imitation landed in the dustbin of history. Conservation, which can hardly exist as an activity without imitation, because it is powerless to do anything if it can't make copies of dilapidated elements, was thus forced in the long run to grub around in this dustbin to save at least something of its *raison d'être* – something it found deeply embarrassing.

An early example of this development was in 1918 when the Modernists denounced the reconstruction of the monuments in Belgium that had been destroyed during the First World War. The vast majority of the local population however called for the ruins to be rebuilt in the former style – something that usually ended up as reconstruction in the traditional local style. Meticulous architectural reproduction was reserved for monuments of special historical value. For ordinary townhouses, the local style was considered sufficient as well as normative, because nobody wanted to return to a style that had never been thought beautiful, such as Classical stucco architecture. From the viewpoint of the preservation of historical buildings, it was impossible to defend this correction of the built past, but in practice, the official bodies concerned hardly raised a murmur against this falsification of history. Since then, many rebuilt Belgian towns have consisted of imitations of what were thought to be the dominant stylistic features. Reconstruction meant that any foreign variants were excluded, as though the devastation of war had provided a unique opportunity for carrying out architectural purges.

At that time an enormous affection for traditionalist architecture prevailed throughout Europe, something that may have been a response to the shock of the war that had devastated not only buildings but the whole civilization of this continent. It may also however have been provoked by a fear of Modernism, which had gained little acceptance among the general public and was thought of as inhumane or even Communist-inspired. This fear melted away like snow before the sun in the years after the Second World War, when Europe began to imitate the modern world according to the American model. It was only in France that this led to a crisis of identity among intellectuals, as one learns from *Le Défi Américain* by Jean-Jacques Servan-Schreiber (1967). In the post-war period, traditionalism in architecture was suspect because it gave rise to memories of the *Blut und Boden* culture of the Third Reich. For this reason, Modernism, which was thought of as uncontaminated, especially where the reconstruction of the cities of Germany was concerned, was given unbridled freedom. This was also true of everything that Modernism implied – an infrastructure that was automobile-friendly, the use of concrete as the sole material for domestic architecture and high-rise developments for offices. The German authority

46 The Technical University, Bandung, Java, by Henri Maclaine Pont (1920)

on architecture, Niels Gutschow, once pointed out that these Modernist urbanist ideas had already been developed and projected on the orders of the Third Reich and were therefore anything but untainted. Nazism, it should be remembered, also had a modern face, characterized mainly by the application of modern technologies to solve social issues.[10]

Copies in Search of an Original

Architectural imitations have the power to conjure up pleasant memories as they allude to major artistic achievements of the past. They can restore our links with the past that have been destroyed in war, and they can also travel – for instance, to the colonies. Colonial architecture, however, was not always a pure reproduction of the architecture of the country of origin. The colonizers often felt a need for an architecture that in some way reflected the character of the colony. This may have been prompted by respect for the local culture, but the architecture of the colonizer was not expected to resemble the indigenous products too closely, because in colonial relations, social distinctions had to be preserved. Even if the colonizer wanted to ignore these differences by imitating local construction traditions, there would still be an inequality because the indigenous characteristics chosen were of course the ones the colonizer preferred. One remarkable example of a somewhat misguided imitation of indigenous architecture is the Technical College in Bandung in Java built in 1920 after a design by the Dutch architect, Henri Maclaine Pont. It is somewhat misguided, because the modern function of the building bears so little relation to its indigenous design, but the architect wanted the building to be a token of his admiration for the architecture of Java. In this way, he aimed to make a contribution to perpetuating local culture.[11] In the 1970s, long after decolonization had taken place, the regionalism of architects like Henri Maclaine Pont began once more to be in vogue and the Indonesian government even encouraged this development so as to protect the identity of the cultural landscape of the nation. People took the idea to such an extreme that traditional roofs were also used for the buildings of the Soekarno-Hatta Airport in Cengkareng, although these were implemented not by local carpenters, but by an architect from France, P. Andreau.[12]

Emigrants can sometimes preserve their own culture for generations. Once they have settled in their adopted country, they will build reproductions of the villages they were forced to leave because of poverty or persecutions. In North America some of the first settlements of European immigrants have been preserved, as one reads in *To Build in a New Land. Ethnic Landscapes in North America* by Allen G. Noble (1992). In Ohio, for instance, there are still some half-timbered houses built by German immigrants, and in Wisconsin, where large settlements of Belgians were established between 1853 and 1857, one can still see brick houses that are very like houses in Belgium, except that in North America, the bricks are no longer used except as a cosmetic decoration for walls that are built of logs. Similarly, there are still Danish houses in Iowa and Minnesota, traditional Czech houses in South Dakota, and Ukrainian houses and churches in the west of Canada. In her article on the German settlements in Texas, Gerlinde Leiding concluded that 'distinctive vernacular architecture still dominates the landscape in a large area of central Texas.' She goes on to say that they have become tourist attractions today – 'the collective charm of the small ethnic buildings in New Braunsfeld and Fredericksburg, together with frequent festivals to celebrate German customs and traditions attract visitors year-round.' This 'little Germany' in Texas suggests a certain resistance on the part of the local population to being absorbed in the celebrated American 'melting pot'. This notion was once the dream of newcomers from Europe, who desired a life free from the restraints of the nationalist and religious traditions that had been such a feature of their existence in the old world. In the New World, after all, there were no longer any social distinctions and a garbage collector could become a millionaire. This ideal of the 'melting pot' is now on the wane, although nobody knows why. Instead a new cult has arisen in America – that of one's 'roots'.

For large groups of Muslims living in Western countries, the mosque is a symbol of their unity. The architect Hasan-Uddin Khan wrote in 1990 that 'the mosque is a very important collective sign of the community's presence, and usually the first public building to be erected'.[13] Gulzar Haider is one of a group of architects who claims that imitations of traditional architecture offer a form of consolation to people who feel deracinated. He

47 *The Faisal mosque, Islamabad (1986)*

designed the Bai'tul Islam Mosque in Toronto especially with a view to this social function, in order, so he said in 1996, to give the Islamic minority a feeling of security.[14]

However, in their own countries as well, Muslims feel that Western influences are eroding their historic traditions. The Pakistani architect Syed Zaigham Shafiq Jaffrey complained a while ago about the lack of a cosy atmosphere in the Modernist mosques in his country. Architects who have been trained in the West want to design modern buildings, but generally speaking, the local population prefers traditional designs for mosques. Modernist architects look down, for instance, on the traditionalist Bhong Mosque in the Punjab in Pakistan, built in 1982 by Ghazi Mohammad Rais, because of its excessive ornament, while they admire the Modernist Faisal Mosque in the Margalla Hills near Islamabad built by the Turkish architect, Vedat Dalokay, because it looks like a space ship which is 'ready to take off'. According to Syed Zaigham, however, most people think the Bongh Mosque is more beautiful because they look for 'familiarity and moorings in a rapidly changing world over which they have no control. They search for their identity.'[15]

The Indian architect A.G. Krishna Menon advises people to encourage local construction traditions so as to restrain the influence of Western architecture.[16] The whole world is inundated with Western buildings, and everywhere one hears complaints about the loss of one's identity. The whole world seems to have become deracinated.

Is there a way of reversing the trend? Maybe the past can only return in disguise. Disguises are usually tasteless, like the new 'neo-Chinese' shopping street in the centre of Shanghai that was built after virtually the whole historical city had been modernized. With the help of the local conservation department, the city authorities ordered a pedestrian shopping street to be built in an Imperial Revival style. The residents of Shanghai had to be content with this – a single street in a style that the city had never had.[17] The residents of Shanghai and other metropolises have become strangers in their own cities and, when they get the chance, they escape the anonymity of urban life and buy a traditional house somewhere in the countryside, or else they commission a new one altogether – one that has a 'local' character.

Interesting examples of this quest for the 'sense of place', for a style that is indigenous and in which the inhabitants can sense ties with the history and customs of a specific area, can be found in *Java Style*, an illustrated book published by Thames and Hudson in 1997. The author, Peter Schoppert, described his work as a voyage of discovery towards 'the feeling for a location that comes from its architecture and landscape, from interiors, views and vistas both intimate and panoramic, furniture and fittings, the domestic settings for the mundane moments that make up a way of life.' This book praises a certain interior because it has 'a striking modern Islamic tropical look'. In itself this is a somewhat paradoxical description, but what is apparently involved is not so much any faithfulness to history or geography as the evocation of an enchanting, Oriental fairy-tale atmosphere for the wealthy cosmopolitan.

Just how besotted some people become over such matters can be seen in an article in the magazine *Residence* of October 1999 about a woman in Maarn, Holland, who has furnished her home as an English manor house with hunting paraphernalia and paintings depicting hounds. She is 'crazy about Scotland' and 'a passionate huntswoman'. She is in love with 'the grandeur of the past', 'of the country life of the upper classes between 1800 and 1940.' All that is antique or antiquated is at her fingertips, so that she may enjoy a lifestyle that she hopes is a true reflection of that of the English country gentry. Life as a copy of another, more beautiful life that, depending on the whim of fashion, will be either elegant or else 'local' – this is something that appeals to all those who feel deracinated or discontented with their home in a modern suburb.

The architectural copy can best be studied with reference to magazines that specialize in elegant or exotic lifestyles. What imitations like this have in common is the zeal with which the original is imitated. In a sense, imitations end up looking more real than their original – to use the well-known term of the French philosopher Jean Baudrillard, they are 'hyperréel'. They are so effective and precise in imitating what their clients have in mind that the imitation overshadows the authentic. It is apparently comforting to live out one's days in an atmosphere of centuries-old traditions and it is also comforting to see how well the imitation adapts itself to the traditional landscape.

48 A Victorian house built in the 1990s (in the Old House Journal from September 1993 new 'old' houses like this are called 'reproduction houses')

A Degenerate Century

Imitation hasn't always been considered tasteless. It only began to be seen as such in the nineteenth century, partly due to the work of innovators such as William Morris. Morris's frustration with the art of his own age is legendary, but due to the new admiration for nineteenth-century Revival styles, his frustration is currently becoming increasingly hard to comprehend. In his eyes the whole nineteenth century was to blame. He called it 'that degenerate century with its pedantic imitations of classical architecture of the most revolting ugliness, and ridiculous travesties of Gothic buildings …'[18] Following in the footsteps of William Morris, the Modernists developed a contempt for the Revival styles that was so profound as to be irrational. One result was that the study of Revival styles as an academic and theoretical discipline ceased to exist. Educated Europeans found the entire artistic production of this 'degenerated' age abhorrent. Architectural imitations represented the absolute nadir of this century. The generation after the Second World War no longer has any first-hand link with William Morris's loathing, but it still recurs in reference works, such as *Changing Ideals in Modern Architecture* (1965) by Peter Collins.

In his discussion of the work of the German architect Leo von Klenze, the creator of the Walhalla in Regensburg, which was built as a copy of the Parthenon in Athens in 1842, Collins wrote that Klenze was actually an artistic charlatan, because it apparently made little difference to him which style he built in. According to Collins, Klenze 'displayed a certain lack of artistic integrity in the indifference with which he indiscriminately adopted various styles in accordance with his clients' wishes.' Elsewhere in this very widely used reference work, Collins said that architects who copy a historical building are behaving unethically: 'The architects who so easily built copies of famous models from antiquity were indifferent as to the ethical implications which the choice of style necessarily raised for their more scrupulous colleagues.' In his eyes, nineteenth-century historicism was a mistake; like every form of 'stylistic imitation', it should be rejected 'as reprehensible for ever.'[19]

Collins did not even entertain the possibility that there might be another viewpoint on the historicizing architecture of the nineteenth century. If one bears in mind that an incredible, almost endless number of buildings were produced in Revival styles in the course of this despised century by the prevailing elite of almost every country in the world, one is bound to think it strange that these styles were held to be nothing more than a fatal mistake to be condemned by scholars to the garbage heap of history. Collins did not even bother to speculate on how it came about that the nineteenth century could have made such a 'fatal mistake'.

It might well be however that nineteenth-century historicism was by no means a symptom of cultural anaemia but the exact opposite; perhaps it was a period when European civilization rested on its laurels. The Romantic Age viewed the past with a new sort of historical awareness and this inspired it to restore the past to celebrate and commemorate it. The average nineteenth-century contractor or designer of a Revival-style building certainly did not see himself as someone who 'displayed a certain lack of artistic integrity', to quote Peter Collins's dismissive verdict on Leo von Klenze. Collins was using the artistic criteria of the twentieth century to condemn those of the nineteenth century. It was the kind of mistake one could forgive an undergraduate for making, whereas Collins had certainly put his student years well behind him. One can only assume then that he was blinkered by a faith in the universal validity of Modernism. What is more, he was not the only one to be so blinkered, with the result that architectural history contains almost no suggestion that there may have been a positive side to the Revival styles.

It is quite possible that historicism was a heroic attempt to prevent a break with the past. It may also have been a way of sublimating the fear of such a break. Perhaps the intention was to build comforting architecture, one of compromise, confronted as one was with the voracious energy of modern times. Perhaps it was intended as an act of homage to the heritage of European architecture. But Modernists like Peter Collins were not interested in the motives of nineteenth-century consumers, and indeed it was only in the 1970s that people began to ask this question. For the Modernists, Revival styles were treated at best as a curiosity.

William Morris's dislike of these styles was still the prevailing view in

1971 when Die Neue Sammlung held a major exhibition in Munich on the legacy of nineteenth-century engineering. The title of the catalogue was ominous: *Die verborgene Vernunft. Funktionale Gestaltung im 19. Jahrhundert*. In 1971, however, a certain reappraisal of Revival styles had already begun and the interesting thing is that the organizers of this exhibition regarded this reappraisal as inexplicable and thus to be avoided. They were willing to give the nineteenth century a fair chance of cultural rehabilitation, but this was not supposed to degenerate into a foolish admiration for bourgeois pseudo-Baroque architecture or other such follies. The organizer of this exhibition, Wend Fischer, wrote in the catalogue that he viewed the recent flurry of interest in the pompous kitsch of the nineteenth century as a 'neues Unrecht', a new injustice being perpetrated on the nineteenth century: 'Die Schwächen der Epoche in Qualitäten umzumünzen, ist keine Rehabilitierung' (presenting the defects of the century as virtues is no rehabilitation). In his opinion, if one wanted to rehabilitate the nineteenth century, the only way to do so was to reappraise the architecture that paved the way for Functionalism. The significance of nineteenth-century architecture lay concealed behind the historicizing false façades, because it was there that the 'Vernunft', or ingenuity, of the iron constructions – rationalism cast in metal – was to be found.[20]

In fact, one of Fischer's older colleagues, Henry-Russell Hitchcock, had already said as much in 1929, when he remarked that the tragedy of the 'Age of Romanticism' was that 'its finest monuments did not belong to the province of architecture, but to the world of technology: 'bridges, for example, and exposition halls … it is nearly true therefore that there was no altogether great Romantic architecture as such.'[21] In 1972, Nikolaus Pevsner wrote that it must have been extremely difficult for the nineteenth century to shake off architectural traditions: 'to break that convention required men of exceptional calibre, and even they could only win after Morris and his followers had softened the defences.'[22] According to Pevsner, the 'Revivalists' had walked in darkness until the dawn of the 'Modern Movement'.

Some people went a step further and accused the nineteenth century of hypocrisy. Historicism in their view was a sublimation of political impotence and a statement of the frustration of the bourgeois class. Klaus Döhmer said something like this in his dissertation of 1976 on the architectural theories of the nineteenth century. His perspective on this period was imbued with Marxist ideas about the false consciousness of an emerging middle class in a capitalist society. The bourgeoisie, he thought, was blinded by false values and false aesthetics. He had presumably read about how the bourgeoisie came to be so degenerate in the *Communist Manifesto* by Marx and Engels, published in 1848.

At the beginning of the nineteenth century, according to Döhmer, the bourgeoisie opted not for what he called 'the early signs of functionalism', but for an imitation of Greek architecture. He condemned this as a regressive choice: 'Gräkoklassizismus und der Rigidität seiner ästhetischen Rückorientierung' (neo-Hellenism and the rigidity of an aesthetic nostalgia).

The functionalism of the turn of the nineteenth century was progressive, and pointed the way towards Modernism, whereas the Revival styles only clung to the past. This is an almost-perfect example of what historians have called the 'Whig interpretation of history' – the tendency to describe the past in terms of the present. As Döhmer saw it, the fact that the bourgeoisie of the nineteenth century opted for a nostalgic architecture merely confirmed that it was a period of decadence, concerned solely with superficial aesthetic sensations. In this way, nineteenth-century society simply postponed the day when the arts would be saved from the clutches of the false precepts of imitation art: 'Einmal mehr zeigt sich hier Ästhetik von ihrer manipulativen, ihrer anti-emancipatorischen Seite' (Once again, aesthetics shows here its manipulative, anti-emancipatory side). This is the last sentence of Klaus Döhmer's book and, were this still necessary, it clearly shows where his hatred came from: of everything that aspired to be beautiful. It would be difficult to find a better spokesman for Modernism.[23]

Architecture, Critical and Uncritical

In 1785, Thomas Jefferson, the architect of Virginia State Capitol, the design of which was based on that of the Maison Carrée in Nîmes, a Roman temple from 16 BC, said that it was much more sensible to take an existing design as one's starting point than to devise something new, because it was 'a model already devised and approved by the general suffrage of the world'. If one asks an architect to invent something himself, the chance is much greater that it will end in failure – 'in which way experience shows that about once in a thousand times a pleasing form is hit upon'. This tale about Jefferson is found in Peter Collins's book mentioned above, *Changing Ideals in Modern Architecture*. Collins had a low opinion of Jefferson, because, in his view, the building in Virginia belonged to the reprehensible category of imitations built with a totally different purpose than its original. Collins thought that imitations like this were absurd, shamelessly displaying as they did the hallmarks of the 'regressive' tendency of historicism.[24]

Maybe Thomas Jefferson was less backward than Collins realized. What is wrong, after all, with repeating a successful design? Why should a client take an unnecessary risk? Apparently, for many people such imitations were not a bad idea at all and throughout the nineteenth century a large number of clients and architects were perfectly happy to draw inspiration from the historical masterpieces of architecture. After all, there was no contemporary style – something that many people deplored. One such person was Sydney Smirke, the architect of the Carlton Club in London (built in 1847 as a copy of the sixteenth-century Biblioteca Marciana by Jacopo Sansovino in Venice). We ought to have a new style, he explained, because the imitation of historical styles was no solution, but he admitted that he had no idea how one was to be developed. Instead he decided, 'to seek rather for that which is good, than for that which is new, and in this search you may perchance fall in with something new which is good'.[25]

Peter Collins was not persuaded by either Jefferson or Smirke. In the last chapter of *Changing Ideals* he returned to the subject of historicism, once more telling his readers that this was 'the worst failing of the early nineteenth century'. But what was an architect supposed to do, Collins asked, when commissioned to design a building in a historical setting? In such cases he should design something that 'harmonizes with earlier forms without sacrificing any of the principles of the modern age.' The architect's task has to do with 'creating a humane environment', and it was thus essential that 'a new building fits harmoniously into the environment into which it is set'. Collins's advice comes down to designing an architecture that would be a sort of compromise between regionalism and Functionalism. The result would be a generally applicable form of architecture, a 'banal architecture', in that it wouldn't draw attention to itself. This would be much better, according to Collins, than 'to seek architectural novelty for its own sake'.

It is perhaps surprising that someone like Peter Collins should give us a lesson in architectural etiquette, because as a principled Modernist he ought not to have made function secondary to the requirement to preserve a 'harmonious cityscape'. He did do so, however, and it is to his credit, even if he didn't say what such an adaptable architecture would look like.

At any rate, both Jefferson and Collins felt that excessive creativity was a risky business – the former because most new designs prove disappointing and the latter because these new designs encroach on the harmony of the cityscape. Jefferson was writing in 1785, when architectural extravagances were still the exception, but in Collins' day, the situation was quite different. By then the triumphal march of Modernism had reached every corner of the globe, making indigenous architecture a rarity. People were beginning to wonder whether the aim of Modernism was to eradicate all local architectural styles from the face of the earth.

Influenced by Gianni Vattimo's book *La fine della modernità* (1985), Kenneth Frampton came to realize that buildings were built in the same way throughout the world. As a result, he wrote, he began increasingly to appreciate 'a self-consciously cultivated regionalism', or what he started calling 'critical regionalism'.[26] He used the term *critical* to distinguish it from the sort of regionalism that promoted local traditions in building or that limited itself to imitating historical styles. The latter variant is mainly fashionable with the *nouveau riche* and, according to Frampton, it is an expression of a neo-Conservative world view, which of course he rejected. He thought that neo-Conservatism was 'culturally and politically retrogressive'. Critical regionalism on the other hand offered the possibility of combining 'the emancipatory and progressive aspects of the modern architectural legacy' with an attempt to do justice to local architectural traditions.

All this sounded very persuasive and, as a result, critical regionalism has gained a large following throughout the world. What exactly did Frampton mean however by the term *critical*? In *Modern Architecture. A Critical History* (1985) he gave some examples – for instance the Bagsvaerd Church by Jorn Utzon, built in 1976 in a suburb of Copenhagen, and the ISM housing development in Barcelona of 1951 by the Spanish architect J.A. Coderch. These are sober buildings in which traditional forms of building are deployed in a serious fashion. Initially, the work of Ricardo Bofill also seemed critical, Frampton explained, but in his later work he indulged in 'a form of kitsch romanticism'. His obsession with castles, according to Frampton, reached a provisional climax in the housing development of Walden 7 in Sant Just Desvern in Barcelona (1970-1975). Here, he said, Bofill's architecture 'marks that unfortunate boundary where what was initially a critical impulse degenerates into highly photogenic scenography'. Frampton rejected this sort of architecture, because it is seductive and narcissistic. It consisted of a 'formal rhetoric', aimed at 'high fashion'; the empty gestures should be thought of as an expression of the mysterious and flamboyant personality that Ricardo Bofill would like to be.[27]

Kenneth Frampton is averse to outward display in architecture and this quality places him firmly in the Modernist tradition. Architecture is supposed to be honest and shouldn't offer any empty display – illusions are forbidden. In this connection it is noteworthy that in his discussion of nineteenth-century architecture in *Modern Architecture. A Critical History*, he is only interested in the technological developments of that period, as though the Revival styles were an irrelevant phenomenon and historicizing architecture was no more than a fancy-dress party.

For the generation that grew up with a culture of social awareness and criticism, it is not sufficient for architecture just to be beautiful. In the first place, it has to be useful and usable – something, however, that one would think was self-evident. In the second place, it has to be instructive, in the sense of exemplary; it should be a model of political correctness. This was also the message of the Belgian architectural historian Hilde Heynen in her book, *Architecture and Modernity* (1999). She wrote that 'providing comfort and convenience for daily life is not architecture's one and only goal', because it also needs to give form to 'a critical dialogue with context and program'. According to her, architecture has to mean more than 'its smoothly fitting into the international magazines'.[28] Fashion is stupid and is not interesting for the serious-minded. Anyone who wants to live consciously has to be critical and engage in a dialogue with one's environment. If you subject the modern architecture of the entire twentieth century to the critical method of Hilde Heynen, all you have left is a handful of buildings. Heynen's thesis, in fact, comes down to the notion that architects should 'disrupt, shock or at least produce difficult architecture', to quote Hans Ibelings, who reviewed her book in *de Volkskrant* (25 August, 2002). Ibelings's conclusion was that she regarded only four architects as having managed to do this – Adolf Loos, Daniel Libeskind, Rem Koolhaas and Constant. 'This is a pretty poor harvest for the whole twentieth century', he wrote. If only four architects succeeded in living up to Heynen's definition, he asked, wasn't there perhaps something wrong with the definition?

49 *Housing block in Barcelona by José Antonio Coderch (1951)*

Peter Collins's Advice

Peter Collins's advice that architects had a duty to design a humane architecture in a 'harmonious cityscape' must have sounded remarkably progressive
in the 1960s. The prevailing notion in that period was that a city could only
survive if it adapted to modern life. Of course, most of the administrators
of large cities and their planning departments understood that they had to
treat historical buildings and the historically evolved structure of the city
with proper respect, but their ideal image in every instance remained that
of Le Corbusier, namely a *tabula rasa*. One interesting ideal image in which
the designer did not need to worry about the past is Jaap Bakema's sketch of
1964 of the high street in his project for Pampus, near Amsterdam where an
entirely new modern town should be built. This new town was never built,
but what makes the sketch so interesting is that forty years later his ideal
image has become reality everywhere in the world – an urban scene with
traffic having free rein and high-rise developments alternating with separate
pedestrian precincts. Moreover, by 1964, this image had already in a sense
become old-fashioned, because it derived from the Modernist projects of

the 1920s and 1930s, for instance from Ludwig Hilberseimer's design of 1924 for a Hochhausstadt. Jaap Bakema's sketch offers us a megastructure, a phenomenon that was exceedingly popular with the members of Team X that Bakema was a member of, the international Modernist group of architects that came into being during the CIAM of 1953. It is hard to believe that architects persisted in designing megastructures in which no human being has ever wanted to live. They can only have been blinkered by the belief that they 'were working in the spirit of the times'. Maybe they thought that their work was dictated by a *Zeitgeist* that was superior to anyone's individual housing needs or desires. This superior attitude must have strengthened their determination to design something that, even on the drawing board, looked relentlessly functional and that proved after implementation to be just that. Bakema's sketch shows a traffic artery that in reality would produce a deafening noise; the buildings on this motorway are, to put it mildly, boring; there is not a tree or park to be seen and the view is the same in all directions. Wherever one looks, one sees identical roads, blocks of flats and bridges. An architect who designs something like this lives in a different, possibly superior, but not necessarily better world than someone who prefers life in a compact historical city centre.

It is possible that architects like Bakema hated historical cities. It could well be that their hatred originated in the dreary image of the polluted, cramped, overcrowded cities they had seen with their own eyes and which the CIAM (Congrès Internationaux d'Architecture Moderne) had campaigned against in order to give humanity a more dignified environment for both work and domestic life – one that was more healthy, manageable and accessible and where air and light were more abundant. Anyone who criticizes the planning ideals of the CIAM ought to remember that its members had seen alleys and slums such as have vanished from the collective image of our historical cities today, at least in Europe. It is thus not so strange that the Modernists wanted to break the historical city open.

Breaking the City Open

In the year 2000, Harper Collins published *Over London. A Century of Change*. The book contains a number of aerial photographs of London from the 1920s and 1930s juxtaposed with recent shots of the same districts. The difference is truly shocking. To the tourist in the vicinity of the major sights, the city may appear fairly unharmed, with the exception of the area around St Paul's Cathedral. From a plane however one can see the extent of the damage immediately. In fact, it would be an endless task to ascertain exactly what has changed in the body of the city, when these changes took place and what the purpose of these changes was. Nonetheless, that is exactly what Harold Clunn tried to do, at least for the years between 1897 and 1927.[29] His book, *London Rebuilt* (1927), shows that even in the first third of the twentieth century, London suffered drastic changes, with parts of it being

50 Design for the new estate of Pampus near Amsterdam by Jaap Bakema (1964)

totally rebuilt, especially those areas where streets had required widening. The aim was always the improvement of traffic circulation. Clunn sums the changes up as follows: 'many street improvements and widening of narrow thoroughfares have been carried out, and progress in this direction has been almost continuous since the closing years of the last century'. He names Kingsway, the wide street that links High Holborn with the Strand, as the first straight thoroughfare, and goes on to mention the broadening of the Strand itself, of Kensington High Street and Knightsbridge and the layout of the Mall. Then there was the broadening of Constitution Hill, of King William Street and so forth. Along all these wider streets new buildings were built, often higher than what was there before. Medieval London was destroyed but, according to the criteria of the time, this was compensated for by the city becoming far more magnificent. It became much more what one would expect the capital of a huge empire to be. After the planning revolution around 1900, one would have assumed or at least hoped that the renovated City District would preserve its grandeur, but that occurred only in part. To a degree, the Blitz was to blame, but to a much greater extent, the contempt for turn-of-the-century architecture was responsible. After the widening of the streets described by Clunn had taken place, the city embarked on its second modern transformation after the Second World War, the results of which can be seen in the book *Over London*.

The actual image of the city would seem to have suffered less than one would expect as a result of all these changes, perhaps because it is determined by a limited number of famous sights which are familiar to everyone and which have remained intact. That which no longer exists and which never formed part of this famous panorama of images is perhaps not all that much missed. For instance, if one doesn't know what Regent Street looked like before 1900 one wouldn't feel any regret, because the street is both imposing and beautiful, something that was to an important extent due to its architect Sir Reginald Blomfield. Harold Clunn, however, remembers Regent Street as it was before. Built between 1813 and 1825 with white stucco neo-Classical buildings after a design by John Nash, it was a masterpiece of city planning. That was especially true of the curved part, the Quadrant as it was called, on the Piccadilly Circus side. All this vanished between 1900 and 1923, despite 'a considerable amount of adverse criticism', according to Clunn.[30] In fact he did not agree with this criticism, because he thought that John Nash's stuccoed architecture was not that well suited to the character of London. It was also expensive to maintain, he argued. 'These were fronted with stucco, which is a material wholly unsuited to the London atmosphere, and which very quickly cracks and gets dirty unless it is repainted at least once every three years …' One of those who resisted the demolition of the old Regent Street was A. Trystan Edwards, the author of *Good and Bad Manners in Architecture* (1924). 'Now, Regent Street', he wrote, 'was the supreme instance of good manners in architecture.' He thought that its demolition was an urban tragedy: 'Regent Street was the most beautiful street in the world. In its quite perfect scale and rare delicacy of Classic detail, in its expression of a spirit most urbane yet intimate and hospitable it had surpassing merit. An assemblage of buildings designed to serve the commonalty was here imbued with aristocratic grace. Moreover, the sensitive texture of the façades enabled them by day to respond to every evanescent change of light or atmosphere, and at night-time to stand radiant against the background of 'Darker London'. No mean skill is required to design a palace, but it is immeasurably more difficult to combine into an harmonious whole a group of purely commercial buildings. Regent Street lent distinction to the very idea of commerce.' With the exception of a few fine photographs, Edwards's eulogy is pretty much all that remains of the street.

All the changes the urban body of London had to suffer in this period, however, were nothing compared with what planners and traffic circulation specialists had in store for it after the Second World War. Many of these plans were not actually implemented, but they remain interesting because they give an idea of the preferential treatment given to motorized traffic, with everything else being sacrificed to it.[31] The traffic circulation plan developed in 1947 by the Improvements and Town Planning Committee and made public in 1951, for instance, included an elevated circular road from Holborn to Aldersgate, the 'Northern Boundary Route'. In order to rebuild the city, the committee wanted to completely transform the structure of the built-up areas. Above all, inner courtyards should receive more light and air. How one should picture this new city was illustrated by Gordon Cullen in a number of drawings. These drawings were really fan-

51   Drawing for a Northern Boundary Route around London by Gordon Cullen (1947)

ROMANTIC MODERNISM

tasies and that is what they remained until the 1970s, at least for a number of architects and planners, as we can see from the designs they made at the time.

The depressing book *The Rape of Britain*, by Colin Amery and Dan Cruickshank (1975), begins by announcing that 'Britain has not been invaded by an enemy power for more than nine hundred years.' According to them, the United Kingdom was still 'remarkably intact' in 1945, despite the Blitz. They have no doubt that the blame for the damage done to our historic cities lies entirely with our generation. All the cities, they said, have been buried under a dense layer of concrete, this 'joyless material', so that everything looks the same and is equally ugly, consisting of 'multiple heaps of prefabricated units that now make up our town centres'. For instance, in London there were still were some beautiful quarters, such as Bloomsbury for example, genuine neighbourhoods with lovely streets and squares. At the beginning of the twentieth century, it was still understood that 'civilization had its roots in the city'. One could still speak of our surroundings being treated with care. Since the 1960s, however, cities have become places where business is done; they are sites of 'material gain'. The book contains a large number of photographs illustrating the grisly consequences of modernization. It is not suitable for over-sensitive readers.

Such readers are also advised not to open the book *Paris Perdu*.[32] This book is one long jeremiad against the generation that was responsible for the destruction of the beautiful nineteenth-century quarters of Paris and for replacing people's familiar surroundings with degrading blocks of flats. This dismal prospect was already dramatically depicted in 1958 by Jacques Tati in *Mon Oncle*. The film concludes with a scene that sends up the dream of Modernism, exposing it as a nightmare. Tati's parody however is sometimes cancelled out by genuinely poetic images of the pure simplicity of modern *design*. There is one sequence where one views a modern neighbourhood from the window of a house that looks out on a typically intimate Parisian square. A squad of chilling tower blocks advances like a concrete army, trampling underfoot everything in its path. When it first came out in 1958, the film achieved instant fame and there would also have been government officials and planners among the audiences who saw it then. At the time it was not yet too late, but even a scene like this seems to have failed to win them over. The reality was much grimmer than the scene in Tati's film because the high-rise buildings there still have a certain appeal, if a somewhat military one.

Take for instance the modern architecture that has replaced the Rue de Flandres. The modern high-rise development that currently stands there is bizarre and even frightening if one looks at photos of the former street. Formerly a street of great charm, it was initially widened in order to improve the traffic flow along Route Nationale 3, after which it was rebuilt in the spirit of the modern age. It is now a fifty-metre-wide racetrack. In discussing plans like these, some critics use terms normally reserved for crime journalism. In his article on the urban renewal programme for the Place

52 *Rue des Amandiers, Paris, about 1955*

53 *New development of 1967 on the site of the Rue des Amandiers, Paris*

des Fêtes, where the townscape of the quarter is now dominated by high-rise blocks, Frédéric Edelmann wrote in *Le Monde* (19 January 1978), 'Sans nécessité, la réalité d'un quartier s'est vue désarticulée au profit d'un urbanisme qui confond modernisme et brutalité, et n'a sans doute d'urbanisme que le nom.' In other words, what was built here was a rape masquerading as planning.

At the beginning of the twenty-first century, Modernist projects like this are no longer in favour and are gradually being consigned to history's chamber of horrors. It is becoming ever harder to understand what on earth possessed these planners. How, for instance, can one account for the primitive sort of iconoclasm that raged in Germany after the Second World War that rejected the façade decoration of the architecture of the *Gründerzeit* – 'purified', to use the word fashionable at the time? This completely exaggerated hatred of late nineteenth-century Renaissance and Baroque revival styles was an outgrowth of Modernism. This dark page in the history of Modernism in Berlin was described by Wolf Jobst Siedler in his book *Die gemordete Stadt* of 1964. Such a fanatical campaign of iconoclastic destruction is almost inexplicable today. 'Denn dies ist es', Siedler wrote, 'was heute von Hamburg über München bis nach Berlin geschieht. Von überallher hämmert und klopft es, allerorten sinken Gesimse und Kapitelle in den Staub, wohin man nur blickt, hauchen Karyatiden und Amoretten unter puristischen Schlägen ihr Leben aus … Ganze Stadtviertel, die den Krieg nur mässig beschädigt überstanden, sind erst in den letzten Jahren zerstört worden, vernichtet in ihrem historischen Charakter und in ihrer architektonischen Einheitlichkeit' (Because this is what is currently going on, from Hamburg via Munich to Berlin. Everywhere things are being chopped down and mouldings and capitals are being demolished; wherever you look caryatids and cupids are succumbing to the onslaughts of the purists … whole neighbourhoods that survived the war reasonably well have been destroyed in recent years and robbed of their historical character and harmony).

What was the origin of this iconoclastic assault, this loathing of the Baroque Revival ornamentation on the facades from Hamburg to Munich? The Revival styles were associated with a world that had gone off the rails, for which there was no cure and which therefore had to be replaced by a better one. That is what all the Modernists wanted, anyway. The original principles of Modernism were humane and humanitarian. Shortly after the war, the mayor of the devastated city of Dresden, Walter Weidauer, said that the basic aim of the rebuilding of the city had to be to achieve a better life, because in former times not everything was as it should have been. What sense did it make then to rebuild in the spirit of the past, when people were again forced to live in uncomfortable houses? 'Was nützt dem Menschen die Tradition, wenn er dadurch in eine Zwangsjacke gesteckt wird, wenn er unbequem wohnt und den Krankheiten Vorschub leistet. Besser wohnen wollen wir, schöner und freier soll unser Leben sich gestalten. Keine Paläste für die Reichen und Hütten für die Armen, sondern Demokratie auch im

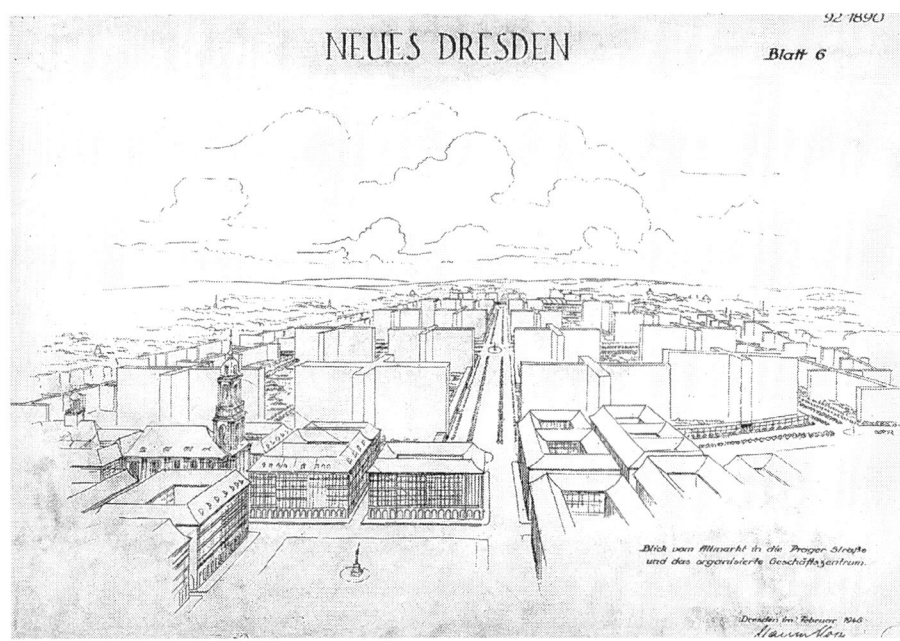

NEUES DRESDEN   *Blatt 6*

Blick vom Altmarkt in die Prager Strasse und das organisierte Geschäftszentrum.

Dresden im Februar 1946

54 *Design for the new city of Dresden by Hanns Hopp (1946)*

Wohnungbau. Je besser und zweckmässiger der Mensch wohnt und lebt, um so grösser seine Leistungsfähigkeit. Nicht eine Residenzstadt mit ihrem starken parasitären Einschlag, sondern eine Stadt der Arbeit, der Kultur, des Wohlstandes für alle muss Dresden werden' (What is the point of tradition, if it forces people into a straitjacket, creating discomfort and encouraging diseases? We want our homes to be better and more beautiful and to have lives that are freer. No more palaces for the rich and cottages for the poor; instead we want democracy in housing. The better and more functional people's domestic situations and daily lives are, the more they will achieve. We don't want a residential city with a parasitic character, but one with work, culture and prosperity for all – that's what Dresden should become).

What would this humane city of the future have looked like then? There was only one existing model and that was the modern, functionalist city with its mixture of urbanity and countryside as developed in the circles of the CIAM. It was not so strange, then, that one of the plans for the rebuilding of Dresden was a more or less literal quotation from Le Corbusier's *Ville Radieuse*. In 1946, the designer of this plan, Hanns Hopp, defended his series of tower blocks with an appeal to the technological character of the modern age: 'hinter dem gewohnten Stadtbild am Ufer des Stromes erhebt sich die rhythmische Reihe der hohen Geschäftshäuser und Wohnblöcke als vernünftige und praktische Form einer Stadt des technischen Zeitalters' (behind the old city on the river rise the rhythmi-

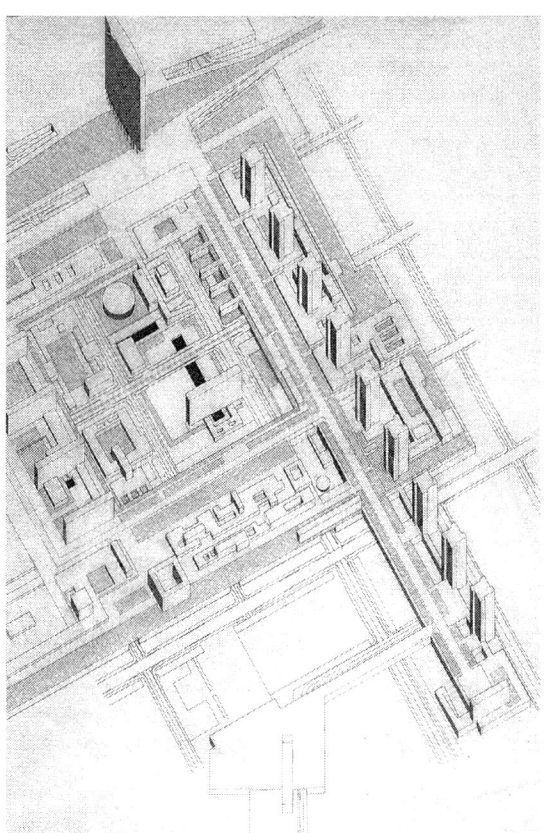

55 Design of 1957 for the new Friedrichstrasse layout in Berlin by Marion Tournon-Brandy

cal rows of towers as the rational form of a city in the machine age). The authors of *Ostkreuz*, the two-volume standard work on the architecture of the former German Democratic Republic, make it clear that Hanns Hopp was no exception. The notion of accentuating the new by placing it next to the old was a commonly applied stylistic device of that period. It was considered interesting to stress the contrasts. Any softening of this contrast was regarded as a form of weakness, as 'Anbiederung', or cosying up to the old.[33]

The happiness of the population was also the prime aim in most of the master plans drawn up in 1957 for the competition for the restructuring of Berlin; today, however, in 2009, these schemes look unreal and, in a sense, old-fashioned.[34] This is particularly true of the design of a group of youthful architects around Marion Tournon-Branly who wanted to design an elevated city after the model of the plan their teacher Auguste Perret had drawn up for Le Havre – a new city to be built some metres above the ruins of the former city destroyed in the Second World War. Why did these pupils choose this model for Berlin, when they must have known that the residents of Le Havre hated Perret's relentlessly Modernist plan and that the city council had finally rejected it? The local population wanted the city to be rebuilt as it had been before the war.[35]

Mirages of the Past

At the end of the twentieth century, when faith in Modernism was on the wane, the monster of imitation reared its head once again. Is this modern historicism an offshoot of neo-Conservatism or commercial postmodernism, or is it a response to the devastating loss of our historical environment?

Most architectural critics view the recent retreat into a sham past as something to be ashamed of. According to Robert Hewison in *The Heritage Industry* (1987), it is no solution 'to retreat into a fake history' as a way of escaping the disastrous consequences of the modern age. The flight into an idealized past, while it might appear to offer some certainty in our bewildering times, is 'a conservative, nostalgic impulse and also a dangerous one'. It is dangerous, he argues, because it makes people blind to reality. The nostalgic retreat into the past is also fertile soil for an odious form of conservatism that rejects everything it doesn't understand and that doesn't fit in with conventional expectations. This flight from reality blocks any attempts at renewal or innovations, dismissing them as deviations from the norm. Hewison fully understands the people's inclination to flee today's chaos and to retreat into a fantasy world, but he still regards it as cowardly and dishonest. Deracinated man, he concludes, has to learn to live with this chaos, however painful that may be.

Robert Hewison refuses to allow modern humanity, living in surroundings that are a grisly nightmare of concrete, asphalt and endless traffic, to seek refuge in a postmodern Potemkin village. Our suffering is simply part of the modern world and we owe it to ourselves to acknowledge the state of affairs. That people display this sort of discreditable escapism is, however, a cause of concern for Hewison.

Hewison seems to me to be a Romantic who continues to lend credence to the Modernist myth of the *Brave New World*. He probably still loathes the Victorian masquerade of Revival styles that hid the real world of iron structures behind a false decor. In the meantime, though, he must have wondered why these built illusions of the nineteenth century or earlier seem today to have a greater appeal than most of the products of the 'machine age'. The answer cannot only have to do with a universal decline in the realism or honesty of the twentieth-century urban dweller.

In the world of conservation, the new historicism has led to a sense of disorientation and uncertainty. Whereas historical architecture has hitherto had to be rescued from the jaws of hell, historical monuments are so much in demand today that additional ones are even being built. In the United States there is a magazine with the title *Old House Journal*, which contains advertisements for homes in historical styles. Anyone wanting to purchase one must first browse through the 'attractive, authentic, and buildable historical designs from all periods of American history' and, having made his or her selection, must call in 'a local mechanical contractor' to implement the design in question. It is easier than one might suppose to live in a historical monument. Ownership of an ancestral château or a substantial villa from 1875 is no longer just the privilege of a small elite.

In our postmodern age we no longer know what is right and wrong in the field of architecture. Is the fake historical hamlet of Poundbury near Dorchester, funded by Prince Charles and based on the designs of an architect from Luxemburg, Leon Krier, modern kitsch or is it a postmodern protest against Modernist monotony and a model of domestic architecture on a human scale?[36] In any case, Poundbury has evolved into a typical old English village with cosy-looking houses built round the village green. A modern housing estate disguised as an old village.

It is undeniable that what we see here is a piece of nostalgic pastiche, but the somewhat insular and smug reference to a supposedly idyllic rural past in the English countryside does not seem to be a problem for the Prince of Wales or his many followers. Since the advance of the New Urbanism that has blown over from America, one can no longer automatically denounce all forms of historicism.[37] In the Netherlands, too, new housing estates are built in the shape of old villages and they do well in the housing market. Examples are the imitation Brabant village of Brandevoort, designed by Rob Krier, and the 1930s-style estate of Dierdonk, both near Helmond.[38]

The past can also be used as a source of inspiration in urban designs. Modern urban planning was recently enriched, for example, by Sjoerd Soeters with an imitation historical canal in the Java Island housing estate in Amsterdam. The same architect also designed the plan for Haverleij, a new development in Den Bosch, conceived of as a collection of dwellings resembling castles in a landscape resembling a park.[39] Can this new historicism perhaps be explained by the downfall of Modernism with its revulsion for the past? This is all very well, but why should the revolt against the ugliness of Modernism itself be so ugly? Why do the products of this revolt always prove to be imitation middle-class cottages or farmsteads? Why are imitations hardly ever built of beautiful Modernist houses like those of Le Corbusier?

Not all imitations are crude and vulgar, however; there are also examples of successful pastiche. Take, for instance, the new development in the Lakensestraat in Brussels, a project carried out a few years ago by Atelier Atlante of the Fondation pour l'Architecture. In the 1960s, the nineteenth century, represented mainly by neo-Classical buildings in this street, was replaced by modern office blocks. These gigantic glass and concrete edifices were in turn demolished when they were no longer needed. From a distance the new development that has stood here since 1995 looks like a neo-Classical copy; as one approaches it, however, one sees that all the details are newly designed. The street is a pastiche, but it is a playful one and beautiful to look at. The finishing has been carried out meticulously and it is even a bit 'upmarket' in places, but that suits neo-Classicism anyway. It is a prime example of New Urbanism. The project was managed by the architect Demetri Porphyrios from London and Maurice Culot, the president of the Fondation.[40] The finished project was even honoured by a visit

56 Historicist-style canal, Java Island, Amsterdam, designed by Sjoerd Soeters (1999)

by Prince Charles and this perhaps explains the lack of interest in it on the part of the critical professional press, because anyone who agrees with the Prince of Wales's ideas is automatically assumed to be against modern architecture.

Recently, the Netherlands' former Chief Government Architect, Wytze Patijn, revealed what the prevailing notion of the past was when he was a student: 'I studied architecture at a time when Modernism was deemed above criticism. Here, in the Netherlands at least, what was involved was a fundamental principle in the debate about architecture. During our training we were told in such fulsome detail about all the benefits that progress would continue to bring us that we quite simply had no eye for everything that had evolved historically in our cities over the past centuries. It was considered suspect to take an interest in such things ... Because of this attitude of systematic rejection, we were never led to ask how one was supposed to approach this past; the basic idea was that everything historical should be demolished and replaced with modern forms.'[41]

By now Modernism itself has become a part of history, but the copying of historical architecture is still deplored by serious architectural criticism; even the copying of the Modernism of the 1920s was lambasted until recently.[42] In the light of the Romantic idea of art, one can perhaps account for the repugnance felt for imitations; nonetheless it has had distressing consequences for the preservation of the cityscape.

Some time ago a city councillor in Groningen proposed restoring part of the northern front of the Grote Markt to its pre-1945 state. He had seen pre-war photo's that showed that prior to 1945 this market square had been extremely beautiful. After the war the mistake was made of not restoring everything to its former state, something that could easily have been done on the basis of the architectural remains and the surveyor's drawings that the Department for Conservation had made of the façades. He wanted the former situation to be restored and had the courage to make his wishes public. Perhaps he would have done better to keep his views to himself, because his proposal received virtually no support, not even from the Heemschut League, an organization concerned with national heritage. The League didn't want to hear anything about a former state and the City Council that was just getting over the disasters of war was similarly unenthusiastic. Anyone who wanted to build a new future after the war had to allow for the requirements that the modern age imposed on a city – that was the universally held view of Dutch officialdom. Any return to a former state was regressive. Anyone who wanted such a thing was considered unworldly. He was just a poor chap who did not realize that times had changed and that fuddy-duddy pre-war attitudes no longer applied. The layout and fabric of a city had to be forward-thinking. In 1946, the mayor of Groningen, P.W.J.H. Cort van der Linden, had said just that. According to him, the havoc of war had offered the city a unique opportunity to solve certain spatial problems. The Dutch Communist Party, the second largest in the new council at the time, spurred on by the doctrine of historical materialism, knew for certain that future society would be determined by economic and social forces. A scientific analysis of the various functions that a city centre was expected to fulfil was all that was needed. The Communists were hardly charmed by M.J. Granpré Molière's reconstruction plans either, because he put the emphasis on spatial compositions. What was involved in his plan was not so much the reconstruction of the buildings that had been bombed, but the improvement of the layout using historical forms. According to the architect, 'The historical shape of the market square will admittedly disappear, but its historical grandeur will return.' One could speak then of a neat compromise, because the modernization of the city could then be combined with a historical outward form. The Department for Conservation thought that this divergence from the existing structure was a violation of the historical meaning of the old city and of course they disagreed with the Communists, too. These differences were hard to overcome and it was not until 1952 that a compromise was finally reached. Molière's reconstruction plan proved to be a historicist mirage, and in this regard it strongly resembles P. Verhagen's plan for the rebuilding of Middelburg.

The councillor's proposal to restore part of the Grote Markt in Groningen to its former state would have put an end to this Mediaeval Revival decor. As one might expect, the proposal received plenty of support from local residents, but none whatsoever from those who represented them on the city council. Even the alderman of the councillor's own party, the liberal

57 New development, Lakensestraat, Brussels (1995)

ROMANTIC MODERNISM

D66 faction, felt that the term 'mock-medieval' was an adequate description of the reconstruction plan. As previously said, the body that should have been the final resort in the battle for the city's historical heritage, the Heemschut League, didn't see any point in imitating historical façades, because they 'do not make any contribution to the atmosphere of our own age.'[43]

The League saw it as its task to defend the existing legacy of the past, not what had already disappeared. Its local representative, Piet Reijenga, added that reconstructing vanished architecture was unethical. An architect should speak the language of his age, he said, just as contemporary composers no longer compose music in the style of Buxtehude. Nor could any support be expected from the Department for Conservation, even though the secretary of the National Historic Monuments Commission, G.W.Van Herwaarden, had let it be known in connection with a comparable issue in The Hague that he was not opposed to reconstructions in every case.[44] He thought that copying historical architecture was permissible when it was possible to restore the historical context by doing so. He also thought that conservation should have nothing to do with pastiche, because this would potentially harm its reputation. It should not be associated with nostalgic imitations, but only with 'authentic remains'.

In The Hague, what was involved was a plan to fill a vacant lot on the Prinsegracht with imitation eighteenth-century houses. The empty space came about due to plans for a hospital building in 1960, the immense Westeinde Ziekenhuis. On the Prinsegracht there still were a number of dilapidated eighteenth-century houses awaiting demolition. Their death sentence was commuted, however, because they were listed historic buildings, protected by the state and thus exempt from capital punishment. Four of them were demolished instead as part of a restoration programme and immediately rebuilt – a procedure that often has to be followed when the frame of a building has also suffered damage. The restoration was carried out in 1994 by the architect Ton Deurloo as a commission of the Stadsherstel, the local corporation for architectural restorations. Shortly afterwards it was decided to build new homes next to these four houses in the empty lot on the Prinsegracht. Deurloo promptly designed a series of imitation eighteenth-century houses to restore the townscape. A housing corporation, the Algemene Woningbouw Vereniging, had also come up with a plan, but one with modern forms. Deurloo's plan was praised by the neighbourhood and was also approved by the Department for Conservation, the building inspectorate and a large majority of the council. Yet the reconstruction didn't take place, because the alderman whose department it was and who apparently knew something about architecture blocked Ton Deurloo's project because he thought that modern architecture was required here, not imitations. Some people have no qualms about taking full advantage of their political position. The Stadsherstel corporation and Ton Deurloo lost out, but to this day they have received no explanation as to why their plan was rejected.

58 Oudekerksplein, Amsterdam shortly before 1900 (photo by Jacob Olie)

59 New development, Oudekerksplein, Amsterdam (2001)

ROMANTIC MODERNISM

Opinions among conservationists are sharply divided when it comes to reconstructions. The Minister of Culture in 1972 ordered a number of houses scheduled for demolition as part of the plans for Amsterdam's first metro line to be reconstructed in their entirety. These were the premises on the Nieuwe Herengracht 45-49 in Amsterdam. Later on, the Amsterdam Council for Conservation declared that it 'felt that a contemporary design was preferable to a historicizing approach.' In other cases, too, the bodies concerned with conservation were opposed to reconstructions. An example was a report from some years back from the now-defunct National Historic Monuments Commission about the country house of Heemstede in Houten which burned down in 1987. The Commission was opposed to any rebuilding, but went along with the plan of the architectural firm Groep 5 in Rijswijk to rebuild the parts that had been lost in steel and reflective glass. The minutes of the Commission's meeting on 27 May 1988 state that some members of the Commission regarded the house as lost because the fire had destroyed a large part of the building that dated from 1645. The building, they argued, had been damaged by fire more than once – at the beginning of the twentieth century and again in 1973 – so there was little original work left. The Commission recommended to the Minister of Culture that it be removed from the list of monuments and that permission should be granted for its rebuilding in steel and glass.[45] The minister kept the building as a listed monument, while still giving his approval to Groep 5's plan. The plan, however, was not implemented because the client and the local government rejected the Commission's advice. The country house has meanwhile been entirely restored.

Another equally instructive controversy arose in 1992 around the rebuilding of some houses in Amsterdam's city centre. Strangely enough, the notorious 'king' of the red light district, Jopie de Vries, who had been murdered a few years previously, deserves an honourable mention here because he took the initiative for the restoration of three listed buildings on the Oudekerksplein. He had drawings and measurements made of the three houses with the aim of giving them a new function in his branch of business. Things never got beyond the planning stage, however, because a short while later the houses were burned to the ground. For years there was a hideous hole in the row of houses on the north side of the Oude Kerk square. One would think that this extremely old site with its virtually intact medieval structure would automatically be at the top of any list of classified monuments. The three façades admittedly only date from the nineteenth century, but the houses themselves must have been a great deal older. Even more important than their historical value was how harmoniously they fitted into the urban context – the relations between the small, narrow houses, the crooked lane in front of them and the enormous hulk of the church. As the owner of the lots, the city of Amsterdam wanted to use them to build a crèche. In 1991, the Afdeling Jeugdzaken (youth department) came up with a plan that showed quite a shocking lack of understanding of city planning. It looked like a 1970s-style clubhouse, outwardly

60 Leidsegracht 106, corner of Raamdwarsstraat in Amsterdam (1995)

61 Leidsegracht 106, after reconstruction (1999)

ROMANTIC MODERNISM

businesslike but displaying a musty functionalism that looked totally out of place on this historical spot. The design was soon withdrawn and replaced with a series of chambered gables, a design rejected by the building inspectorate with the argument that they looked like 'Almere gables'. Jeugdzaken responded by improving the appearance of the gables, for instance, by sketching in a cornice front next to three gables and providing all the windows with nineteenth-century casements. One gets the impression that it didn't really matter to Jeugdzaken all that much what the façade looked like. Maybe they felt that exteriors in architecture are only an expression of the interior and that the only rule of thumb to be complied with was that one shouldn't indulge the typically Dutch passion for façade tourism. After this design, too, was rejected, Jeugdzaken contacted the famous architect Sjoerd Soeters, who had the local building inspectorate in the palm of his hand. His design, implemented in 1999, is perhaps just about acceptable but the question remains of why the charred gables were not simply rebuilt. That was what Stadsherstel (the Amsterdam society for urban heritage rehabilitation) wanted. Jeugdzaken had rejected this with the argument that old houses like these could not possibly be adapted to the needs of modern children. Stadsherstel received backing in 1992 from the Koninklijk Oudheidkundig Genootschap (Royal Antiquarian Association), the Genootschap Amstelodamum (a local antiquarian society), the Heemschut League, the Hendrick de Keyser Society, the Vrienden van de Binnenstad (Society for the Friends of Amsterdam) and the Monumentenfonds. These bodies asked the alderman Louis Genet to support the reconstruction plan. And then something happened that nobody could have anticipated – the Netherlands Department for Conservation also joined the fray, adopting a diametrically opposite position to these bodies. It found the notion of a reconstruction totally unacceptable, declaring in its letter to the Council that it was confident that 'the urban planning problem in this historically sensitive situation can be solved using contemporary architectural means'. How is one to explain such a wide divergence in viewpoints? Surely the nature of the bodies just mentioned was not so different from that of the Department for Conservation. What was the Department's argument? In its letter, it said that the historical value of the listed monuments had been destroyed in the fire and that no amount of reconstruction could restore that value.

In the dispute over the rebuilding of a dwelling at Leidsegracht 106 in Amsterdam, the Department for Conservation arrived at a comparable verdict. In Stadsherstel's annual report from 1997, one reads the sorry tale of this neglected historical monument. Only two storeys remained, but it was still on the list of historic monuments. It was decided to restore it and plans had been drawn up, when, totally unexpectedly, the floor of the main storey caved in, with the result that the house had to be totally demolished to prevent it collapsing. As if this weren't bad enough, another setback occurred. The bodies in charge felt that the dismantling of the house meant that it no longer had the normal status of a listed monument. The annual report described the painful situation as follows: 'Despite the fact the re-building will take place in compliance with a survey conducted by the architect with the utmost care, using the materials of the old building which have been set aside, the officials of the Department for Conservation are of the opinion that this no longer provides any guarantee that its status as a listed monument can be maintained.' There was still no certainty that the rebuilding would be subsidized. The officials concerned took the position that a monument had to be at least fifty years old to be legally protected and that a monument that had been totally renovated did not meet with this requirement. The Department for Conservation felt that there was no longer any basis for letting the reconstruction go ahead and giving it a grant. Stadsherstel appealed the Department's decision on the following grounds: 'The notion that a building can no longer have any value as a historical monument if it needs to be almost entirely replaced has no basis in the law. All that the law says is that something must be over fifty years old to be declared a national historical monument. According to legal history, the reason why this term was set was to allow a sufficient distance of time to be taken from the architecture of a property to judge whether it deserves to be listed or not. The law therefore does not protect materials that are older than fifty years, but it does aim to maintain valuable buildings. For this to be possible, grants are provided for the replacement of the materials of these buildings in the context of a restoration. The preservation of valuable historical properties can mean that the object has to be totally renewed. There are abundant instances of this…'[46] Despite its long-winded preamble, Stadsherstel had hit the nail on the head. The Appeals Committee of the Ministry of Education, Culture and Science had to acknowledge this and a subsidy was granted after all. Several years later, the result is a building on the corner of the Raamdwarsstraat and the Leidsegracht that, although it is entirely new, displays a striking resemblance to the monument that formerly occupied this site.

Bombed Cities

Of course, the loss of historical buildings is nothing compared with the human suffering caused by the Second World War, but the fact that it will never again be possible to stroll through Dresden as it was – this city that once was described by Johann Gottfried Herder as 'Florence on the Elbe' – is shocking and will remain so a hundred years hence, when the human suffering occasioned by the collective memory of that event has faded. But the memory of the beauty of Dresden as it was has not been lost, above all due to the city scenes by the eighteenth-century painter, Bernardo Bellotto, who depicted both Dresden and Warsaw with great accuracy. Unlike Dresden, however Warsaw was rebuilt, and Bellotto's paintings played a key role in that city's reconstruction.[47]

Why was Warsaw rebuilt, whereas most of the German cities were not?

In Germany, a large number of memorable historic buildings were admittedly reconstructed, because this was seen as part of the cultural duty of a state that wanted, at any cost not to be thought barbaric. These reconstructions were intended to show that Germany had not reneged on its responsibilities. More important, however, was the endeavour to bury the past and to rebuild the bombed cities as modern ones. The rubble covered the doomed past, and once that had been cleared away, space was made for a new future; the new modern cities would stand as symbols of a Germany that had overcome its past. From 1939 onwards, Warsaw was systematically bombed on Hitler's orders with the aim of wiping out the history and culture of Poland and annexing the country to the Third Reich. When Eisenhower visited the city immediately after the war he expressed his profound shock. 'I have visited many cities that have been bombed', he said on the occasion, 'but nowhere has it been so terrible and bestial'. The city was bombed house by house, and the decision to reconstruct it in its entirety was an understandable response to the German attempt to destroy the Polish nation. The only way that the Poles could cope with their humiliation was to completely rebuild their ancient capital.

Dresden, on the other hand, was expected to behave as a model of the Communist ideal of society in the post-war period. The debate about the reconstruction of the city was endless and, as the result testifies, also fruitless. Once one of the most beautiful cities of Europe, Dresden has become a cheerless conglomerate of inhuman Stalinist concrete blocks. There was, however, an important difference between the destruction of Dresden and that of Warsaw. The former city had been bombed by the Allies in the struggle against Nazism, whereas the latter was destroyed by the Germans and, what was more, the destruction was implemented not as part of a military campaign but, as just said, in order to destroy Polish culture. The Poles did not think twice about rebuilding their lost city – reconstruction for them was almost a form of revenge. There were some architects who boggled at the thought of such a gigantic project, especially as it was in conflict with the ethics of restoration. It was, for instance, at odds with the well-known principle stated by the German art historian Georg Dehio in 1905 – 'Konservieren, nicht restaurieren'. The Polish architect Jan Zachwatowicz confessed in 1974 that he was at that time 'torn by conflicting feelings', because by reconstructing the city of Warsaw 'we acted in conflict with the principles of restoration as applied so far'.[48]

Jan Zachwatowicz was apparently incapable of appreciating at the time – and he wasn't in 1974 either – that the principles of restoration had been drawn up as a response to the historicizing restorations of the nineteenth century. Around 1900, those who had to combat all those fanciful interpretations of medieval architecture, such as Georg Dehio, could not have foreseen the possibility that only a little while later whole cities would be destroyed. Fortunately Warsaw was rebuilt and after such a vast undertaking it seemed almost improper to ask critical questions about the 'scientific soundness' of the reconstruction. Nonetheless, that is precisely what has to be done if one is to understand what the Poles thought important to restore and what they did not want to see rebuilt – how they saw their own city, that is. Contrary to what might have been expected – that the city would be rebuilt exactly how it was before the war – they sometimes opted for ideal images over the actual pre-war reality. What ideal image could have appealed to them more than that of the urban scenes Bellotto depicted between 1767 and 1780? The city was at its most beautiful at that time; it was calm, harmonious and untouched by modernity. This is the image the modern stress-ridden city dweller has longed for since the Industrial Revolution. We view the work of Bellotto with romantic eyes, with that longing for the ideal city that, again by no coincidence, is always an eighteenth-century city, because it was in that period that the most beautiful urban scenes were painted. But even a romantic has to admit that plenty of beautiful buildings were built in the city after Bellotto's time, especially in the nineteenth century. The people who rebuilt Warsaw ignored that, and the Cathedral of St John, for instance, was given a different front façade. Adam Idzikowski's Gothic Revival front of 1840 was not rebuilt, but replaced by its fifteenth-century precursor, and the east gable of the nave was restored to its former state as depicted in one of Bellotto's scenes. The director of the National Museum (Muzeum Narodowe) in Warsaw, Stanislaw Lorentz, could still recall in 1963 the cases where Bellotto was invoked. A corner house on Senator Street which had been totally altered in the nineteenth century was restored to its state as depicted in one of his paintings. The bishop's palace, too, and Jan Klemens Branicki's house on the Miodowa Street weren't rebuilt in their pre-war forms, but as Bellotto had depicted them, down to the smallest detail. A work by Bellotto also served as a model for the rebuilding of the market square of the Nowe Miasto with the Classical Church of the Nuns of the Holy Sacrament, a design from 1680 by the Dutch architect Tilman van Gameren. The same was also the case with the reconstruction of the Royal Palace, another work by Van Gameren. All the towers were rebuilt on the basis of the great panorama of Warsaw painted by Bellotto in 1778. Lorentz acknowledged that 'gefühlsbetonte Momente' – an emotionally charged conjuncture – had played a decisive role in the return of the eighteenth-century cityscape. People simply felt a desire to see the old glory restored and not have to be confronted with any signs of decay. In this effort to attain urban harmony, even a building that had miraculously been spared by the bombs was demolished because it didn't fit into the schemes of those in charge of the reconstruction. What made the gallery on Freta Street in the Nowe Miasto unsuitable, for instance, was not its date – 1823 – but the Gothic Revival style of its architecture. The house of the court physician Jozef Skalski at 45 Krakówskie was rebuilt in loving detail because it dated from 1780, but the adjacent neo-Renaissance house from 1890 was not allowed back. In its stead there is now a house in a vaguely eighteenth-century style. An extreme form of hatred for all the Revival styles was evident in the Saint Alexander Church on the Square of the Three Crosses. This neo-Classical church of 1825 was subjected to a neo-Renaissance enlargement in 1894, with the semicircular dome being replaced by a high full dome in the style of Saint Peter's in Rome. The reconstruction overlooked all this, so what we see today is the church as it was in 1825.

This attitude towards the Revival styles, treating them like a symptom of an architectural plague, was of course not confined to Warsaw or Poland. What was typically Polish was the hostility towards architectural Russianization. Whenever they saw a chance, the Poles liberated themselves from the hated Russian architecture. One such opportunity was after the First World War, when the country became an independent state. Immediately after independence, the Poles demolished the Greek-Orthodox church of Alexander Nevsky. This church that stood on Victory Square (the former Saxon Square), was built by the Russians after the uprising of 1863 as a symbol of Russian rule. After 1921, the Russian towers of the Church of the Virgin on Krasinski Square were also demolished as detested symbols of the Russianization that took place subsequent to the revolt of 1830.[49]

After the Second World War, Russian power was restored, and with it came new Russian edifices, but now their style was no longer Greek Orthodox or Tsarist but Stalinist. This style naturally fell out of favour after the non-violent revolution of 1989 and it is likely that buildings in this style will be demolished because architecture is political in Warsaw. Bellotto's city scenes were also political instruments of a people who wanted to restore their past, preferring beauty to honesty in their quest. Honesty, after all, has a lower priority for a people that have lived on the edge of an abyss.

In Dresden, a number of important monuments were rebuilt, such as the Zwinger complex and Semper's Opera House (Gottried Semper was popular with the Communists, because he chose the side of the revolutionaries in 1848), but little was done in this area till the fall of the Berlin Wall in 1989. Once the decision had been taken, however, to rebuild the Frauenkirche, it seemed more or less logical to bring back the square on which the church had stood. In fact, everyone agreed that it was a good idea to restore the form of the façades of the former square, but there was disagreement about the design of these walls. Should they be a replica of the former façades or should something new be built? A number of study days were devoted to this problem in the autumn of 2000 and a competition was also held. In 2001, both the discussions and the designs, complete with commentaries, were published in the book *Atelier Neumarkt Dresden 2000*. All the different viewpoints were given generous coverage and all the designs were illustrated with comments by the architects. The charm of this book is added to by the fact that it does not include any official viewpoint or general attitude held by the local authorities. A second, equally excellent work was published in 2000 by the Sächsische Akademie der Künste of Dresden with the title *Stadtplanung und Stadtentwicklung in der Kernstadt Dresden*. It consists of a detailed account of a debate on the subject organized by the academy in the spring of 1999.[50]

62 *The Neumarkt in Dresden in 1910*

In the discussions on the rebuilding of the Neumarkt, two distinct parties can be discerned. On one hand there is the Gesellschaft Historischer Neumarkt Dresden that believes that the square should be restored to its pre-war form. This society argues for a reconstruction based on old photographs and other documentary sources. Its viewpoint is represented in the book by Stefan Hertzig, the society's president. Hertzig's opponents reject the building of imitation architecture. One such opponent was Annette Friedrich of the Dresden Planning Department. She rejected the idea of the future square being nothing more than a pretty picture of the former one: 'In der Zukunft aber nur ein Abbild der Vergangenheit zu sehen, erscheint zumindest aus unserer Sicht dann doch zweifelhaft.' She added that restoring a city district on the basis of suppositions and personal interpretations was not exactly a meaningful or inspiring task.

The director of the Deutsches Architektur Museum in Frankfurt am Main, Ingeborg Flagge, also spoke out against Hertzig's plan. She said that she was shocked by the view of the traditionalists present at the debates who were incapable of imagining anything beyond the restoration of the old square. She said that this attitude was entirely alien to her, stating: 'I live in the present; I have to give a form to the city of today, to create something that belongs to our age. Architecture has in fact always been the expression of *Zukunftwillen*, or a will to the future.' She continued by arguing that it was a mistake to view the city's planning as having been harmonious throughout history , because 'mit Harmonie hatte die alte Stadt recht wenig zu tun' (the historical city had little to do with harmony). The historical city was an assemblage of divergent architectural styles and these differences were noticed by her contemporaries, but 'wir tun heute so, als gäbe es sie nicht'. We behave as though these differences don't exist, as though things were in harmony in the past. According to the Director of the Architectural Museum of Frankfurt am Main, this was a modern error.

Nobody contested this thesis at the discussions in Dresden, but I suspect that Ingeborg Flagge may have given a distorted picture of the state of affairs. First of all, architects in the past have always taken more account of their surroundings than she thinks, and secondly, just because people tend to speak of a historical city as a harmonious whole, that doesn't mean they are mistaken, let alone deluding themselves. The concept of harmony that Flagge is referring to has less to do with stylistic similarities than with the impression that a historical city makes on people today. A cityscape is spoken of as being intact and harmonious today when it is not encroached upon by modern, twentieth-century alterations.

To return to the viewpoint of Stefan Hertzig's opponents, some of the architects who submitted entries for the competition also turned against the notion of erecting stage sets from another age. Thomas Will and Andreas Rieger had made a design for a number of houses on the Rampische Strasse. Some superb photos of this street had been preserved from before the Second World War. Nonetheless, they still opted for modern architecture, not out of any submission to the principles of Modernism, but 'aus Achtung vor den verbliebenden Kunstwerken der Geschichte' (out of a respect for the historical artworks that have survived). Those monuments which are authentic would be harmed by the 'Musealisierung der Innenstadt'; they would be 'entwertet', or devalued. Imitation casts a stain on the authentic; it is an insult, not a tribute.

Thomas Will and Andreas Rieger rejected beautiful but empty cityscapes. In this they were supported by the majority of Hertzig's opponents. The *Landeskonservator* Gerhard Glaser, shared their view, although he made an exception for buildings that could be faithfully reconstructed. According to him, reconstructing a building on the basis of photo's was unacceptable, because 'eine zweidimensionale Bildinszenierung kann nicht das Ziel für die Schaffung des angemessenen Umfeldes für die Frauenkirche sein' (a two-dimensional stage set cannot provide a suitable surrounding for the Frauenkirche). The scientific reconstruction of the Frauenkirche would clash with others that were insufficiently scientific. If the designs for the rebuilding of the façades were only based on what we know from old photographs, there was, in Glaser's view, a danger that the Neumarkt would not recover its former identity. It would be nothing more than a commercially attractive site with a nostalgic value. Glaser also thought that rebuilding using Hertzig's method would cast doubt on the ruins of war elsewhere in the city that had been restored with such care – for instance the Zwinger

complex and Semper's Opera House, the Johanneum, the Stallhof, the Co-
sel Palace, the city palace and the chancellery building.

Most of Hertzig's opponents thought that architecture should convey
the atmosphere of our own age and that a return to the past would indicate
a regressive culture, one that had abandoned all hope for the future and
had turned to the past for consolation. They also saw it as unacceptable
to build historical pieces of scenery, because it was obvious that the houses
could not be reconstructed internally any more. Hertzig, for his part, also
acknowledged that behind these historical pieces of scenery modern homes
will have to be built, something his opponents saw as dishonest.

Hertzig defended himself by saying that he understood perfectly well
that a copy of a historical building was something different from the building itself. A copy was a repetition and as such it was a picture or image of
something that no longer existed. In his view, this was exactly the point of
a copy, namely that the lost building could be restored in the form of an
'Erscheinungsbild', a pictorial image, for those who mourned the loss of
the original. Their grief remained and the only thing that could ease it was
a 'bildhafte Vergegenwärtigung' (representation in the form of an image)
of the lost original. Once this historical-philosophical background was understood, the ever-optimistic Hertzig argued, there would no longer be any
reason for opposing reconstructions.

Discussions like this are held in other cities and other countries too, but
in Germany these matters tend to be a little bit more sensitive. In his recently published book *Munich and Memory*, Gavriel D. Rosenfeld describes
how painful it was for the Germans to confront their past, taking the reconstruction of Munich as his example. But he also looks at what he calls
postmodernist historicism, the building of imitation historical architecture
for the sake of creating a harmonious cityscape. He mentions, for instance,
the city museum on the Jakobsplatz built in 1977 by Martin Hofmann and
Tilmann Erdle and the main offices of the Deutsche Beamtenversicherung
on the Lenbachplatz of 1981. The latter instance of postmodernist historicism was built after a design by Erwin Schleich, the author of a book which
is extremely famous in Munich, *Die zweite Zerstörung Münchens* (1978),
which argues that Modernism is a danger for the harmony of the cityscape.
Historical copies, such as Schleich's design, were much admired by the general public, although they were despised by all self-respecting intellectuals,
architects and other connoisseurs of art. In Munich, however, this conflict
took on a bitter undertone due to some of the critics trying to give the war
a prominent role in the debate. In 1977, Christoph Hackelsberger wrote in
the *Münchner Stadtanzeiger* that the mendacity of the historical imitations
built on the Jakobsplatz obscures reality, just as the historicism of the nineteenth century masked the social problems of that time with 'the historic
waste of centuries'. He goes on to say something genuinely provocative –
that the mendacity of the nineteenth century led to the First World War,
and that National Socialism continued with lies like this in their architecture and that the postmodernists with their historicizing architecture

were reverting to these lies. In other words, postmodernist historicism is a repetition of the fake architecture of the National Socialists. This line of argument was obviously over the top; nonetheless, it was in this tone that the debate was conducted.[51]

Trauma and Therapy

In a discussion between Michel Foucault and Paul Rabinow about post-modernism in architecture, the latter argued that 'some postmodernists have claimed that historical references *per se* are somehow meaningful and are going to protect us from the dangers of an overly rationalized world.' Irritated by what he saw as a naïve suggestion, Foucault said, amongst other things, that 'one should totally and absolutely suspect anything that claims to be a return. One reason is a logical one; there is in fact no such thing as a return.'[52] Nobody would disagree that it is sensible to be suspicious, but the fact that references to the past can in certain cases offer consolation is something that maybe did not occur to Foucault. Nonetheless it is a general human characteristic to want to compensate for a trauma. This is the function of monuments to the dead. They keep memories alive. If the loss of an artwork can be compensated for by a copy or by an architectural quotation, many people will have no problem with that.

It is understandable that Hamid Karzai, the current prime minister of Afghanistan, set great store by the restoration of the two celebrated gigantic statues of the Buddha in the region of Bamiyan. These statues, dating from the fourth century AD, were blown up by the Taliban in 2001. During a conference in Tokyo, Karzai spoke about this loss as follows: 'It's like you lose a member of your family every day. It's a loss that we have not been able to reconcile.' Meanwhile, Paul Bucherer, the director of the Afghan Institute in Switzerland, has been given the contract to prepare the building of two replicas. 'Money is no object', according to Bucherer. 'There are plenty of Buddhist foundations that will be eager to finance the project.'[53]

For Afghanistan, the statues were a cultural symbol and that of course was reason enough for the terrorists to destroy them, something that according to Bucherer they did 'in an extremely professional manner', leaving virtually no trace. The world experienced a far greater shock on 11 September 2001, when Al-Qaeda terrorists, who had received protection under the Taliban, demolished the two towers of the World Trade Center in New York with similar professionalism. After a year of clearing the rubble and assimilating the shock, many New Yorkers felt that the only way of reaching closure for their humiliation was by rebuilding the towers. Salman Rushdie recently wrote on the subject as follows, 'If we are to believe a recent opinion poll, a majority of New Yorkers thinks in exactly the same way [as the people of Warsaw]. They say that we should build the Twin Towers again just as they were, or in any case just as high and imposing. Make our city whole once again. We cannot undo the past, but we can remove the scar that it has left.' Given the choice, Rushdie said that he would 'presumably go for the side of those who think that the new buildings ought to look like the towers that had been demolished, at least outwardly. The people who destroyed the towers wanted to carry out a symbolic act and we must give them a symbolic answer.' Salman Rushdie went on to launch his own design that consisted of rebuilding the hundred and ten storeys of one or perhaps both towers, while leaving the top thirty or forty floors empty but lit up inside, so as to mark the spot in the sky where the attacks took place, a monument in the form of a lighthouse.[54]

At this point it is perhaps relevant to quote a sentence from *Social Memory* by James Fentress and Chris Wickam (1992), in which the authors argue that the role the past plays in the collective memory is much greater than sociologists generally realize. 'Analyses of social identity of all kinds', they argue, 'could well give more attention to memory as one of its major constituent elements, and as one of the clearest guides to its configuration.'[55]

Despite their absence, the memory of the Twin Towers remains intact, and perhaps this memory of their arrogant height has turned their absence into a permanent presence in the collective memory of New Yorkers and of all other Americans. The towers were already a symbol of a sort of power that the United States has tended to display and perhaps their very destruction, aimed at wounding the pride of this superpower, has actually increased their symbolic importance. It is not yet clear what action New York will take to replace them; the New World has after all less experience of the afflictions that the past can impose on an urban body.

Unlike the Americans, the people of Berlin are all too familiar with past traumas – traumas moreover of a quite different order, more comparable with the problems of Dresden as described above. In Berlin too, architectural references to the pre-war city have met with fierce opposition. After the fall of the Wall and its actual demolition, the old, seriously damaged city centre was once again to be made whole. At the point when discussions on the subject were at their most heated, the former director of the Deutsches Architekturmuseum, Vittorio M. Lampugnani, made the case for a return to traditional pre-war architectural conventions. He felt completely at odds with the prevailing architectural culture that held that the only thing people were interested in was building something spectacular. 'Die Begeisterung für das Neue um des Neuen willen ist eine der verhängnisvollsten Erbschaften aus der Epoche der Avantgarden' (The passion for the new for its own sake is one of the most fatal legacies of the epoch of the avant-garde), he wrote in 1993.[56]

With these words he brought down the wrath of the German intelligentsia on his head. They accused him of calling for a return to a sort of architecture that they had always associated with a kind of conservatism that had the Nazis' seal of approval. His colleague from Munich, Winfried Nerdinger, thought that Lampugnani's solution was culpable from the outset because it ignored the complexity of the contemporary world. He also thought that architecture had to be a social criticism and that Lampugnani's interest in forms and styles was out of date. 'Am Anfang kann also nur eine Gesellschaftkritik stehen. Sie aber schreiben lediglich von Stilen, Formen und Fassaden und rufen nach dem traditionsfähigen Architekten' (First of all it has to be a form of social criticism. You write, however, about empty matters such as styles, forms and facades and you appeal to traditional architects)[57]. Of all Lampugnani's critics, however, the most hostile was Daniel Libeskind. He said that his article concealed something else, and that was 'ein gefährliches und autoritäres Verständnis von Politik' (a dangerous and authoritarian political idea). In the professional journal *Arch +* (1994), Philipp Oswalt, who published a book six years later, *Berlin – Stadt Ohne Form*, wrote that Lampugnani's thesis displayed a reactionary temperament that 'die Gegenwart ablehnt und den Mythos einer idealisierten Vergangenheit als Utopie für die Zukunft beschwört' (denies the present and believes in the myth of an idealized past as a utopian model for the future). In Oswalt's view, the past could never serve as a model and that this had been the great mistake of the nineteenth century. It was a demonstrable fact that the twentieth century was far superior to the nineteenth and it was also his view that a harmonious city was only possible if a 'Stildiktat' was imposed, something that was against everything that a 'liberal, open society' stood for. Unity on the basis of master plans was only possible in an authoritarian state. As an example he named the Stalinallee in East Berlin, that a supporter of Lampugnani, Hans Kollhoff, much to Philipp Oswalt's fury, had called 'eine wahrhaft grossstädtische Anlage' (a genuine big-city layout). All this was merely a prelude to a debate that one finds summarized by Gert Kähler in 1995 in *Einfach schwierig. Eine deutsche Architekturdebatte*, a book in the series *Bauwelt Fundamente*.

Lampugnani's viewpoint resembled what Josef Paul Kleihues had called 'critical reconstruction'. In his contribution to the *Internationale Bauausstellung Berlin* (1984-1987) this architect had argued that the reconstruction of Berlin Mitte had to take the planning history of the city into account; at the same time however it should not be allowed to degenerate into nostalgic imitation. It had, in other words, to be critical.[58] The proposal bears a striking similarity to Kenneth Frampton's critical regionalism discussed above, and it displays a similar anxiety to avoid evoking the wrong type of memories. At the same time, Kleihues's proposal to take the historical layout of the city and the pre-war planning structure of the city centre as his starting point was a revolution in thinking about the future of the city. How the architectural avant-garde felt about Berlin's future became clear in 1991 with the exhibition in the museum of German architecture in Frankfurt am Main, *Berlin morgen – Ideen für das Herz einer Grosstadt*. All the designs in this exhibition were based on a vision of a radically modern city free of all memory of the atmosphere of pre-war Berlin.

The place of the past in the new Berlin was also the issue in a debate on the concept of identity between Tom Fecht of *Kunstforum International* in 1997 and Rem Koolhaas. Fecht put the question as follows, 'Since architecture is a very important element of storing memory and history, what

63 The Friedrichstrasse in Berlin (1925)

64 The Friedrichstrasse in 2000

ROMANTIC MODERNISM

function could memory have in the context of architecture from your point of view looking at the next century?' Koolhaas answered that he expected the memory of the past to be banished from the architecture of the future. He took Berlin as an example, saying that, '...to the extent that architecture embodies memory the present reconstruction of Berlin is a kind of blatant attempt to extinguish and to eliminate certain kinds of memories, the memories of communism, the memories of the fifties, the memories of a kind of sober, optimistic moment of modernity'. He expressed his intense dislike of this kind of selective conservation of the past, calling it 'a single empty memory operation'. It had no charm for him whatsoever, but he admitted that this was probably because, as he put it, 'I think I have an obsession with the present.' The fact that historicist architecture has almost never been free of manipulations aiming to make an image that fitted in neatly with ideological or artistic doctrines drove Koolhaas to a radical and total negation of the past. And Koolhaas had no lack of people who agreed with him, just as after 1918 it felt preferable to build a new world that bore no trace of the old, fundamentally corrupt Europe of around 1900. The only trouble with this approach is that the past cannot be repressed like this, however much one might like.

The avant-garde with their old-fashioned ideas about urban design originating with the CIAM failed to get a hearing in Berlin; the devastated city was therefore rebuilt on the basis of its eighteenth and nineteenth-century structure. By the 1990s, this sort of idea about urban design was no longer an entirely new one, but once it acquired the title of *critical reconstruction*, it suddenly became universally popular. One of its principal advocates was the celebrated architectural critic, Dieter Hoffmann-Axthelm. In his view, it was meaningless to design a new city because the structure of the historical city, despite all the damage it had suffered, was still in a condition that would allow for restoration.[59] Hoffmann-Axthelm's viewpoint was adopted by the municipal authority. Senatsbaudirektor Hans Stimmann argued that the future planning of Berlin should be based on the lots, street profiles, building heights and shapes of blocks, squares and other elements of the historical city: 'Die historische Grundstruktur der Stadt muss als Konstante zur Grundlage der Stadtentwicklung werden' (The historical structure of the city must serve as the foundation for urban development). Even though they were reluctant to admit it, the opponents of this approach could not deny that it was based on a definite historical image of the city. It did, it is true, present a rather one-sided picture of Berlin, but that is true of every picture that people form of the past. Unwelcome images are therefore ruled out, even though these too form part of the history of the city. 'Der Mythos der Vergangenheit dient als Vision für die Zukunft' (The myth of the past serves as a vision for the future) – this was Philipp Oswalt's verdict in 1994 on critical reconstruction. The rebirth of the severely damaged body of the city is only possible on the basis of an idealized picture of the city's history and in Oswalt's view an operation like this played into the hands of conservative and nationalist forces. Giving Berlin its Prussian identity once more meant rejecting all international tendencies in architecture; an introverted architectural approach policy like this was in sharp conflict with the idea of a new capital of a united Germany being rooted in a western and European culture. Philipp Oswalt feared the decline of the 'Westbindung Deutschlands', a Germany that is tied to the West rather than eastward-looking. It is clear where his fear comes from, but it is equally clear that it has no bearing on discussions about the rebuilding of other cities, such as Sarajevo or Beirut. It is a typically German fear and one that determined the debate on the future of Berlin. Some other aspects of the debate in Germany however are of a more general relevance, as one can see from Gert Kähler's analysis of the issue.

In *Stadt der Architektur. Berlin 1900-2000*, Kähler wrote that the *Berliner Architekturstreit* of the early 1990s had perhaps been totally pointless because it was concerned solely with the outward appearance of the city (nur eine Frage der Dekoration) and not with social matters. Berlin today, according to Kähler, is being rebuilt as a beautiful shape, but this shape is hollow and empty, a hostage to 'tourists and investors'. The building body has been healed and it has acquired an urban design (not an architectural one) inspired by the pre-war state of the city. This design however doesn't take account of the residents and is convenient solely for large businesses, or shoppers and tourists. These categories apparently could not count on Gert Kähler's blessing. He had hoped for a social-democratic municipal policy, in which there would be less room for a property market that seems incapable of producing anything other than 'Urban Entertainment Centers'.

Had Gert Kähler really expected the debate not to be concerned with the external form of the city? Once again, outward appearance, the aesthetics, the charm or beauty of the architecture or of an urban image are not only depicted as superficial minor considerations but even dismissed as hollow, meaningless and even reprehensible. Once again we hear the voice of the honest romantic, who is repelled by outward forms and thinks that art must present us with the actual and thus, by implication, ugly reality. This romantic viewpoint is defended by Philipp Oswalt and Gert Kähler and by plenty of others too, with an appeal to honesty; they forget however that in the arts – and one should include urban planning here – the notion of *honesty* has always played a subordinate role, except for dyed-in-the-wool Functionalists.

In rebuilding a city – any devastated city, that is – the first concern is the shape, the design and layout of the urban body. Everything else is secondary. If one judges the results of the 'Heilung' of Berlin on the basis of traditional planning requirements according to the principles of critical reconstruction, in the Friedrichstrasse, the Gendarmenmarkt and the Pariser Platz for instance, then these results might be appreciated – that at least was Michael Hesse's conclusion. According to him, these requirements do not exclude 'Geniestreiche' (strokes of genius), but they do also make the mediocrity bearable.[60] There are some who disagree with him. The former director of the Netherlands Architectural Institute in Rotterdam, Kristin Feireiss, told Hans Verbeek of the Amsterdam daily, *Het Parool*, that in the rebuilding of the Friedrichstrasse and the Gendarmenmarkt, the new architecture was carried out in total compliance with 'the old alignments and the traditional block structure'. In her view Berlin had missed many opportunities – 'almost no room was allowed for innovative concepts'.[61] Kristin Feireiss appears only to be interested in architecture that is spectacular. It is true that few architects are interested in harmonious, unremarkable edifices that fit in with the street where they are built, buildings based on Lampugnani's concept of a *Neue Einfachheit* (new simplicity). The thing that they see as being especially contemptible is buildings that are more or less directly based on historical examples – uncritical buildings, that is, like the historical Revival buildings on the Gendarmenmarkt (the former Platz der Akademie) designed by Manfred Prasser and Günter Boy or the Hotel Adlon on the Pariser Platz by the architectural firm of Patzschke, Klotz and Partner.

The design of this hotel is based on the former Hotel Adlon built in 1906, but it is much larger and higher than its predecessor. The old hotel was a myth, Christine Waiblinger-Jens writes in her book about the new Pariser Platz, *Der Pariser Platz in Berlin von der Nachkriegszeit bis zur Gegenwart – Städtebau und Architektur* (1999). The name Adlon had a magic ring; it was a synonym for luxury and naturally the new manager wanted to exploit that. And the new hotel aimed to evoke that old-fashioned luxury in every detail. It proclaimed this bygone glory and this is exactly what Peter Rumpf denounced as 'platt historistisch' – vulgar historicism.[62] Then there is Heinrich Wefing, who wrote in the *Frankfurter Allgemeine Zeitung* (12 May 1997) that 'at least the postmodernists use irony when they quote, but the new Adlon hotel wants to conjure up those spirits of former ages in all seriousness'. The design also provoked Christine Waiblinger-Jens's indignation. She argued that on a historical site like this a suitable building should have been put up and not just a collage of styles ('Anstatt diesem geschichtsträchtigen Ort eine angemessene architektonische Identität zu verleihen, ist eine Stilcollage aus postmodernen und historisierenden Versatzstücken entstanden'). She also said that the rebuilding of the Pariser Platz may well have been based on the historical layout, but that this wasn't the case with the separate buildings. It was right to restore the contours of the square, its urban form, that is, but 'ihre abbildhafte Wiederherstellung kann nur als oberflächliche Evokation realitätsferner Träume betrachtet werden' (the reproduction of the individual buildings can never be more than a superficial evocation of deluded dreams). After having put the dreamy hotel manager in his place, Christine Waiblinger-Jens scolded him for publishing a brochure with all the famous visitors to the hotel since 1907, 'so, als hätte es die fünfzig Jahre ohne das Adlon nie gegeben' – as though there had never been a period of fifty years when there was no Adlon Hotel at all. The manager pretended that the period of Communism had never happened and that was a bare-faced lie. The architects too should take their share of blame, she

65 Adlon Hotel, Berlin,1914

66 The new Adlon Hotel building, Berlin (1997)

ROMANTIC MODERNISM

said, for deviating in an irresponsible way from the design of the old hotel, with some of the parts not getting enough emphasis, or else using proportions which are simply wrong. She saw the copy as having failed as a copy, while admitting that the architects never intended to build a replica. Their idea had always been to make a 'version' of the old hotel.

Nonetheless, Christine Waiblinger-Jens admitted that the general public was enthusiastic when the hotel was opened in 1997. One could even speak of an 'Adlon mania', with the hotel representing a provisional climax in the 'hauptstädtischer Sehnsucht nach Verlorenen' – the nostalgia in the German capital for all that had been lost. The professionals were of course left speechless and *Landeskonservator* Helmut Engel said that ordinary people's enthusiasm had to be accepted as a reflection of the current state of society. In other words, not only were the board of the Adlon and its architects blind, the same was true of the public at large. According to Christine Waiblinger-Jens, this was proof, if proof were needed, that a modern design would have been more appropriate.

The criticism of the building in professional circles may appear somewhat over the top. After all, architecturally speaking, the building is nothing special. It isn't very beautiful, but it isn't particularly ugly either. All it is, is a big luxury hotel, executed in a style that is well suited to Berlin. The only problem with it is that it is too large and high. The critics would have done better to have addressed these issues and not aimed their shafts at the pretence and luxury. It was petty, for instance, of Heinrich Wefing to talk in a superior tone about the fact that at least three different materials were used for the walls of all the toilets or to say, as Gerwin Zohlen did, that the design for the façade was like a fashion show. The new building does recall the famous hotel of 1906 and in that sense it does make a contribution to inserting the past in the new Berlin. Was it such a mistake to attempt that? Admittedly, the design is not exactly critical in the sense that Daniel Libeskind's buildings are. Does anyone have any objection to that? Does architecture always have to be critical? This, however, is not a question that Christine Waiblinger-Jens asks. She deplores architecture such as this because it is an unbridled celebration of bygone glory. Why, however, shouldn't a commercial enterprise do such a thing? Probably she feels uncomfortable with the openly displayed *Sehnsucht* for a period that she saw as suspect, the age of gaudy nationalism that preceded the First World War.

The discussions over the rebuilding of the city palace of Berlin, blown up in 1950 on the orders of Walter Ulbricht, were also coloured by unresolved traumas concerning the German past. Both the Adlon Hotel and the *Schloss* were viewed as architectural expressions of all that was dubious in German history, of the authoritarian, militarist and totalitarian Germany. No pains should be spared to prevent this past from returning, whether as replica or as pastiche. Times, however, are changing and so are opinions. Initially everyone, following the example of the critical intellectuals, was opposed to the palace being rebuilt. To their astonishment however, the experts in the fields of architecture and conservation, who had poured scorn on the reconstruction plans, had the experience of seeing their own arguments dismissed as irrelevant.[63]

On 16 April 2002, Peter Stephan reported in the *Frankfurter Allgemeine Zeitung* that a majority of the government's Historische Mitte Berlin Commission had come out in favour of rebuilding the former royal and imperial palace, built for the most part in about 1700 and which, while it suffered serious damage, was not a total ruin in 1945. As said above, it was only completely destroyed in 1950. Furthermore there was a practical problem in that the Palast de Republik had been built on the site of the palace in 1976 and this building was seen as a monument of the Communist age by a portion of the population of the former German Democratic Republic. This was mainly a political problem, of course, since what was involved was deciding between two conflicting interests, a task that is generally thought to belong to the political bodies concerned. The plan to rebuild the palace then was complicated enough, both politically and practically, but the main issue in the present context was the historical or art-historical grounds on which the opponents to the plan supported their case. In 1993 the *Förderverein Berliner Stadtschloss* had held an exhibition about the reconstruction that gave plenty of space to tried and tested opponents, among them Julius Posener, Wolfgang Pehnt and Kristin Feireiss.[64]

Posener for his part said that he was against the plan, because the city's future would not be served with the reconstruction of a former memory. Pehnt wrote that it would be 'zutiefst ahistorisch' (deeply ahistorical) to ignore the historical development of so many years: 'Geschichte ist nicht abwählbar, sondern nur forsetzbar' (you can't choose history, it just advances). Feireiss said that it was mistaken 'to resort to nostalgia' and that what was needed was to rebuild the empty spot in the centre of the city as a manifesto of 'contemporary architectural culture.' This, however, was just the sort of thing that Wolf Jobst Siedler felt was going too far. Despite its admirable architectural achievements, he argued, the twentieth century hadn't provided any instance of a successful intervention in a historical environment – 'nirgendswo ist es dieser Generation gelungen, die Mitte einer Stadt zu formen'. All this was anathema to the architectural and conservationist experts, but the general public had no problem in understanding what Siedler meant.

Strong arguments were raised against the reconstruction. In *Die Zeit* of 26 July 2001, Jens Jessen wrote that a reconstruction of the palace would be a 'Denkmal der Geschichtslosigkeit' (a monument to an ignorance of history), because all it would be would be an expression of a conservative petty bourgeois attitude that is not interested in real history, but is quite happy with a sort of waxworks museum. Arguments like this, however, failed to convince the advocates of the palace, because they knew perfectly well that there have always been reconstructions, especially after wars and natural disasters, and that a copy is only a copy and that a copy shouldn't be mistaken for a political interpretation of the past. Was it the fault of the seventeenth-century architects of the palace, Andreas Schlüter and Eosander von Göthe that their building served as a backdrop for a gang of murderous dictators?

As just said, a new wind was blowing in the discussions about the rebuilding of the palace; a change in mood had occurred, as strikingly represented by Konrad Schuller in the *Frankfurter Allgemeine Zeitung* (26 May 2000). He begun by saying: 'Berlin is in the throes of nostalgia – a nostalgia for the palace ... this nostalgia is a nostalgia for the centre. Because just as the axes of the city, point now as ever like index fingers towards that empty square ... the nervous system of the political climate also points towards that centre ... a city whose main thoroughfares have for half a century ended in a windswept bombsite, this city longs to be healed, it wants its heart restored to it' (Eine Sehnsucht geht um in Berlin: die Sehnsucht nach dem Schloss ... Diese Sehnsucht ist eine Sehnsucht nach Mitte. Denn wie die Achsen der Stadt, heute wie eh und je, wie gestreckte Zeigefinger auf jenen leeren Platz weisen ... so streben die Nervensysteme des politischen Sentiments einem Zentrum zu ... Eine Stadt, deren Magistralen ein halbes Jahrhundert lang auf einen windigen Sprengplatz zustreben, dürstet nach Heilung, will ihren Kern wieder haben).

The nostalgia for this former central point had overruled all objections and sidelined the hopes of architects for an architectural manifesto for our own age. Berlin certainly has its topography of terror, but it also has one of nostalgia for the years around 1900 that have been recorded in marvellous photographs.[65]

It is as though Berlin's architectural debt for its dubious past could never fully be paid off. It was as though it was offered no alternative to this guilt-ridden form of *Vergangenheitsbewältigung*, of managing the past. Jürgen Trimborn too, the author of a long and detailed article in the journal *Die alte Stadt*, appears to have suffered a similar difficulty. He thinks that the present wave of reconstructions is even politically dangerous and puts the following question to his readers: 'Is it proper, in the light of increasing European unity, to honour and pay tribute once again to these documents of imperial ambition, these monuments of militarism and the lust for power, these symbols of the gradually eroding ties of nationalism, instead of drawing attention to the democratic tradition in Germany – no matter how short – and to the existing and prospective future democracy of the German Federal Republic?' (Ist es heute – angesichts eines immer weiter zusammenwachsenden Europas – angebracht, diese Dokumente kaiserzeitlicher Geltungssucht, diese Monumente des Militarismus und Grossmachtdenkens, diese Symbole einer doch wohl obsolet gewordenen nationalstaatlichen Orientierung, wieder auf den Sockel zu heben und verklärend zu glorifizieren, anstatt sich auf die – wenn auch kurze – Tradition der Demokratie auf deutschem Boden und auf die Gegenwart und Zukunft der bundesdeutschen Demokratie zu besinnen?).[66]

Trimborn sees the imperial palace as a symbol of Germany's dubious heritage and therefore concludes that it should not be reconstructed. Is it true that buildings can be innocent or guilty in themselves? Can a building from 1700 be guilty of crimes committed in the twentieth century by the people who lived or resided in them then? If buildings can be guilty because their occupants or visitors had committed crimes, are any historical monuments still innocent? Jürgen Trimborn's train of thought is reminiscent of the moralistic ideas about architecture so typical of the nineteenth century, of Eugène Viollet-le-Duc's contempt for instance for the palace of Versailles because he saw it as standing for the bombastic and dictatorial regime of the Bourbon monarchy.

The rebuilding of the city palace is as ahistorical as any other reconstruction of the architecture destroyed in the war, such as the palace of Charlottenburg in Berlin. Every reconstruction is a form of rebellion, a revolt against time. Reconstructions are nothing new, but since the rise of history as a science, no one ever lets us forget that reconstructions are ahistorical. What the historians do forget, however, is that these reconstructions nearly always have a social or socio-psychological function. They can soften the blow of a sudden loss through war or natural disaster. Reconstructions can restore one's ties with the past and evoke a feeling of continuity as though a magic wand has been waved. In this they may have a useful function in restoring the identity of a city, a region or a country. The rebuilding of the royal palace in Berlin might serve to heal the trauma of the horrors with which it is associated. A resurrected palace might evoke the memories of better times, of the centuries before the atrocities, and thus stand as a symbol of a fresh start, of a victory over evil. The resurrection of this monument might contribute to giving the city a face once more; it might be a token of faith that it wasn't Germany's historical destiny to perpetrate the atrocities of the twentieth century. It is perhaps a mistake to include previous centuries in the work of overcoming the trauma of two world wars. A new city palace then could serve as a kind of triumph, a victory over German susceptibilities. In this sense it could be therapeutic just because it is a copy. An architectural cure for a ruined spot might help heal the wounds of the city as a whole. According to Gavriel D. Rosenfeld, this was the achievement of the reconstruction of Munich. In the post-war period even Third Reich buildings were rebuilt straightway and used again as government offices. Examples are the Haus des Deutschen Rechts, built by Oswald Bieber in 1939, the Zentralministerium building by Friedrich Gablonsky, also built in 1939, and the Luftgaukommando building by German Bestelmeyer (1938). Rosenfeld argues that this strategy has effectively immunized these buildings against their National Socialist past. The director of the Bavarian Department for Conservation, Georg Lill, thought the Luftgaukommando so beautiful and imposing that in 1948 he proposed that this masterpiece of German Bestelmeyer should be put on the list of protected monuments. [67]

In the publications on the rebuilding of Berlin after the fall of the Wall there is hardly any reference to what happened elsewhere. There is, however, much to learn from other debates in other cities. The history of the former market square in Hildesheim, for instance, is extremely educational.

The square was destroyed in the war and was then rebuilt with modern buildings and a more spacious layout. Around 1990 all this had to yield to the complete reconstruction of the medieval market. Martin Thumm, who has written the recent history of the market in Hildesheim, presumes that the historicizing new development of the square will be counted as one of the most important architectural achievements of our age, because it testifies to the 'wundersamen Fähigkeit einer Gesellschaft mit Bildern und Illusionen der Vergangenheit Probleme der Gegenwart zu lösen' – the marvellous skill of a society in resolving the problems of the present by drawing on the images and illusions of the past. Perhaps, Thumm hopes, these reconstructions and built illusions will also finally be able 'to overcome the disaster of the total loss of identity.'[68]

In Beirut, too, where the civil war in Lebanon (1975-1990) had destroyed virtually the entire historical city centre, the debate about reconstruction was prolonged and wide ranging. The result is comparable to the rebirth of the Adlon Hotel. Beirut was not rebuilt as it was before the war, but resurrected as a pastiche. The aim of this imitation was to provide an attractive backdrop for shoppers and create an entertainment quarter. The reconstruction has not yet been completed and will probably only be so in 2015. According to the architect, Hüsnü Yegenoglu, Beirut will be a 'model of optimism and a symbol of a restored identity'; at the same time, however, the city is an allusion 'to a past that has never existed'. [69]

According to him, the plan for the new city was 'a mixture of nostalgia, kitsch and fantasy', and he did not intend these terms as compliments. As just said, the future of Beirut had been the subject of intense and widespread discussion, with some parties arguing that any attempt to recreate the former atmosphere of the city was in conflict with the values of modern culture that are less and less concerned with the identity of a place. According to Jean Franco, professor in comparative literature at Columbia University in New York, the new culture is a global one, 'resulting in the collapse of time-hallowed ties between a physical place and the social, collective and cultural memory'. In Beirut this image of a hybrid city, which bears some resemblance to Rem Koolhaas's generic city, was fiercely contested, among others by Robert Saliba, one of the best-known local planners. According to Saliba, local residents felt deracinated and were eager to see the restoration of the neighbourhood that they knew. After a lengthy civil war nobody wants something hybrid. The war itself was hybrid enough. A return to normality would perhaps have been better served by strengthening one's ties with the past than by breaking with it completely.

Jean Franco's dream is reminiscent of that of a new and better world cherished by both Communists and Modernists. This dream in turn was a continuation of that of the Enlightenment and the fact that it remained unrealized does not mean that the dream itself was a nightmare. The world might well have been a better place if people had set less store by their own identity. Once again, what is at issue is identity. First of all, wars were fought in the name of identities, then ethnic cleansings were carried out for similar reasons, and. Finally. architecture is required to adapt to what is considered a politically correct identity.

Notes

Introduction

1   *NRC Handelsblad*, 20 December 2002.
2   David Watkin, *Morality and Architecture*, 1977.

Sentimentality and the City

1   Kees van der Ploeg, *Beeld van de stad*, 1992, 255.
2   Niels Gutschow, *Hamburg*, 1990, 114-130.
3   Winfried Nerdinger, *Aufbauzeit*, 1984, 10 and 11.
4   *Wonen TABK* 19 (1978), 16.
5   Reyner Banham, *New Brutalism*, 1966, 73.
6   Helena Webster, *Modernism without Rhetoric*, 1997, 60.
7   Quotation from *Wonen TABK* 19 (1978), 16.
8   Kenneth Frampton, *Modern Architecture*, 1980, 265.
9   Nigel Whiteley, *Reyner Banham*, 2002, 22.
10 Rutger A.F. Smook, *Binnensteden veranderen*, 1984, 11 and 255.
11 Wolfgang Pehnt, *Gottfried Böhm*, 1999, 86.
12 *Archithese* 14 (1988), 77-88.
13 Rem Koolhaas, *S,M,L,XL*, 1995, 1248.
14 Ton Koopman in his commentary on the CD of the *St Mark's Passion* (Paris, Erato Disques, 2000).
15 Bernhard Colenbrander, Referentie OMA, 1995, 18.
16 *Primeur*, April 1993.
17 *Blauwe Kamer* 3 (2002), 21.
18 *NRC Handelsblad*, 3 May 1991.
19 *Archis* 8 (1991), 17.
20 *Intermediair*, 8 August 1980, 9.
21 I owe all my information here about Bruges to Lori van Biervliet.
22 *Bouwen door de eeuwen heen. Stad Brugge*, 1999, 203.
23 Gavin Stamp, *History in the Making*, 1989, 40.
24 Vincent van Rossem, *De oude binnenstad vernieuwd*, 2000, 36-58.
25 Paul Meurs, *De moderne historische stad*, 2000, 303.
26 Paul Meurs, 305.
27 See the *Architecture Memorandum* of the two ministries (Planning and Culture) of 1992.
28 Monumentenzorg, 1996, 249.
29 *NRC Handelsblad*, 23 November 1992.

30 Ed Taverne, *Carel Weeber*, 1989, 9.
31 *Binnenlands Bestuur*, 12 April 2002.
32 *NRC Handelsblad*, 24 February 2002.
33 *Bouwkundig Weekblad* (1884), 319.
34 Wolfgang Herrmann, *Gottfried Semper*, 1984, 161.
35 Michel Foucault, *Politics*, 1988, 83.

The Rectangular Sickness

1   Alain Paucard, *Les Criminels du Béton*, 1991.
2   Tom Wolfe, *From Bauhaus to Our House*, 1983, 26.
3   Henry-Russell Hitchcock and Philip Johnson, *The International Style*, 1932.
4   Charles A. Jencks, *The Language of Postmodern Architecture*, 1977, 31.
5   Karin Kirsch, *Die Weissenhofsiedlung*, 1987.
6   Julius Posener, *Funktionalismus*, 1977.
7   Wolfgang Pehnt, *Das Ende der Zuversicht*, 1983, 74.
8   Auke van der Woud, *Het Nieuwe Bouwen Internationaal*, 1983, 12.
9   Gérard Monnier, *Histoire Critique*, 1990, 331.
10 Quoted by Manfred Bock, *Van het Nieuwe Bouwen*, 1983, 157.
11 Francine Houben in: *De Architect* (December 1987), 41-49.
12 Philippe Boudon, *Pessac*, 1969.
13 Hans van Dijk, *Onderwijzersmodernisme*, 1990.
14 Leen van Duin, *Postmodernisme*, 1988, 17-34.
15 Wolfgang Welsch, *Unsere postmoderne Moderne*, 1988, 92 and 99.
16 Richard Pommer, *Ludwig Hilberseimer*, 1988.
17 Malcolm MacEwen, *Crisis in Architecture*, 1974.
18 David Harvey, *The Condition of Postmodernity*, 1989, 116.
19 Jürgen Habermas, *Moderne und postmoderne Architektur*, 1985, 11-29 (lecture, 1981).
20 *Werk-Archithese*, 3 (1977). Heinrich Klotz wrote a response to Habermas in *Arch+* 63/64 (1982), 92-93.
21 *Berliner Tageblatt* 522, 1927 (Karin Kirsch, *Die Weissenhofsiedlung*, 1987, 206).
22 Peter Meyer, *Moderne Architektur*, 1928.
23 M. Bock, *Nieuwe Bouwen*, 1982, 14.
24 Fritz Neumeyer, *Mies van der Rohe*, 1986, 305.
25 Marcel Breuer, *Where do we stand?*, 1935.
26 Walter Gropius, *Bilanz*, 1934.
27 Sir James Richards, *The Hollow Victory*, 1972, 192-197.
28 Lewis Mumford, *The Highway and The City*, 1964, 155 and 156.
29 Buckminster Fuller, *Ideas and Integrities*, 1969, 30-32.
30 Philip Johnson, *Where Are We At?*, 1960, 173-175.
31 Lecture, 1959 (*Philip Johnson, Writings*, 1979, 232).
32 Robert Venturi, *Complexity*, 1966, and *Learning from Las Vegas*, 1977.
33 London, Studio Vista, 1976.
34 Peter Blake, *Form Follows Fiasco*, 1977.
35 Peter Blake, *The Master Builders*, 1961.
36 Julius Posener, *Funktionalismus*, 1977, 20.
37 The letter was also published in the *Bouwkundig Weekblad* of 1929, 105-111.
38 Peter Hall, *Cities of Tomorrow*, 1988, 240.
39 Johan van de Beek and Gerrit Smienk, *J.B. van Loghem*, 1971, 50 and 51.
40 J. Buit, *Hoogbouw*, 1988 and *Hoog in Nederland*, 1986.
41 Auke van der Woud, *Het Nieuwe Bouwen Internationaal*, 1983, 132.
42 Idem, 120.

43 Conrad Jameson, *British Architecture - Thirty Wasted Years* (1977), 1980, 80.

44 Niek de Boer and Donald Lambert, *Woonwijken*, 1987.

45 August Willemsen, *Braziliaanse Brieven*, 1985, 12.

46 Wolfgang Sofsky, *Schreckbild Stadt*, 1986, 1-21.

47 Laura Starink, 'Kommoenalka's in Moskou een bron van haat en nijd', *NRC Handelsblad*, 14 November, 1990.

48 L. M. Hermans, *Krotten en sloppen*, 1901.

49 J.B. van Loghem, *Krotwoningen*, 1933, 83-87.

50 Alexander Schwab, *Das Buch vom Bauen*, 1930.

51 Anatole Kopp, *L'Architecture stalinienne*, 1978.

52 *Wonen in het Verleden*, 1987.

53 V. Sackville-West, *The Edwardians*, 1930, 128-133.

54 Mark Adang, ' 'Breng me in uw huis, laat me uw woonkamer zien en ik zal zeggen wie gij zijt!' [Invite me home and show me your living room, and I'll tell you who you are], *Nederlands Kunsthistorisch Jaarboek 1977. Kunst en Kunstbedrijf Nederland 1914-1940*. Haarlem, Fibula-Van Dishoeck, 1978, 209-259.

55 Nancy Stieber, *Housing Design*, 1998, 191.

56 Barbara W. Tuchman, *The Proud Tower*, 1962, 11 and 242-243.

57 Stephan Zweig, *Die Welt von Gestern*, 1944.

58 Hans Redeker, *De dagen der artistieke vertwijfeling*, 1950, 18. The years after the Second World War were as different from those that followed the First World War, 'as exhaustion compared with vitality and a noisy recklessness, as lack of colour with a motley and passionate life, as resignation with a focused and committed choice of stance…'.

59 Ger Harmsen, *De Stijl en de Russische revolutie*, 1982, 45.

60 Johan van de Beek and Gerrit Smienk, *J.B. van Loghem*, 1971, 38.

61 Barbara Miller Lane, *Architecture and Politics in Germany, 1918-1945*, 1968, 45.

62 Cor de Wit, *Johan Niegeman*, 1979, 23.

63 William Gaunt, *The March of the Moderns*, 1949, 105 and 164.

64 Willemijn Stokvis, *Totalitair denken en kunst*, 1990, 3-16.

65 Theo van Doesburg, *De Stijl*, 1924-1931, 71 and 79.

66 Adolf Loos, *Hands Off*, 1917.

67 Hermann Czech and Wolfgang Mistelbauer, *Das Looshaus*, 1968, 22.

68 Hans Cürlis and H. Stephany, *Die Irrewege*, 1916, 11.

69 Sigfried Giedion, *Space, Time and Architecture*, 1949, 414.

70 Idem 19.

71 David Watkin, *Morality and Architecture*, 1977.

72 Henry-Russell Hitchcock and Philip Johnson, *The International Style*, 1932, 28.

73 Le Corbusier, *Oeuvre Complet*, 1956, 45.

74 The declaration came out of the first International Congress of Modern Architecture (CIAM) held in La Sarraz in Switzerland in 1928.

75 Peter Blake, *The Master Builders*, 1961, 57.

76 Reyner Banham, *Theory and Design in the First Machine Age*, 1960, 235 and 329.

77 Robert Mens in: *Le Corbusier en Nederland*, 1985, 19-20.

78 Manfred Bock, *Nieuwe Bouwen*, 1983, 36 and 87.

79 J.J.P. Oud, *Nieuwe Zakelijkheid*, 1935, 8.

80 Ton Idsinga and Jeroen Schilt, *W. van Tijen*, 1987, 153 and 166.

81 J.P. Kloos, *Architectuur*, 1985, 36, 44 and 49.

82 *Five Architects*, 1975 (preface).

83 Robert Mens, *Mies van der Rohe*, 1986, 35-37.

84 Adolf Behne, *Der moderne Zweckbau*, 1926, 66-68 (written in 1923).

85 Walter Gropius, *Bilanz des neuen bauens*, 1934, 159.

86 Ulrich Conrads, *Programs and manifestoes*, 1970, 117.

87 *8 en Opbouw* (1932), 231-233.
88 J.B. van Loghem, *Bouwen*, 1932, 21.
89 From a lecture by J.B. van Loghem (2 December 1930): *Plan* 12 (1971), 39.
90 Henri Labrouste (1830), letter quoted in *Verborgene Vernunft*, 1972, 41.
91 Nikolaus Pevsner, *Some Architectural Writers*, 1972, 284.
92 Klaus Döhmer, *In welchem Style*, 1976, 120.
93 Roger Scruton, *The Aesthetics of Architecture*, 1979, 7.
94 Emil Kaufmann, *Architecture in the Age of Reason*, 1955, 10.
95 Hans Sedlmayr, *Verlust der Mitte*, 1948, 106. See also his analyses in *Die Revolution der modernen Kunst* (1955) and *Der Tod des Lichtes* (1964).
96 *De Stijl. Maandblad voor de Beeldende Vakken*, 6 (1918).
97 H.T. Zwiers, *Bouwkunst en crisis*, 1934, 524-525.
98 *Moderne Bouwkunst in Nederland*, 1932 (introduction).
99 J. Huizinga, *In the shadow of tomorrow*, 1936.
100 Nic. Molenaar, *De nationalistische strooming*, 1934, 53-55.
101 Hans Mulder, *Ontaard en gezond*, 1982, 314-323.
102 Richard Hamann and Jost Hermand, *Stilkunst um 1900*, 1967, 40-81 and A. Labrie, *Zuiverheid*, 1994.
103 Paul Schultze-Naumburg, *Kunst und Rasse*, 1928, 135.
104 Shulamit Volkov, *The Rise of Popular Antimodernism*, 1978, 297-325.
105 Fritz Stern, *The Politics of Cultural Despair*, 1963, 122.
106 Anna Teut, *Architektur im Dritten Reich*, 1967, 79 and Barbara Miller Lane, *Architecture and Politics in Germany*, 1968.
107 Anna Teut, 1967, 121.
108 Paul Schmitthenner, *Baugestaltung*, 1932, 6.
109 Paul Mebes, *Um 1800*, 1908.
110 Alexander von Senger, *Krisis der Architektur*, 1928.
111 Norbert Huse, *Neues Bauen*, 1975, 87.
112 David Watkin, *The Rise of Architectural History*, 1980, 94-144.
113 Reginald Blomfield, *Modernismus*, 1933, Preface.
114 W.R. Lethaby, *Form in Civilization*, 1922, 5 and 6.
115 Wolfgang Sofsky, *Schreckbild Stadt*, 1986, 1-21 and Peter Hall, *Cities of Tomorrow*, 1988.
116 *Exceptions: Moderne Architektur in Deutschland,* 1992 and Hans Ibelings, *Het andere modernisme*, 1988, 36-51.
117 Falko Herlemann, *Zwischen unbedingter Tradition,* 1989, 95 and 119.
118 Rob Kroes, *Amerika*, 1993, 79-84.

Romantic Modernists

1   Jozef Keulartz, *Strijd om de natuur*, 1995, 195.
2   *Natuurbeleidsplan*, 1990, 2-3.
3   Henny J. van der Windt, *Natuurbescherming*, 1995, 191.
4   *Notulen van de vergaderingen van de Rijkscommissie voor de Monumentenzorg.* Department B, 1920, 246-248.
5   *Grondbeginselen*, 1917.
6   Raymond Williams, *Culture and Society*, 1958, 54.
7   From a lecture by C. Blok, 14 March 1997, at the University of Leiden.
8   Stendhal, *Mélanges d'Art*, 1932, 44 and David Wakefield, *Stendhal*, 1973, 101 and 102.
9   Charles Baudelaire, *Oeuvres*, 1976, II, 696.
10 Ernst H. Gombrich, *Kunst und Fortschritt*, 1978, 84 and 107.
11 Raymond Williams, *The Country and the City*, 1973, 172.

12 Charles Baudelaire, *'Salon de 1846': Oeuvres*, 1976, II, 421.

13 Godfried Bomans, *Nieuwe Buitelingen*, 1955, 163.

14 J.A.C. Tillema, *Schetsen*, 1975, 474.

15 Ineke Pey, *Torenprijsvragen*, 1995, 184-203.

16 C. Peeters and W.F. Denslagen, *Antwoord*, 1980, 103-113, 110.

17 *The Charter of Venice* (1964): *Il Monumento*, 1971, LXIX-LXXII.

18 C.J.A.C. Peeters and W.F. Denslagen, *Restauratienota*, 1984, 89-134, 113.

19 *Meinungsstreit Wiederaufbau Frauenkirche*, 1991, 79-90.

20 *Deutsche Kunst und Denkmalpflege* (1991), 96.

21 Hanno-Walter Kruft, *Rekonstruktion als Restauration?* 1993, 582-589.

22 Jörg Traeger, *Ruine und Rekonstruktion*, 1992, 217-232 and *Zehn Thesen*, 1992, 629-633.

23 Georg Mörsch, *Zu den 10 Thesen*, 1992, 634-638.

24 Manfred F. Fischer, *Non Possumus*, 1993, 589-604.

25 Achim Hubel, *Konservieren und Rekonstruieren*, 1993, 134-154.

26 Jörg Traeger, *Ruine und Rekonstruktion*, 1994, 288-296.

27 C'est dans les parties essentielles que consistent toutes les beautés, dans les parties introduites par besoin consistent toutes les licenses, dans les parties ajoutées par caprice consistent tous les défauts (Laugier, Essay, 1755, 10). The quoation from E.E. Viollet-le-Duc is found in the entry on 'Architecture' in his *Dictionnaire Raisonné*, 1854.

28 Wim Denslagen, *Romantische ondergang*, 1996, 189-209.

29 Ernst H. Gombrich, *Kunst und Fortschritt*, 1978, 29.

30 Caroline van Eck, *Organicism*, 1994, 187.

31 Klaus Döhmer, *In welchem Style*, 1976.

32 Paul Mebes, *Um 1800*, 1908, 9.

33 Sigfried Giedion, *Space, Time and Architecture*, 1962, 226.

34 John Ruskin, *The Seven Lamps*, 1849, 353.

35 Georg Hager, *Denkmalpflege und moderne Kunst*, 1905, 21-41.

36 *Der Wiederaufbau der St. Michaeliskirche in Hamburg*, 1909, 79-103.

37 Hermann Muthesius, *Kunstgewerbe und Architektur*, 1907, 47 and 155.

38 Jan Kalf, *Van Oude en Nieuwe Kunst*, 1908, 3-18.

39 E.R.M. Taverne, *Bouwen zonder make-up*, 1983, 8-22.

40 Idem, 18.

41 Cord Meckseper, *Architekturrekonstruktionen*, 1984, 18.

42 Herman Stynen, *De hal te Ieper*,1983, 32-43. *Resurgam* 1985. Pieter Uyttenhove and Jo Celis, *Louvain*, 1991.

43 Jo Celis, *De wederopbouwarchitectuur*, 1985, 135 and 132.

44 Rudy Koshar, *Germany's Transient Pasts*, 1998.

45 Werner Durth and Niels Gutschow, *Träume in Trümmern*, 1993, 314-318.

46 Hartwig Beseler and Niels Gutschow, *Kriegsschicksale Deutscher Architektur*, 1988, Vol. 1, XLII.

47 Dieter Hoffmann-Axthelm, *Krieg & Architektur*, 1983, 14-18.

48 Hartwig Beseler and Niels Gutschow, *Kriegsschicksale Deutscher Architektur*, 1988, XLIV.

49 H.G. Burkhardt, *Freudenstadt*, 1988.

50 Günter Bandmann, *Wandel der Materialbewertung*, 1971, 129-157.

51 Jürgen Paul, *Knochenhaueramtshaus*, 1980, 64-76.

Self-seeking Romantics

1 Proceedings of the Nara Conference on Authenticity, 1995.

2 Geert Bekaert, *Erfgoedzorg*, 2000, 15-22

3   Derek Linstrum, *Giuseppe Valadier*, 1982, 44-69.
4   Viollet-le-Duc, *Dictionnaire Raisonné*, 1866, 31.
5   Thomas Nipperdey, *Kirche und Nationaldenkmal*, 1979, 175-202.
6   Jane Fawcett, *Restoration Tragedy*, 1976, 90.
7   Wim Denslagen, *Architectural Restoration*, 1994, 86.
8   Dehio, *Denkmalschutz*, 1905 and Marion Wohlleben, *Konservieren oder restaurieren*, 1989.
9   Wolfgang Götz, *Denkmalpflege des 16. Jahrhunderts*, 1959, 45-52. Nikolaus Pevsner, *Historismus*, 1965, 13-24. Arnold Wolff, *Kölner Dombau*, 1974, 137-150. Peter Kurman and Dethard von Winterfeld, *Gautier de Varinfroy*, 1977, 101-159. Georg Germann, *Konformität*, 1966, 119-143. Rudolf Wittkower, *Gothic versus Classic*, 1974. Erwin Panofsky, *The First Page of Giorgio Vasari*, 1955, 169-225.
10 Paul Clemen, *Ein Bekenntnis*, 1933, 36.
11 Nobuo Ito, *Authenticity*, 1995, 35-45.
12 Adolf W. Ehrentraut, *Symbols of Nostalgia*, 1994, 1-23.
13 Siegfried Enders and Niels Gutschow, *Hozon*, 1998, 54.
14 Joris Luyendijk, *de Volkskrant*, 6 March 1999.
15 Hartwig Schmidt, *Wiederaufbau*, 1993.
16 John Papadopoulos, *Conservation of Archaeological Sites*, 1997, 93-125.
17 Viollet-le-Duc, *Dictionnaire Raisonné*, 1866, 14.

Bad-mannered Buildings

1   *NRC Handelsblad*, 15 August 1986.
2   From *Architecture Must Blaze* (www.greatbuildings.com/buildings/Office Extension in Vienna).
3   Jaap Huisman, *Lelijk gebouwd Nederland*, 1991, 65
4   *NRC Handelsblad*, 30 March 1990.
5   *Monument en Binnenstad*, 1976, 210.
6   Geurt Brinkgreve, *Amsterdam verdient beter,* 1997, 62.
7   *Stadhuis Zutphen*. Amsterdam, Rau & Partners, 1999.
8   Verbal account of P.C. Wieringa, then a staff member of the Department for Conservation who was responsible for the case.
9   *Report of SB4*, 1996, commissioned by the Stichting Buitengoed Overijssel.
10 Archive of the Rijksdienst voor de Monumentenzorg.
11 Lydia Lansink, *Stationsplein*, 1982.
12 *Bulletin van de Koninklijke Nederlandse Oudheidkundige Bond* (1990), 6.
13 Gert Urhahn, *Stadsontwerp Amsterdam*, 1990, 109-123.
14 *Bouwkundig Weekblad* 9 (1969), 12.
15 Ab Warffemius in: *Bouwkunst*, 1993, 597.
16 *Bouwkundig Weekblad* 9 (1969), 209.

The Revival Styles and Time Regained

1   Gerard Brom, *Herleving*, 1933, 49, 50, 69, 70, 304 and 308.
2   Harald Bodenschatz, *Berlin West*, 1992, 58-77. *Paris Perdu* 1991.
3   Klaus Döhmer, *In welchem Style*, 1976, 34, 55, 64 and 65.
4   *Annales Archéologiques* (1846), 325-353.
5   Pierre Bourdieu, *The Rules of Art: Genesis and Structure of the Literary Field*, 1996, 95.

6   Raymond Williams, *Culture and Society*, 1960, 130. Michael J. Lewis, *Politics of German Revival*, 1993. Jan De Maeyer, *Katholiek reveil*, 1992, 81-97.

7 Peter Collins, *Changing Ideals*, 1965, 143.
8 Eugène Viollet-le-Duc, *Entretiens*, 1863, 449-451.
9 Hermann Fillitz, *Der Traum vom Glück*, 1996.
10 Hans Curjel, *Henry van de Velde, Zum Neuen Stil*, 1955.
11 J.J.P. Oud, *Over de toekomstige bouwkunst*, 1921, 25.
12 Walter Gropius, *Grundlagen für Neues Bauen, 1925-1926*, 134-147.
13 *Bouwkundig Weekblad* (1908), 824-826.
14 Bruno Taut, *Nieder der Seriosismus*, 1920, 11.
15 Jan Gratama in: K.P.C. de Bazel, *Dr. H.P. Berlage*, 1916, 26.
16 J.G. Wattjes, *Moderne Architectuur*, 1927 (introduction).
17 Wolfgang Herrmann, *Gottfried Semper*, 1984, 161.
18 Adolf Loos, *Ornament und Verbrechen* (1908) and *Heimatkunst* (1914) in *Sämtliche Schriften*, 1962. Volume I, 276 and 331.
19 H.P. Berlage, 'Amsterdam en Venetië', 1883, 217-234.
20 H.P. Berlage, *Gedanken über Stil in der Baukunst* , 1904, 53 and 61.
21 Vincent van Rossem, *De Stad gebouwd*, 2000, 36-58.
22 Sergio Polano, *Berlage*, 1988, 92: *De ontwikkeling der moderne bouwkunst in Holland* (1924).
23 Gottfried Semper, *Kulturzuständen*, 1884, 351.
24 Henry-Russell Hitchcock, *Modern Architecture*, 1929, 18.
25 Hitchcock, 1929, 30.
26 Wilfried van Leeuwen, *Het schilderachtige*, 1994, 95-105,102.
27 Auke van der Woud, *Waarheid en Karakter*, 1997, 263.
28 Idem, 110.
29 *Bouwkundig Weekblad* (1884), 264-268, 268.
30 Wilfried van Leeuwen, *Jan Springer*, 1991, 3-23.

Nostalgia and Imitation

1 D. Raoul-Rochette, *Style Gothique*, 1846, 326-333.
2 Richard Krautheimer, *The Carolingian Revival*, 1942, 1-38, 29 and *Iconography of Mediaeval Architecture*, 1942, 1-33, 4.
3 Henri Focillon, *The Art of the West*, 1963, 36 (volume 2).
4 Francis Haskell and Nicholas Penny, *Taste and the Antique*, 1981.
5 Elizabeth Gilmore Holt, *The Triumph of Art for the Public*, 1979, 289.
6 Stendhal, Salon de 1824, in *Mélanges d'Art*, 1932, 21 and David Wakefield, *Stendhal and the Arts*, 1973, 101-102.
7 Klaus Döhmer, 'In welchem Style sollen wir bauen?', 1976, 32.
8 Viollet-le-Duc, *Entretiens sur l'Architecture*, 1863, 450 (volume I).
9 *Bulletin Monumental* (1880), 421.
10 Jeffrey M. Diefendorf, *Rebuilding Europe's Bombed Cities*, 1990 and Werner Durth and Niels Gutschow, *Träume in Trümmern*, 1993.
11 Ben F. van Leerdam, *Henri Maclaine Pont*, 1995.
12 Gunawan Tjahjono, *Indonesian Heritage*, 1998, 133.
13 *Expressions of Islam*, 1990,120.
14 Gulzar Haider, *Muslim Space*, 1996, 31-45.
15 *Expressions of Islam*, 1990, 186 and Martin Frishman, *The Mosque*, 1994.
16 A.G. Krishna Menon, *Conservation in India*, 1989, 22-27.
17 I am indebted to Marieke Kuipers for this information.
18 E.P. Thompson, *William Morris*, 1977, 90.
19 Peter Collins, *Changing Ideals in Modern Architecture*, 1965, 69, 89 and 297.
20 *Die verborgene Vernunft*, 1972, 6.

21 Henry Russell Hitchcock, *Modern Architecture*, 1929, 18.
22 Pevsner, *Some Architectural Writers*, 1972, 237.
23 Klaus Döhmer, 'In welchem Style sollen wir bauen?, 1976, 46, 48, 81 and 141.
24 Peter Collins, *Changing Ideals in Modern Architecture* , 1965, 77 and 299.
25 Nikolaus Pevsner, *Some Architectural Writers*, 1972, 227 and 242.
26 Kenneth Frampton, *Place, Form and Cultural Identity*, 1988, 51-65.
27 Kenneth Frampton, *Modern Architecture*, 1980, 316 and 327.
28 Hilde Heynen, *Architecture and Modernity*, 1999, 224.
29 Harold Clunn, *London Rebuilt*, 1927.
30 Hermione Hobhouse, *Lost London*, 1971.
31 *The City of London*, 1951.
32 *Paris Perdu*, 1991.
33 Werner Durth, Jörn Düwel and Niels Gutschow, *Ostkreuz*, 1999, I, 211 and 214.
34 Hauptstadt Berlin, 1990.
35 Koos Bosma and Helma Hellinga, *De regie van de stad*, 1997, 266.
36 Dick Wittenberg, *NRC Handelsblad*, 15 May 1998.
37 Peter Katz, *The New Urbanism*, 1994.
38 John Cüsters in *Bouw* 10 (1998) 44 and Tracy Metz, *NRC Handelsblad*, 9 June 1999.
39 Bernard Hulsman, *NRC Handelsblad*, 5 January 2001.
40 *Oproep*, 1995.
41 Wytze Patijn, *Jonge monumenten*, 1996, 63.
42 Hans van Dijk, *Het onderwijsersmodernisme*, 1990, 8-12.
43 *Heemschut* 6 (1995), 19.
44 *Heemschut* 6 (1995), 21.
45   B. Olde Meierink, *Kastelen*, 1995, 247.
46 Letter to the Ministry of Education, Culture and Science, 17 October 1997.
47 Stanislaw Lorentz, *Bernardo Bellotto*, 1964.
48 Cord Meckseper, *Architekturrekonstruktionen*, 1984, 17-24.
49 Alberto Rizzi, *Varsovia Resurrecta*, 1987.
50 Dresden. *Stadtplanung*, 2000
51 Gavriel D. Rosenfeld, *Munich and Memory*, 2000, 241.
52 Michel Foucault, *Space, Power and Knowledge*, 1984.
53 *De Volkskrant*, 31 January 2002.
54 Article by Salman Rushdie, *de Volkskrant*, 10 August 2002.
55 James Fentress and Chris Wickam, *Social Memory*, 1992.
56 Gert Kähler, *Einfach schwierig*, 1995, 25
57 *Baumeister* 8 (1994), 46-50.
58 Thorsten Scheer, Josef Paul Kleihues and Paul Kahlfeld, *Stadt der Architektur*, 2000, 382
59 *Bauwelt* 82 (1991), 565.
60 *Architektur der Stadt. Berlin 1900-2000*, 327.
61 *Het Parool*, 29 November 2001.
62 *Stadt der Architektur. Berlin 1900-2000*, 366.
63 Wilhelm v. Boddien and Helmut Engel, *Die Berliner Schlossdebatte*, 2000.
64 *Das Schloss?* 1993
65 Brian Ladd, *The Ghosts of Berlin*, 1997, 230.
66 Jürgen Trimborn, *Schlussstrich*, 2001, 102.
67 Gavriel D. Rosenfeld, *Munich and Memory*, 2000, 102.
68 Martin Thumm, Achim Hubel, *Denkmalpflege*, 1993, 50.
69 Hüsnü Yegenoglu, 'The Torn Metropolis: Explorations in Beirut', *Archis* 1 (2000), 69-78.

Bibliography

Ackbar Abbas, *Hong Kong: Culture and the Politics of Disappearance*. Minneapolis, Minnesota University Press, 1997.

Yoshio Abé, 'Les débuts de la conservation au Japon moderne: idéologie et historicité', in Irving Lavin, *World Art. Themes of Unity in Diversity. Acts of the XXVIth International Congress of the History of Art*. Pennsylvania State University Press, 1989. Volume III, 855-859.

Gerrie Andela, *Kneedbaar landschap, kneedbaar volk. De heroïsche jaren van de ruilverkavelingen in Nederland*. Bussum, Thoth, 2000.

Arjun Appadurai, *Modernity at Large: Cultural Aspects of Globalization*. Minneapolis, University of Minnesota Press, 1997.

Celia Applegate, *A Nation of Provincials. The German Idea of Heimat*. Berkeley, University of California Press, 1990.

Jay Appleton, *The Experience of Landscape*. Chichester, John Wiley, 1986.

Donald Appleyard, *The Conservation of European Cities*. Cambridge MA, The MIT Press, 1979.

Dana Arnold, *The Metropolis and Its Images. Constructing Identities for London c. 1750-1950*. London, Blackwell, 1999.

Clive Aslet, *Quinlan Terry: The Revival of Architecture*. London, Viking, 1986.

Atelier Neumarkt Dresden 2000. Dresden, Stadtplanungsamt, 2001.

Günter Bandmann, 'Der Wandel der Materialbewertung in der Kunsttheorie des 19. Jahrhunderts', *Beiträge zur Theorie der Künste im 19. Jahrhundert*. Volume 1. Frankfurt on Main, Vittorio Klostermann, 1971, 129-157.

Reyner Banham, *The New Brutalism. Ethic or Aesthetic?* Stuttgart, Karl Krämer, 1966.

Reyner Banham, *Theory and Design in the First Machine Age*. London, The Architectural Press, 1960.

Stephen Bann, *The Inventions of History. Essays on the Representation of the Past*. Manchester University Press, 1990.

Diane Barthel, *Historic Preservation. Collective Memory and Historical Identity*. New Brunswick, Rutgers University Press, 1996.

Charles Baudelaire, *Oeuvres complètes*. Paris, Gallimard, 1976.

Jean Baudrillard, *Simulacres et Simulations*. Paris, Editions Galilée, 1981.

K.P.C. de Bazel and others, *Dr. H.P. Berlage en zijn werk*. Rotterdam, Brusse, 1916.

Johan van de Beek and Gerrit Smienk, 'ir. j.b. van loghem b.i. architect', *Plan* 12 (1971), 2-64.

Adolf Behne, *Der moderne Zweckbau*. Munich, Drei Masken Verlag, 1926 (new edition, 1964, Frankfurt am Main, Verlag Ullstein).

Geert Bekaert, 'Kan het erfgoed de architectuur redden?', *Erfgoedzorg in de 21ste*

eeuw. Kritische Beschouwingen. Ghent, Koning Boudewijnstichting, 2000, 15-22.

Françoise Bercé, *Des monuments historiques au patrimoine: ou les égarements du coeur et de l'esprit. Du XVIIIe siècle à nos jours*. Paris, Flammarion, 2000.

H.P. Berlage, 'Amsterdam en Venetië. Schets in verband met de tegenwoordige veranderingen van Amsterdam', *Bouwkundig Weekblad* (1883), 217-234.

H.P. Berlage, 'Gedanken über Stil in der Baukunst' (1904) in: Bernhard Kohlenbach, *Hendrik Petrus Berlage. Über Architektur und Stil. Aufsätze und Vorträge 1894-1928*. Berlin, Birkhäuser, 1991, 53 and 61, published as 'Beschouwingen over Stijl' in 1922 in the collection *Studies over Bouwkunst Stijl en Samenleving*, Rotterdam, Brusse.

Marshall Berman, *All that is Solid Melts into Air. The Experience of Modernity*. Penguin Books 1988 (first edition, 1982).

Azadine Beschaouch, 'Les archéologues dans la reconstruction de l'identité', *Patrimoine et Passions Identitaires. Actes des Entretiens du Patrimoine sous la présidence de Jacques Le Goff*. Paris, Fayard, 1998, 327-336.

Hartwig Beseler and Niels Gutschow, *Kriegsschiksale Deutscher Architektur. Verluste – Schäden – Wiederaufau. Eine Dokumentation für das Gebiet der Bundesrepublik Deutschland*. Two volumes. Neumünster, Karl Wachholtz, 1988.

Klaus von Beyme, *Architektur und Städtebaupolitik in beiden deutschen Staaten*. Munich, Piper, 1987.

Klaus von Beyme and others, *Neue Städte aus Ruinen. Deutscher Städtebau der Nachkriegszeit*. Munich, Prestel, 1992.

Peter Blake, *The Master Builders*. New York, Knopf, 1961.

Peter Blake *Form Follows Fiasco. Why Modern Architecture Hasn't Worked*. Boston, Little, Brown and Company, 1977.

Reginald Blomfield, *Modernismus*. London, Macmillan, 1933.

M. Bock, 'Hoe nieuw en wat is het Nieuwe Bouwen?' *Het Nieuwe Bouwen. Voorgeschiedenis*. Delft, University Press, 1982, 6-22.

Manfred Bock and others, *Van het Nieuwe Bouwen naar een Nieuwe Architectuur. Groep '32: Ontwerpen, gebouwen, stedebouwkundige plannen 1925-1945*. The Hague, Staatsuitgeverij, 1983.

Wilhelm v. Boddien and Helmut Engel, *Die Berliner Schlossdebatte – Pro und Contra*. Berlin, Verlag 2000.

Harald Bodenschatz, 'Berlin West: Abschied von der steinernen Stadt', *Neue Städte aus Ruinen. Deutscher Städtebau der Nachkriegszeit*. Munich, Prestel, 1992.

Niek de Boer, 'Dilemma's van dynamisch behoud. Ideevorming over restaureren en beschermen van stadsgezichten', *Wonen TABK* 15 (1984), 19-27.

Niek de Boer and Donald Lambert, *Woonwijken. Nederlandse stedebouw 1945-1985*. Rotterdam, 010, 1987.

Godfried Bomans, *Nieuwe Buitelingen. Facetten en Aspecten*. Amsterdam, Elsevier, 1955.

René Boomkens, *Een drempelwereld. Moderne ervaring en stedelijke openbaarheid*. Rotterdam, Nai, 1998.

Nicola Borger-Keweloh, *Die mittelalterliche Dome im 19. Jahrhundert*. Munich, C.H. Beck, 1986.

C. Bos and others, *Successen en mislukkingen in de Nederlandse ruimtelijke ordening. Een evaluatie van 11 inrichtingsprincipes*. Amsterdam, Planologisch en Demografisch Instituut, 1988.

Koos Bosma, *Ruimte voor een nieuwe tijd: vormgeving van de Nederlandse regio 1900-1945*. Rotterdam, Nai, 1993.

Koos Bosma and Cor Wagenaar, *Een geruisloze doorbraak. De geschiedenis van architectuur en stedebouw tijdens de bezetting en de wederopbouw van Nederland*. Rotterdam, Nai, 1995.

Philippe Boudon, *Pessac de Le Corbusier*. Paris, Dunod, 1969.

Pierre Bourdieu, *Les Règles de l'Art. Genèse et structure du champ littéraire*, Paris, Seuil, 1992.

Vincent Bouvet, 'Le château de Voisins', *Monuments Historiques de la France* 142 (1986), 81-96.

Bouwkunst. Studies in vriendschap voor Kees Peeters. Amsterdam, Architectura & Natura Pers, 1993.

M. Christine Boyer, *The City of Collective Memory. Its Historical Imagery and Architectural Entertainments*. Cambridge, MA, MIT Press, 1994.

Marcel Breuer, 'Where do we stand?', *The Architectural Review* (1935). Reprinted in: *The Rationalists. Theory and Design in the Modern Movement*. Ed. Dennis Sharp. London, The Architectural Press, 1978.

Martin S. Briggs, *Goths and Vandals. A Study of the destruction, neglect and preservation of historical buildings in England*. London, Constable, 1952.

Geurt Brinkgreve, Wiek Röling and Max van Rooy, *Amsterdam verdient beter*. Bussum, Thoth, 1997.

Ingrid Brock, *Probleme des Wiederaufbaus nach 1945*. Bamberg, Arbeitskreis Theorie und Lehre der Denkmalpflege, 1991.

Gerard Brom, *Romantiek en Katholicisme in Nederland*. Two volumes. Volume I (*Kunst*). Groningen, Wolters, 1926.

Gerard Brom, *Herleving van de kerkelike kunst in katholiek Nederland*. Leiden, Ars Catholica, 1933.

Wolfgang Brönner, 'Geschichte als Grundlage und Kategorie des heutigen Denkmalbegriffs', *Die Alte Stadt* (1986), 286-294.

G. Baldwin Brown, *The Care of Ancient Monuments*. Cambridge, University Press, 1905.

Dick de Bruin and others, *Ooievaar. De toekomst van het rivierengebied*. Arnhem, Stichting Gelderse Milieufederatie, 1987.

J. Buit, 'Woningen in Hoogbouw', *Successen en mislukkingen in de Nederlandse ruimtelijke ordening*. Planologische Studies no. 7. Amsterdam, Planologisch en Demografisch Instituut, 1988, 90-110.

Jan Erik Burger and others, *Visies op het landschap*. Amsterdam, Op Lemen Voeten, 1989.

Hans-Günther Burkhardt and others, *Stadtgestalt und Heimatgefühl. Der Wiederaufbau von Freudenstadt 1945-1954. Analysen, Vergleiche und Dokumente*. Hamburg, Christians, 1988.

Ian Buruma, *The Missionary and the Libertine. Love and War in East and West*. London, Faber and Faber, 1996.

Jo Celis, 'De wederopbouwarchitectuur tussen inhoud en vorm' in: *Resurgam*, 1985, 131-152.

Dipesh Chakrabarty, 'Postcoloniality and the Artifice of History: Who Speaks for "Indian Pasts"?', *Representations* 37 (1992), 1-26.

Charter of the New Urbanism. New York, McGraw-Hill, 2000

François Chaslin, *Une haine monumentale*. Paris, Editions Descartes et Cie, 1997.

François Chaslin, 'Patrimoine yougoslave et purification ethnque', *Patrimoine et Passions Identitaires. Actes des Entretiens du Patrimoine sous la présidence de Jacques Le Goff*. Paris, Fayard, 1998, 337-348.

Francoise Choay, *L'Allégorie du Patrimoine*. Paris, Seuil, 1992.

Dimitri Chvidkovski, 'Le cas des églises de Moscou', *Patrimoine et Passions Identitaires. Actes des Entretiens du Patrimoine sous la présidence de Jacques Le Goff*. Paris, Fayard, 1998, 321-326.

The City of London. A Record of Destruction and Survival. London, Shenval Press, 1951.

Kenneth Clark, *The Gothic Revival. An Essay in the History of Taste*. London, John

Murray, 1962 (first edition 1928).

Paul Clemen, *Die deutsche Kunst und die Denkmalpflege. Ein Bekenntnis*. Berlin, Deutscher Kunstverlag, 1933.

James Clifford, *The Predicament of Culture: Twentieth-Century Ethnography, Literature, and Art*. Cambridge, Harvard University Press, 1988.

Harold Clunn, *London Rebuilt 1897-1927*. London, John Murray, 1927.

Bernhard Colenbrander, *Referentie: Oma: de sublieme start van een architectengeneratie*. Rottterdam, Nai, 1995.

Peter Collins, *Changing Ideals in Modern Architecture 1750-1950*. London, Faber and Faber, 1965.

Ulrich Conrads, *Programs and manifestoes on 20th-century architecture*. Cambridge, MA, MIT Press, 1970.

John Cornforth, *The Inspiration of the Past. Country House Taste in the Twentieth Century*. New York, Viking, 1985.

Hans Cürlis and H. Stephany, *Die künstlerischen und wirtschaftlichen Irrwege unserer Baukunst. Vergleichende kritische Studien deutscher und belgischer Architektur*. Munich, R. Piper, 1916.

Hermann Czech and Wolfgang Mistelbauer, *Das Looshaus*. Vienna, 1968 (typescript, Literature Faculty library, Rijksuniversiteit Utrecht), 22.

Fred Davis, *Yearning for Yesterday: A Sociology of Nostalgia*. New York, Free Press, 1979.

Régis Debray, *Contre Venise*. Paris, Gallimard, 1995.

Georg Dehio, *Denkmalschutz und Denkmalpflege im neunzehnten Jahrhundert*. Strasbourg, Heitz/Mündel, 1905.

Georg Dehio, *Alois Riegl. Konservieren, nicht restaurieren. Streitschriften zur Denkmalpflege um 1900. Mit einem Kommentar von Marion Wohlleben und einem Nachwort von Georg Mörsch*. Braunschweig, Vieweg, 1988.

Charles Dellheim, *The Face of the Past. The Preservation of the Medieval Inheritance in Victorian England*. Cambridge, University Press, 1982.

Denkmalpflege heute. Akten des Berner Denkmalpflegekongresses Oktober 1993. Published by Volker Hoffmann and Hans Peter Autenrieth. Berne, Peter Lang, 1996.

W. F. Denslagen, *Omstreden herstel. Kritiek op het restaureren van monumenten. Een thema uit de architectuurgeschiedenis van Engeland, Frankrijk, Duitsland en Nederland (1779-1953)*. The Hague, Staatsuitgeverij, 1987.

Wim Denslagen, 'Een crèche aan het Oudekerksplein in Amsterdam', *Kunstschrift* 6 (1992).

Wim Denslagen, 'Restoration Theories, East and West', *Transactions of the Association for Studies in the Conservation of Historic Buildings* 18 (1993), 3-7.

Wim Denslagen, *Architectural Restoration in Western Europe: Controversy and Continuity*. Amsterdam, Architectura & Natura, 1994.

Wim Denslagen, '"That we are to endure more". De romantische ondergang van de classicistische architectuur' in: Jo Tollebeek, Frank Ankersmit and Wessel Krul, *Romantiek en Historische Cultuur*. Groningen, Historische Uitgeverij, 1996, 189-209.

Wim Denslagen, *Architectural Restoration in Western Europe: Controversy and Continuity*. Amsterdam, Architectura & Natura, 1994.

W.F. Denslagen, 'Een crèche aan het Oudekerksplein in Amsterdam', *Kunstschrift* 6 (1992).

Wim Denslagen, '"That we are to endure more". De romantische ondergang van de classicistische architectuur' in: Jo Tollebeek, Frank Ankersmit and Wessel Krul, *Romantiek en Historische Cultuur*. Groningen, Historische Uitgeverij, 1996, 189-209.

Die Denkmalpflege als Plage und Frage. Festgabe für August Gebessler. Munich, Deutscher Kunstverlag, 1989.

Herman Diederiks and others, *Het platteland in een veranderende wereld: boeren en het proces van modernisering*. Hilversum, Verloren, 1994

Die Dresdner Frauenkirche. Jahrbuch zu ihrer Geschichte und zu ihrem archäologischen Wiederaufbau. Weimar, Böhlau, 1996.

Jeffry M. Diefendorf, *Rebuilding Europe's Bombed Cities*. New Hampshire, Macmillan, 1990.

Hans van Dijk, 'Het onderwijsersmodernisme. Van inspiratiebron tot ballast: de moderne traditie in Nederland', *Archis* 6 (1990), 8-12.

H. Dijkstra and J. A. Kleijn, *Kwaliteit en waardering van landschappen*. Wageningen, DLO-Staring Centrum, 1992 (report 229).

Johannes Dobai, *Die Kunstliteratur des Klassizismus und der Romantik in England*. Three volumes. Berne, Benteli Verlag, 1974-1977.

Theo van Doesburg, *De Stijl en de Europese architectuur. De architectuuropstellen in Het Bouwbedrijf 1924-1931*. With a foreword by Cees Boekraad. Nijmegen, Sun, 1986.

Klaus Döhmer, *'In welchem Style sollen wir bauen? Architekturtheorie zwischen Klassizismus und Jugendstil*. Munich, Prestel Verlag, 1976.

Dresden. Stadtplanung und Stadtentwicklung in der Kernstadt Dresden. Dresden, Sächsische Akademie der Künste, 2000.

P. P. J. Driessen, *Landinrichting gewogen. De plaats van de milieu-, natuur- en landschapsbelangen in het landinrichtingsbeleid*. Zeist, Kerckebosch, 1990.

Leen van Duin, 'De Januskop van het postmodernisme. Vier Nederlandse architecten', *De bevrijding van de moderne beweging. Een dialoog met de modernen*. Nijmegen, SUN, 1988.

Louis Dumont, *La Civilisation Indienne et Nous*. Paris, Armand Colin, 1964.

Werner Durth, Jörn Düwel, Niels Gutschow, *Ostkreuz. Architektur und Städtebau der DDR*. Frankfurt on Main, Campus Verlag, 1999 (two volumes).

Werner Durth and Niels Gutschow, *Träume in Trümmern. Stadtplanung 1940-1950*. Munich, Deutscher Taschenbuch Verlag, 1993.

Werner Durth, Jörn Düwel, Niels Gutschow, *Ostkreuz. Architektur und Städtebau der DDR*. Frankfurt on Main, Campus Verlag, 1999 (two volumes).

Claus-Peter Echter, *Das geschichtliche Bild der Staedte: Grosstadt und Denkmalpflege*. Berlin, Deutsches Institut fuer Urbanistik, 1991.

Caroline van Eck, *Organicism in nineteenth-century architecture. An inquiry into its theoretical and philosophical background*. Amsterdam, Architectura & Natura Press, 1994.

Umberto Eco, *Travels in Hyperreality*. London, Picador, 1986.

A. Trystan Edwards, *Good and Bad Manners in Architecture*. London, Tiranti, 1946 (first edition, 1924).

Adolf W. Ehrentraut, 'Symbols of Nostalgia: the Reconstructed Castles of Japan', Paper presented at the XIIIth World Congress of Sociology in Bielefeld (1994), 1-23.

Mircea Eliade, *Le Mythe de l'Eternel Retour: Archétypes et Répétition*. Paris, Gallimard, 1947.

John Elsner, 'Pausanias: A Greek Pilgrim in the Roman World', *Past and Present* (1992), 3-29.

Siegfried R.C.T. Enders and Niels Gutschow, *Hozon. Architectural and Urban Conservation in Japan*. Stuttgart, Axel Menges, 1998.

John Evans, *A History of The Society of Antiquaries*. Oxford, The University Press, 1956.

Nicole Ex, *Zo goed als oud. De achterkant van het restaureren*. Amsterdam, Amber, 1993.

Expressions of Islam in Buildings. Proceedings of an International Seminar sponsored by the Aga Khan Award for Architecture (Jakarta, 1990). Geneva, Aga Khan Award for Architecture, 1990.

Façadisme et Identité Urbaine. Idées et Débats. Editions du Patrimoine 1999.

Jane Fawcett, 'A restoration tragedy: cathedrals in the eighteenth and nineteenth centuries', *The Future of the Past. Attitudes to Conservation 1174-1974.* London, Thames and Hudson, 1976, 75-115.

James Fentress and Chris Wickam, *Social Memory. New Perspectives on the Past.* Oxford, Blackwell, 1992.

Françoise Fichet, *La Théorie Architecturale à l'âge classique.* Brussels, Pierre Margada, 1979.

Hermann Fillitz and others, *Der Traum vom Glück. Die Kunst des Historismus in Europa.* Vienna, Christian Brandstätter Verlag, 1996.

Manfred F. Fischer, 'Non Possumus. Zur Phantomsimulation von drei Fassaden des ehem. Stadtschlosses am Marx-Engels-Platz in Berlin', *Kunstchronik* (1993), 589-604.

Manfred F. Fischer and others, *Architektur und Denkmalpflege. Neue Architektur in historischer Umgebung.* Munich, Heinz Moos, 1975.

Five Architects. New York, Oxford University Press, 1975.

Henri Focillon, *The Art of the West.* London, Phaidon, 1963.

Michel Foucault, *Politics, Philosophy, Culture. Interviews and other writings 1977-1984.* New York, Routledge, 1988.

Kenneth Frampton, *Modern Architecture. A Critical History.* London, Thames and Hudson, 1985 (first edition 1980).

Etienne François, 'Reconstruction allemande: les monuments de Berlin, de la guerre à la réunification', *Patrimoine et Passions Identitaires. Actes des Entretiens du Patrimoine sous la présidence de Jacques Le Goff.* Paris, Fayard, 1998, 311-320.

Hartmut Frank, 'Auf der Suche nach der alten Stadt. Zur Diskussion um Heimatschutz und Stadtbaukunst beim Wiederaufbau Freudenstadts' in: Hans-Günther Burkhardt, *Stadtgestalt und Heimatgefühl*, 1988, 1-31.

Paul Frankl, *The Gothic. Literary Sources and Interpretations through Eight Centuries.* Princeton University Press 1960.

Edward A. Freeman, *The Preservation and Restoration of Ancient Monuments.* Oxford, John Henry Parker, 1852.

John Frew, 'An Aspect of the Early Gothic Revival: The Transformation of Medievalist Research, 1770-1800', *Journal of the Warburg and Courtauld Institutes* (1980), 174-185.

Martin Frishman and Hasan-Uddin Khan, *The Mosque.* London, Thames and Hudson, 1994.

Walter Frodl, *Idee und Verwirklichung. Das Werden der staatlichen Denkmalpflege in Österreich.* Vienna, Böhlau, 1988.

Buckminster Fuller, *Ideas and Integrities. A Spontaneous Autobiographical Disclosure.* Ed. Robert W. Marks. Toronto, The Macmillan Company, 1969 (first edition, 1963).

William Gaunt, *The March of the Moderns.* London, Jonathan Cape, 1949.

Clifford Geertz, *The Interpretation of Cultures.* New York, Basic Books, 1973.

Frank O. Gehry and Associates, *Architecture + process / gehry talks*. New York, Rizzoli, 1999.

Georg Germann, 'Konformität: ein Begriff aus Historiographie und Architekturtheorie', *Denkmalpflege heute. Akten des Berner Denkmalpflegekongresses. Oktober 1993*. Berne, Peter Lang, 1996, 119-143.

Sigfried Giedion, *Space, Time and Architecture. The Growth of a New Tradition*. Cambridge, Harvard University Press, 1949.

Aleksander Gieysztor, 'La reconstruction polonaise d'après guerre', *Patrimoine et Passions Identitaires. Actes des Entretiens du Patrimoine sous la présidence de Jacques Le Goff*. Paris, Fayard, 1998, 303-310.

E. H. Gombrich, 'In Search of Cultural History', *Ideals and Idols. Essays on values in history and art*. Oxford, Phaidon, 1979, 24-59.

Ernst H. Gombrich, *Kunst und Fortschritt. Wirkung und Wandlung einer Idee*. Cologne, DuMont, 1978.

Roger Goodman and Kirsten Refsing, *Ideology and Practice in Modern Japan*. London, Routledge, 1991.

Wolfgang Götz, 'Zur Denkmalpflege des 16. Jahrhunderts in Deutschland', *Österreichische Zeitschrift für Kunst und Denkmalpflege* (1959), 45-52.

Stephen Jay Gould, *Time's Arrow, Time's Cycle. Myth and Metaphor in the Discovery of Geological Time*. London, Penguin Books, 1987.

Grondbeginselen en voorschriften voor het behoud, de herstelling en de uitbreiding van oude bouwwerken. Leiden, G. H. Théonville, 1917.

Walter Gropius, 'Bilanz des neuen bauens' (1934), in: Hartmut Probst and Christian Schädlich, *Walter Gropius*. Volume 3: *Ausgewählte Schriften*. Berlin, Ernst & Sohn, 1988, 155.

Walter Gropius, 'Grundlagen für Neues Bauen', *Bau- und Werkkunst* (1925-1926), 134-147. Reprinted in: Hartmut Probst and Christian Schädlich, *Walter Gropius. Ausgewählte Schriften*. Berlin, Ernst & Sohn, 1988. Volume 3, 107.

Niels Gutschow, 'Stadträume des Wiederaufbaus – Objekte der Denkmalpflege?', *Deutsche Kunst und Denkmalpflege* (1985), 9-18.

Niels Gutschow, 'Gedanken zum Wiederaufbau Helgolands', *Deutsche Kunst und Denkmalpflege* (1989), 129-147.

Niels Gutschow, 'Idee und Substanz – Konflikte in der Denkmalpflege Japans und Nepals', *Mitteilungen des österreichischen Kunsthistorikerverbandes* 15 (1999), 44-50.

Niels Gutschow, 'Rekonstruktion im Kontekst von Städtebau Wiederherstellung – Kopie – Rekonstruktion: Wiederaufbauüberlegungen in Kassel, Rostock, Münster, Freudenstadt und Neubrandenburg 1944-1955', *Rekonstruktion in der Denkmalpflege. Überlegungen Definitionen Erfahrungsberichte*. Bonn, Deutsches Nationalkomitee für Denkmalschutz, 1997, 30-40.

Niels Gutschow, 'Restaurierung und Rekonstruktion. Gedanken zur Gültigkeit der Charta von Venedig im Kontext Südasiens', *Deutsche Kunst und Denkmalpflege* 49 (1991), 156-160.

Jürgen Habermas, 'Moderne und postmoderne Architektur', *Die Neue Unübersichtlichkeit*. Frankfurt on Main, Suhrkamp, 1985, 11-29.

Georg Hager, 'Über Denkmalpflege und moderne Kunst', *Sechsten Tag für Denkmalpflege* (Bamberg, 1905). Stenographischer Bericht. Berlin, Wilhelm Ernst, 1905, 21-41.

Gulzar Haider, 'Muslim Space and the Practice of Architecture: A Personal Odyssey', *Making Muslim Space in North America and Europe*. Edited by Barbara Daly Metcalf. Berkeley, University of California Press, 1996, 31-45.

Maurice Halbwachs, *La Mémoire Collective*. Paris, Presses Universitaires de France, 1950.

Peter Hall, *Cities of Tomorrow. An Intellectual History of Urban Planning and Design in the Twentieth Century*. Oxford, Basil Blackwell, 1988.

Richard Hamann and Jost Hermand, *Stilkunst um 1900*. Berlin, Akademie Verlag, 1967.

Ger Harmsen, 'De Stijl en de Russische revolutie', Exhibition catalogue, *De Stijl: 1917-1931*. Amsterdam, Stedelijk Museum, 1982, 45.

David Harvey, *The Condition of Postmodernity. An Enquiry into the Origins of Cultural Change*. Oxford, Blackwell, 1989.

Francis Haskell, *History and its Images. Art and the Interpretation of the Past*. Yale University Press, 1993.

Francis Haskell and Nicholas Penny, *Taste and the Antique. The Lure of Classical Sculpture 1500-1900*. Yale University Press 1981.

Rainer Haubrich, *Berlin Auf der Suche nach der Stadt. Gestern – Heute – Morgen*.

Berlin, Nicolai, 1999.

Hauptstadt Berlin. Internationaler städtebaulicher Ideenwettbewerb 1957/58. Berlin, Mann, 1990.

Volker Helas and Franz Zadnicek, *Das Stadtbild von Dresden. Stadtdenkmal und Denkmallandschaft*. Dresden, Landesamt für Denkmalpflege Sachsen, 1996.

Falko Herlemann, *Zwischen unbedingter Tradition und bedingunslosem Fortschritt. Zur Auseinanderstzung um die moderne Kunst in der Bundesrepublik Deutschland der 50er Jahre*. Frankfurt on Main, Peter Lang, 1989.

L. M. Hermans, *Krotten en sloppen*. Amsterdam, S.L. van Looy, 1901 (reprint:, Amsterdam, Van Gennep, 1974).

Wolfgang Herrmann, *Gottfried Semper. In Search of Architecture*. Cambridge MA, MIT Press, 1984.

Robert Hewison, *The Heritage Industry. Britain in a climate of decline*. London, Methuen, 1987.

Hilde Heynen, *Architecture and Modernity. A Critique*. Cambridge, MIT Press, 1999.

Henry-Russell Hitchcock, *Modern Architecture. Romanticism and Reintegration*. New York, Hacker Art Books, 1970, 18 (first edition, 1929).

Henry-Russell Hitchcock and Philip Johnson, *The International Style*. New York, Norton, 1966 (first edition, 1932).

Hermione Hobhouse, *Lost London. A Century of Demolition and Decay*. London, Macmillan, 1971.

Eric Hobsbawm and Terence Ranger, *The Invention of Tradition*. Cambridge University Press, 1983.

Godehard Hoffmann, *Rheinische Romanik im 19. Jahrhundert. Denkmalpflege in der Preussischen Rheinprovinz*. Cologne, J.P. Bachem, 1995.

Dieter Hoffmann-Axthelm, 'Krieg & Architektur', *Arch* + (1983), 14-18.

Anique Marie Hommels, *Unbuilding Cities. Obduracy in Urban Sociotechnical Change*. Maastricht, University Press, 2001.

Yap Hong Seng, 'Orde en chaos in stedebouw en planologie. Op zoek naar "morfologische resistentie"' in: N. de Vreeze, *Orde & chaos in de stadsontwikkeling*. Rotterdam, 010, 1994, 63-80.

Yap Hong Seng, *De stad als uitdaging*. Rotterdam, Nai, 2000.

Hoog in Nederland. Een onderzoek naar motieven achter hoogbouw. Amsterdam, Kunsthistorisch Instituut, 1986.

Egbert J. Hoogenberk, *Het idee van de Hollandse stad*. Delft, Delft University Press, 1980.

Michael Hough, *Out of Place. Restoring Identity to the Regional Landscape*. New Haven, Yale University Press, 1990.

E. S. Houwaart, *De hygiënisten. Artsen, staat en volksgezondheid in Nederland 1840-1890*. Dissertation Maastricht University 1991.

Achim Hubel, *Denkmalpflege zwischen Konservieren und Rekonstruieren*. Bamberg, Arbeitskreis Theorie und Lehre der Denkmalpflege, 1993. Also in: *Zeitschrift für Kunsttechnologie und Konservierung* (1993), Volume 1, 134-154.

Achim Hubel and Hermann Wirth, *Wiederaufgebaute und Neugebaute Architektur der 1950er Jahre*. Weimar, Arbeitskreis Theorie und Lehre der Denkmalpflege, 1997.

Jaap Huisman, *Lelijk gebouwd Nederland*. The Hague, SDU, 1991.

J. Huizinga, *In de schaduwen van morgen. Een diagnose van het geestelijk lijden van onzen tijd*. Haarlem, Tjeenk Willink, 1935.

Michael Hunter, *Preserving the Past. The Rise of Heritage in Modern Britain*. Gloucestershire, Alan Sutton, 1996.

Norbert Huse, *'Neues Bauen' 1918 bis 1933. Moderne Architektur in der Weimarer Republik*. Munich, Heinz Moos, 1975.

Norbert Huse, *Denkmalpflege. Deutsche Texte aus drei Jahrhunderten*. Munich, C.H. Beck, 1984.

Hans Ibelings, 'Het andere modernisme. Traditionalistische architectuur in Nederland 1900-1960', *Archis* 6 (1988), 36-51.

Hans Ibelings, *Van den Broek en Bakema 1948-1988. Architectuur en Stedenbouw*. Rotterdam, Nai, 2000.

Ton Idsinga and Jeroen Schilt, *Architect W. Van Tijen 1894-1974*. The Hague, Staatsuitgeverij, 1987.

Nobuo Ito, 'Authenticity Inherent in Cultural Heritage in Asia and Japan', *Proceedings of the Nara Conference on Authenticity in relation to the World Heritage Convention* (Nara, Japan, 1994). ICOMOS 1995, 35-45.

Jane Jacobs, *The Death and Life of Great American Cities*. New York, Vintage Books, 1961.

W. Jäger and C. A. Brebbia, *The Revival of Dresden*. WIT Press, 2000.

Conrad Jameson, 'British Architecture – Thirty Wasted Years', *Sunday Times Magazine* (Feburary 1977). From: *In Opposition zur Moderne. Aktuelle Positionen in der Architektur*, G.R. Blomeyer and B. Tietze. Braunschweig, Vieweg, 1980, 80.

Charles A. Jencks, *The Language of Post-Modern Architecture*. London, Academy Editions, 1977.

Philip Johnson, 'Where Are We At?', *Architectural Review* CXXVII (September 1960), 173-175. Republished in: *Philip Johnson Writings*. Oxford University Press 1979.

Mark Jones, *Why Fakes Matter. Essays on Problems of Authenticity*. London, British Museum Press, 1992.

Gert Kähler, *Einfach schwierig. Eine deutsche Architekturdebatte. Ausgewählte Beiträge 1993-1995*. Braunschweig, Vieweg, 1995.

Jan Kalf, *Van Oude en Nieuwe Kunst*. Amsterdam, C.L. van Langenhuysen, 1908.

Herman Kampinga, *Opvattingen over onze Vaderlandse Geschiedenis bij de Hollandse Historici der XVIe en XVII eeuw*. The Hague, Martinus Nijhoff, 1917 (reprint: Utrecht, HES Publishers, 1980).

Peter Katz, *The New Urbanism. Towards an Architecture of Community*. New York, McGraw-Hill, 1994.

Emil Kaufmann, *Architecture in the Age of Reason*. New York, Dover, 1955.

Anthony Kemp, *The Estrangement of the Past. A Study in the Origins of Modern Historical Consciousness*. Oxford University Press, 1991.

Jozef Keulartz, *Strijd om de natuur. Kritiek van de radicale ecologie*. Amsterdam, Boom, 1995.

Gottfried Kiesow, *Einführung in die Denkmalpflege*. Darmstadt, Wissenschaftliche Buchgesellschaft, 1982.

Gottfried Kiesow, 'Die Neubebauung des Dom-Römerberg-Bereiches in Frankfurt am Main', *Deutsche Kunst und Denkmalpflege* 42 (1984), 1-10.

Karin Kirsch, *Die Weissenhofsiedlung*. Stuttgart, Deutsche Verlags-Anstalt, 1987.

Barbara Kirschenblatt-Gimblett, *Destination Culture – Tourism, Museums and Heritage*. Berkeley, University of California Press, 1998.

Renata Klée-Gobert, 'Der Wiederaufbau der Grossen St. Michaeliskirche in Hamburg nach der Brandzerstörung von 1906 und die zeitgenössische Kritik', *Deutsche Kunst und Denkmalpflege* (1973), 131-139.

L.A. de Klerk, *Op zoek naar de ideale stad*. Deventer, Van Loghum Slaterus, 1980.

R.H.J. Klok and J. A. J. Vervloet, 'Pleidooi voor de bescherming van cultuurhistorische of historisch-landschappelijke structuren', *Bulletin van de Koninklijke Nederlandse Oudheidkundige Bond* (1983), 2-21.

J.P. Kloos, *Architectuur, een gewetenszaak*. The Hague, Staatsuitgeverij, 1985.

Rem Koolhaas and Bruce Mau, *Small/Medium/Large/Extra Large. OMA*. Rotterdam, 010 Publishers, 1995.

Ton Koot, *Strijd om Schoonheid. 50 Jaar Heemschut*. Amsterdam, Ploegsma, 1961.

Ton Koot, *Help! Ze verpesten ons land*. Naarden, Strengholt, 1973.

Anatole Kopp, *L'Architecture de la période stalinienne*. Presses Universitaires de Grenoble, 1978.

Reinhart Koselleck, *Vergangene Zukunft. Zur Semantik geschichtlicher Zeiten*. Frankfurt on Main, Suhrkamp, 1995.

Rudy Koshar, *Germany's Transient Pasts. Preservation and National Memory in the Twentieth Century*. Chapel Hill, University of North Carolina Press, 1998.

Richard Krautheimer, 'The Carolingian Revival of Early Christian Architecture', *The Art Bulletin* (1942), 1-38.

Richard Krautheimer, 'Introduction to an Iconography of Mediaeval Architecture', *Journal of the Warburg and Courtauld Institutes* (1942), 1-33.

A. G. Krishna Menon, 'Conservation in India. A Search for Direction', *Architecture + Design* (1989), 22-27.

A.G. Krishna Menon, 'Rethinking the Venice Charter: The Indian Experience', *South Asian Studies* 10 (1994), 37-44.

Rob Kroes, 'Hoeveel Amerika zit er in de Nederlandse cultuur?', *De Gids* 1 (1993), 79-84.

Hanno Walter Kruft, 'Rekonstruktion als Restauration? Wiederaufbau zerstörter Architektur', *Kunstchronik* (1993), 582-588.

Dieter Krull and Dieter Zumpe, *Memento Frauenkirche*. Berlin, Verlag Bauwesen, 2001.

Peter Kurman and Dethard von Winterfeld, 'Gautier de Varinfroy, ein "Denkmalpfleger" im 13. Jahrhundert', *Festschrift für Otto von Simson zum 65. Geburtstag*. Edited by Lucius Grisebach and Konrad Renger. Berlin 1977, 101-159.

A. Labrie, *Het verlangen naar zuiverheid. Een essay over Duitsland*. Maastricht, Uniprint RL, 1994.

Brian Ladd, *The Ghosts of Berlin. Confronting German History in the Urban Landscape*. University of Chicago Press, 1997.

Heinz Ladendorf, *Antikenstudium und Antikenkopie. Abhandlung der sächsichen Akademie der Wissenschaften zu Leipzig*. Berlin, Akademie Verlag, 1953.

Landschap als geheugen. Opstellen tegen de dijkverzwaring. Amsterdam, Cadans, 1993.

Het Landschap in 2010. Essays over vormgeving en inrichting. Utrecht, Landinrichtingsdienst, 1994.

Lydia Lansink, *Geschiedenis van het Amsterdamse Stationsplein*. Amsterdam, Raad voor de Stedebouw, 1982.

Le Corbusier, *Le Corbusier et Pierre Jeanneret. Oeuvre complète de 1910 - 1929*. Zurich, Girsberger, 1956.

Le Corbusier en Nederland. Utrecht, Kwadraat, 1985.

Ben F. van Leerdam, *Architect Henri Maclaine Pont. Een speurtocht naar het wezenlijke van de Javaanse architectuur*. Dissertation, Delft Technical University, 1995.

Andrew Lees, *Cities Perceived. Urban Society in European and American Thought, 1820-1940*. Manchester University Press, 1985.

A.J.C. van Leeuwen, *De maakbaarheid van het verleden. P.J.H. Cuypers als restauratiearchitect 1850-1918*. Zwolle, Waanders, 1995.

Wilfried van Leeuwen, 'Tussen droom en daad. Jan Springer als kwartiermaker van een visionaire architectuur', *De Sluitsteen* (1991), 3-23.

Wilfried van Leeuwen, 'Ut pictura architectura. Het schilderachtige en de schilderkunst als bronnen van de Hollandse renaissance', *Het schilderachtige. Studies over het schilderachtige in de Nederlandse kunsttheorie en architectuur 1650-1900*. Amsterdam, Architectura & Natura Pers, 1994, 95-105.

Jean-Michel Leniaud, *L'Utopie Francaise. Essai sur le Patrimoine*. Paris, Menges, 1992.

Paul Léon, *La Vie des Monuments Francais. Destruction Restauration*. Paris, Picard, 1951.

W.R. Lethaby, *Form in Civilization*. London, Oxford University Press, 1922.

Michael J. Lewis, *The Politics of the German Gothic Revival. August Reichensperger*. New York, The Architectural History Foundation, 1993.

Hugo Licht (ed.), *Architektur der Gegenwart. Uebersicht der hervorragendsten Bauausfuehrungen der Neuzeit*. Four volumes. Berlin, Wasmuth, 1892-1894.

Vincent Ligtelijn, *Aldo van Eyck. Werken*. Bussum, Thoth, 1999.

Derek Linstrum, 'Coup d'oeil rétrospectif. Giuseppe Valadier et l' Arc de Titus', *Monumentum* (1982), 43-71.

Wilfried Lipp, *Denkmal-Werte-Gesellschaft. Zur Pluralität des Denkmalbegriffs*. Frankfurt, Campus Verlag, 1993.

Sebastian Loew, *Modern Architecture in Historic Cities. Policy, planning and building in contemporary France*. London, Routledge, 1998.

J.B. van Loghem, 'Krotwoningen', *De 8 en Opbouw* (1933), 83-87.

J.B. van Loghem, *Bouwen, bauen, bâtir, building*. Amsterdam, Kosmos, 1932 (reprint, Nijmegen, SUN, 1980).

Adolf Loos, 'Hands Off' (1917) in: *Sämtliche Schriften in zwei Bänden*. Vienna, Herold, 1962.

Stanislaw Lorentz, 'Die Bedeutung der Bilder von Bernardo Bellottto für den Wiederaufbau Warschaus', Exhibition catalogue: *Bernardo Bellotto genannt Canaletto in Dresden und Warschau*. Dresden, Albertinum, 1964, 151-17.

Han Lörzing, *De angst voor het nieuwe landschap. Beschouwingen over landschapsontwerp en landschapsbeheer*. The Hague, Staatsuitgeverij, 1982.

Han Lörzing, 'Het landschap als plandrager. Oude tegenstellingen lijken opgeheven', 'Stad en Landschap', no. 40, *De Architect* (1990), 7-13.

David Lowenthal, *The Past Is a Foreign Country*. Cambridge University Press, 1985.

David Lowenthal, *Possessed by the Past. The Heritage Crusade and the Spoils of History*. New York, The Free Press, 1996.

Dean MacCannell, *The Tourist: A New Theory of the Leisure Class*. New York, Schochen, 1976.

Dean MacCannell, *Empty Meeting Grounds. The Tourist Papers*. New York, Routledge, 1992.

Malcolm MacEwen, *Crisis in Architecture*. London, RIBA, 1974.

Stephan Tschudi Madsen, *Restoration and Anti-Restoration. A Study in English Restoration Philosophy*. Oslo, Universitetsforlaget, 1976.

Jan De Maeyer, 'Katholiek reveil, kerk en kunst', in: *J.A. Alberdingk Thijm 1820-1889. Erflater van de negentiende eeuw*. Baarn, Arbor, 1992.

Heinrich Magirius, 'Der Wiederaufbau zerstörter Baudenkmäler – dargestellt an der Wiederherstellung von vier Dresdner Monumenten: Zwinger, Oper, Residenzschloss und Frauenkirche' in: *Denkmalpflege heute. Akten des Berner Denkmalpflegekongresses Oktober 1993*. Berne, Peter Lang, 1996, 83-104.

Udo Mainzer, 'Geschichte aus dem Baukasten oder: Von der Lust zum Rekonstruieren', *Rheinische Heimatpflege* 29 (1991), 170-181.

Paul Mebes, *Um 1800. Architektur und Handwerk im letzten Jahrhundert ihrer traditionellen Entwicklung*. Munich, F. Bruckmann, 1908.

Cord Meckseper, 'Architekturrekonstruktionen in der Geschichte', *Deutsche Kunst und Denkmalpflege* (1984), 17-24.

Hans-Rudolf Meier and Marion Wohlleben, *Bauten und Orte als Träger von Erinnerung. Die Erinnerungsdebatte und die Denkmalpflege*. Zurich, Institut für Denkmalpflege, 2000.

'Meinungsstreit: Wiederaufbau der Dresdner Frauenkirche oder Erhaltung der Ruine als Denkmal', *Deutsche Kunst und Denkmalpflege* (1991), 79-90.

Robert Mens, 'Mies van der Rohe. Na honderd jaar terug in Aken', *De Architect* (September 1986), 35-37.

M.A. Mentzel, *Bijlmermeer als grensverleggend ideaal. Een studie over de Amsterdamse stadsuitbreidingen*. Delft, Delft University Press, 1989.

F.A.M. Messing, 'De stad in de Nederlandse literatuur van het laatste kwart der negentiende eeuw', *Bewogen en Bewegen. De historicus in het spanningsveld tussen economie en cultuur*. Tilburg, Gianotten, 1986, 61-79.

Barbara Daly Metcalf, *Making Muslim Space in North America and Europe*. Berkeley, University of California Press, 1996.

Michael Metschies, 'Von der bösen Lust zum Rekonstruieren. Denkmalpflege vor dem Sündenfall?', *Rheinische Heimatpflege* 29 (1992), 91-104.

Paul Meurs, *De moderne historiche stad. Ontwerpen voor vernieuwing en behoud, 1883-1940*. Rotterdam, Nai, 2000.

Peter Meyer, *Moderne Architektur und Tradition*. Zurich, Girsberger, 1928.

F. Mielke, 'Preussische Monarchen und ihre denkmalpflegerische Ambitionen' *Die Alte Stadt* (1981), 133-151.

Friedrich Mielke, *Die Zukunft der Vergangenheit. Grundsätze, Probleme und Möglichkeiten der Denkmalpflege*. Stuttgart, Deutsche Verlags-Anstalt, 1975.

Barbara Miller Lane, *Architecture and Politics in Germany, 1918-1945*. Cambridge, MA, Harvard University Press, 1968.

Mikhaïl Miltchik, 'Original ou copie? Les dilemmes de la restauration', *Monuments Historiques* 179 (1992), 104-108.

Partha Mitter, *Much Maligned Monsters. History of European Reactions to Indian Art*. Oxford, Clarendon Press, 1977.

Moderne Architektur in Deutschland 1900 bis 1950. Reform und Tradition. Stuttgart, Hatje, 1992.

Moderne Bouwkunst in Nederland. Rotterdam, W.L. & J. Brusse, 1932.

Nic. Molenaar, 'De nationalistische strooming in Duitschland en haar invloed in de bouwkunst', *Het R.K. Bouwblad*, 4 (1934), 53-55.

B. Monnet, 'L'Architecture contemporaine dans les monuments et ensembles historiques en France', *Monumentum* (1975), 35-39.

Gérard Monnier, *Histoire Critique de l'Architecture en France 1918-1950*. Paris, Sers, 1990.

Claude de Montclos, *La Mémoire des ruines. Anthologie des monuments disparus en France*. Paris, Mengès, 1992.

Monument en Binnenstad. Discussion document of the Council of European Municipalities. Maastricht, 1976.

Il Monumento per l'Uomo. Atti del II Congresso Internazionale del Restauro. Padua, ICOMOS and Marsilio Editori, 1971.

Monumentenzorg. Dynamiek in behoud. The Hague, Sdu, 1996.

Nay Morris, *William Morris. Artist, Writer, Socialist*. Oxford, Blackwell, 1936 (two volumes).

Georg Mörsch, 'Zu den 10 Thesen zum Wiederaufbau zerstörter Architektur', *Kunstchronik* (1992), 634-638.

Georg Mörsch and Richard Strobel, *Die Denkmalpflege als Plage und Frage*. Festgabe für August Gebessler. Munich, Deutscher Kunstverlag, 1989.

F. W. Mote, *A Millennium of Chinese Urban History: Form, Time and Space Concepts in Soochow*. Rice University Studies. 1973.

Hans Mulder, 'Ontaard en gezond. Nationaal-socialistische kunstkritiek in Nederland', *Berlijn-Amsterdam 1920-1940. Wisselwerkingen*. Amsterdam, Querido, 1982, 314-323.

Gerhard Müller-Menckes, *Neues Leben für Alte Bauten. Über den Continuo in der Architektur*. Stuttgart, Koch, 1977.

Lewis Mumford, *The Highway and The City*. London, Secker & Warburg, 1964.

Hermann Muthesius, *Kunstgewerbe und Architektur*. Jena, Eugen Diederichs, 1907 (Kraus Reprint 1976).

Nara Conference on Authenticity in Relation to the World Heritage Convention (Nara, Japan, 1994). Ed. Knut Einar Larsen. Unesco World Heritage Centre, 1995.

Natuurbeleidsplan (government decision). Netherlands Chamber of Deputies, session 1989-1990, 21 149.

Winfried Nerdinger, *Aufbauzeit. Planen und Bauen. München 1945-1950*. Exhibition catalogue. Munich Technical University, 1984.

Winfried Nerdinger, *Leo von Klenze. Architekt zwischen Kunst und Hof 1784-1864*. Munich, Prestel, 2000.

Neues Bauen in alter Umgebung. Eine Ausstellung der Bayerischen Architek-
turkammer und der Neuen Sammlung München (1978).

Fritz Neumeyer, *Mies van der Rohe – Das kunstlose Wort. Gedanken zur
Baukunst.* Berlin, Siedler, 1986.

Thomas Nipperdey, 'Kirche und Nationaldenkmal. Der Kölner Dom in
den 40er Jahren', *Staat und Gesellschaft im politischen Wandel. Beiträge
zur Geschichte der modernen Welt.* Stuttgart, Klett-Cotta, 1979, 175-202.

Allen G. Noble, *To Build in a New Land. Ethnic Landscapes in North America.* Baltimore, Johns Hopkins University Press, 1992.

Pierre Nora, 'Comment écrire l'histoire de France?', *Les Lieux de Mémoire.*
Volume 3, *Conflits et Partages.* Paris, Gaillimard, 1992, 11-32.

B. Olde Meierink and others, *Kastelen en ridderhofsteden in Utrecht.* Utrecht,
Matrijs, 1995.

Omstreden ruimte. Een discussie over de toekomst van het landelijk gebied.
Volume of articles, Ed. J.N.H. Elerie and C.A.M. Fleischer-van Rooi-
jen. Groningen, REGIO-PRojekt, 1994.

*Oproep aan de jonge Europese architecten 1989-1995. De wederopbouw van een
historische straat in het centrum van Brussel.* Brussels. Fondation pour
l'Architecture, 1995.

Philipp Oswalt, *Berlin – Stadt Ohne Form. Strategien einer anderen Architektur.* Munich, Prestel, 2000.

J.J.P. Oud, 'Over de toekomstige bouwkunst en haar architectonische
mogelijkheden' (1921). Herdrukt in: *Ter Wille van een Levende Bouwkunst.* The Hague, Nijgh and Van Ditmar, no date, 20-30.

J.J.P. Oud, *De 'Nieuwe Zakelijkheid' in de Bouwkunst.* Amsterdam, De
Driehoek, 1935 (reprint, Van Gennep, Amsterdam 1981).

Erwin Panofsky, 'The First Page of Giorgio Vasari's "Libro"', *Meaning in
the Visual Arts.* New York, Anchor Books, 1955, 169-225 (first edition,
1930).

J. K. Papadopoulos, *The Conservation of Archaeological Sites in the Mediter-
ranean Region.* Los Angeles, The Getty Conservation Institute, 1997.

Maurice Parturier, *Prosper Mérimée. Correspondance Générale.* Paris, Le Divan, 1941-1947 (6 volumes).

Wytze Patijn, 'Jonge monumenten en het keetje van Oud', in: Johan de
Koning, *Het traditionalisme overwonnen.* Middelburg 1996, 63.

*Patrimoine et Passions Identitaires. Actes des Entretiens du Patrimoine sous la
présidence de Jacques Le Goff.* Paris, Fayard, 1998.

Alain Paucard, *Les Criminels du Béton.* Paris, Les Belles Lettres, 1991.

Jürgen Paul, 'Die Streit um das Knochenhaueramtshaus in Hildesheim',
Deutsche Kunst und Denkmalpflege 38 (1980), 64-76.

C. Peeters, 'De Doorwerth als toetssteen van restauratiebeginselen' *Bouwen
in Nederland.* Leids Kunsthistorisch Jaarboek 1984. Delft, 1985, 331-359.

C. Peeters, 'De neogotiek tussen nijverheid en kunst', *Tijdschrift voor Geschiedenis* (1991), 356-380.

C.J.A.C. Peeters and W.F. Denslagen, 'Antwoord van de Rijkscommissie
voor de Monumentenzorg op enige recentelijk gepubliceerde bezwaren

tegen het huidige rijksmonumentenbeleid', *Bulletin van de Koninklijke Nederlandse Oudheidkundige Bond* (1980), 103-113, 110.

C. Peeters, 'De Doorwerth als toetssteen van restauratiebeginselen' *Bouwen in Nederland*. Leids Kunsthistorisch Jaarboek 1984. Delft, 1985, 331-359.

C.J.A.C. Peeters and W.F. Denslagen, 'Restauratienota 1982', *Jaarboek 1984 van de Monumentenraad* (1984). Published by the Ministry of Welfare, Health and Cultural Affairs.

Wolfgang Pehnt, *Das Ende der Zuversicht. Architektur in diesem Jahrhundert. Ideeen – Bauten – Dokumente.* Berlin, Siedler Verlag, 1983.

Wolfgang Pehnt, *Gottfried Böhm*. Basle, Birkhäuser Verlag, 1999.

Nikolaus Pevsner, 'Modern Architecture and the Historian or the Return of Historicism', *Riba Journal* (1961), 230-240.

Nikolaus Pevsner, 'Möglichkeiten und Aspekte des Historismus. Versuch einer Frühgeschichte und Typologie des Historismus', *Historismus und bildende Kunst*. Munich, 1965, 13-24.

Nikolaus Pevsner, *Some Architectural Writers of the Nineteenth Century*. Oxford, Clarendon, 1972.

Ineke Pey, *Herstel in Nieuwe Luister. Ideeën en praktijk van Overheid, Kerk en Architecten bij de restauratie van het middeleeuwse katholieke kerkgebouw in Zuid-Nederland (1796-1940)*. Nijmegen, Stichting Nijmeegse Kunsthistorische Studies, 1993.

Ineke Pey, 'Torenprijsvragen in de eerste jaren na de Tweede Wereldoorlog, in het bijzonder voor de vieringtoren van de St. Willibrorduskerk te Hulst', *Jaarboek Monumentenzorg 1995. Monumenten en oorlogstijd.* Zwolle, Waanders, 1995, 184-203.

Paul Philippot, 'Historic Preservation: Philosophy, Criteria, Guidelines', *Preservation and Conservation: Principles and Practices*. Washington, DC, The Preservation Press, 1976, 367-382 (Proceedings of the North American International Regional Conference, Williamsburg, Virginia, and Philadelphia, Pennsylvania, September 10-16, 1972).

Pierre Pichard, 'Can Tradition be Enforced? Architectural Design in Bhutan Today', in: Jackie Assayag, *The Resources of History. Tradition, Narration and Nation in South Asia*. Paris, Ecole française d'Extrême-Orient de Pondichéry, 1999, 247-260.

Kees van der Ploeg, 'Het beeld van de stad en de monumentenzorg', *Holland* (1992), 249-269.

Henri Polak, *Het kleine land en zijn groote schoonheid*. Amsterdam, Querido, 1929.

Sergio Polano, *Hendrik Petrus Berlage. Complete Works*. New York, Rizzoli, 1987.

Sergio Polano, *Hendrik Petrus Berlage. Het complete werk*. Alphen aan den Rijn, Atrium, 1988.

Richard Pommer, *Ludwig Hilberseimer. Architect, Educator and urban Planner*. Chicago, The Art Institute, 1988.

Julius Posener, 'Kritik der Kritik des Funktionalismus', *Werk-Archithese* 3 (1977), 16-22.

Philip Pregill and Nancy Volkman, *Landscapes in History. Design and Planning in the Western Tradition*. New York, Van Nostrand Reinhold, 1993, chapter 25.

Nicholas Stanley Price, M. Kirby Talley, Jr. and Alessandra Melucco Vaccaro, *Historical and Philosophical Issues in the Conservation of Cultural Heritage*. Los Angeles, The Getty Conservation Institute, 1996.

D. Raoul-Rochette, 'Considération sur la question de savoir s'il est convenable, au XIXe siècle, de bâtir des églises en style gothique', *Annales Archéologiques* (1846), 326-333.

Louis Réau, *Histoire du Vandalisme. Les Monuments Détruits de l'Art Français*. Paris, Laffont, 1994 (first edition, 1959)

Reconstructions et Modernisation. La France après les Ruines 1918 ... 1945 ... . Exhibition catalogue, Archives Nationales in the Hôtel de Rohan (1991).

Hans Redeker, *De dagen der artistieke vertwijfeling. Een essay over de crisis van het kunstenaarschap*. Amsterdam, De Bezige Bij, 1950.

A.L. de Regt, 'Kleinschalig landschap in een grootschalig Europa', *Ruimtelijke Verkenningen 1989*. The Hague, Rijksplanologische Dienst, 1989, 12-44.

Rekonstruktion in der Denkmalpflege. Überlegungen/Definitionen/Erfahrungsberichte. Bonn, Deutsches Nationalkomitee für Denkmalschutz, 1997.

Resurgam. De Belgische Wederopbouw na 1914. Brussels, Gemeentekrediet, 1985.

Sir James Richards, 'The hollow victory: 1932-72', *Journal of the Royal Institute of British Architects* (1972), 192-197.

Paul Ricoeur, 'Universalization and National Cultures', *History and Truth*. Evanston, Northwestern University Press, 1961, 276-283.

Alberto Rizzi, 'Varsavia ressurecta: realtà e mito della riconstruzione postbellica', *Varsavia. Immagine e storia di una capitale*. Exhibition catalogue, Ferrara, 1987, 171-201.

Jennifer Robertson, 'Furusato Japan: The Culture and Politics of Nostalgia', *Politics, Culture, and Society* (1988), 494-518.

John Martin Robinson, *The Latest Country Houses*. London, Bodley Head, 1984.

Romantik und Restauration. Architektur in Bayern zur Zeit Ludwigs I. 1825-1848. Edited by Winfried Nerdinger. Munich, Hugendubel, 1987.

Gavriel D. Rosenfeld, *Munich and Memory. Architecture, Monuments and the Legacy of the Third Reich*. Los Angeles, University of California Press, 2000.

Vincent van Rossem, 'Waar wij wonen', *Architectuur in Nederland*. Nai Yearbook 1991/1992, 16-22.

Vincent van Rossem, 'De stad gebouwd. De oude binnenstad vernieuwd', *Amsterdam in de Tweede Gouden Eeuw*. Bussum, Thoth, 2000, 36-58.

Michael Roth and Charles Salas, *Disturbing Remains. Memory, History and Crisis in the Twentieth Century*. Los Angeles, Getty Research Institute, 2001.

Michael S. Roth, *The Ironist's Cage. Memory, Trauma, and the Construction of History*. New York, Columbia University Press, 1995.

Christopher Rowell and John Martin Robinson, *Uppark Restored*. London, The National Trust, 1996.

P. de Ruijter, *Voor volkshuisvesting en stedebouw*. Utrecht, Matrijs, 1987.

John Ruskin, 'The Lamp of Memory', in: *The Seven Lamps of Architecture* (1849). London, Allen and Unwin, 1925, 353-359.

Pierre Ryckmans, 'The Chinese Attitude towards the Past', *World Art. Themes of Unity in Diversity*. Pennsylvania State University Press, 1989, 809-812.

V. Sackville-West, *The Edwardians*. London, The Hogarth Press, 1930.

Edward W. Said, *Culture & Imperialism*. London, Vintage, 1994.

Andrew Saint, *The Image of the Architect*. New Haven/London, Yale University Press, 1983.

Simon Schama, *Landscape and Memory*. London, Harper Collins, 1995.

Thorsten Scheer, Josef Paul Kleihues and Paul Kahlfeldt, *Stadt der Architektur. Berlin 1900-2000*. Berlin, Nicolai, 2000.

L.S.P. Scheffer, 'De Amsterdamse Wederopbouwplannen', *Tijdschrift voor Volkshuisvesting en Stedebouw* (1954), 1-11.

Marijke van Schendelen, *Natuur en Ruimtelijke Ordening in Nederland. Een symbiotische relatie*. Rotterdam, Nai, 1997.

Ingeborg Schild, 'Über Nachbildungen und Rekonstruktionen als Methoden der Denkmalpflege', *Rheinische Heimatpflege* 28 (1991), 247-258.

Erwin Schleich, *Die zweite Zerstörung Münchens*. Stuttgart, Steinkopf, 1978.

Hartwig Schmidt, *Wiederaufbau*. Stuttgart, Konrad Theiss Verlag, 1993.

Paul Schmitthenner, *Baugestaltung. Erste Folge. Das deutsche Wohnhaus*. Stuttgart, Konrad Wittwer, 1932.

Peter Schoppert, *Java Style*. London, Thames and Hudson, 1997.

Paul Schultze-Naumburg, *Kulturarbeiten*. Nine volumes. Munich, Callweg, 1901-1917.

Paul Schultze-Naumburg, *Kunst und Rasse*. Munich, Lehmann, 1928.

Schutz und Pflege von Baudenkmälern in der Bundesrepublik Deutschland. Ein Handbuch. Published by August Gebessler. Cologne, Kohlhammer, 1980.

Alexander Schwab, '*Das Buch vom Bauen'. Wohnungsnot/ Neue Technik/ Neue Baukunst/Städtebau aus sozialistischer Sicht*. Düsseldorf, Bertelsmann, 1973 (published in 1930 under the pseudonym of Albert Sigrist).

Science et Conscience du Patrimoine. Entretiens du Patrimoine. Paris, 1994.

Geoffrey Scott, *The Architecture of Humanism. A Study in the History of Taste*. London, Constable, 1914 (reissued by the Architectural Press in London in 1980 with a foreword by David Watkin).

Roger Scruton, *The Aesthetics of Architecture*. Princeton University Press, 1979.

Hans Sedlmayr, *Verlust der Mitte*. Salzburg, Otto Müller, 1948.

Gottfried Semper, 'Über den Zusammenhang der architektonischen Systeme mit allgemeinen Kulturzuständen', in: *Kleine Schriften*. Berlin, Spemann, 1884, 351.

Alexander von Senger, *Krisis der Architektur*. Zurich, Rascher, 1928.

Christopher Shaw and Malcolm Chase, *The Imagined Past. History and Nostalgia*. Manchester University Press, 1989.

Rob Shields, *Places on the Margin – Alternative Geographics of Modernity*. London, Routledge, 1991.

Wolf Jobst Siedler and Elisabeth Niggemeyer, *Die gemordete Stadt. Abgesang auf Putte und Strasse, Platz und Baum*. Munich, Herbig, 1964. Reprinted 1978.

H. T. Siraa, *Een miljoen nieuwe woningen. De rol van de rijksoverheid bij de wederopbouw, volkshuisvesting, bouwnijverheid en ruimtelijke ordening (1940-1963)*. The Hague, Sdu Uitgeverij, 1989.

Camillo Sitte, *De Stedebouw volgens zijn artistieke grondbeginselen. Vertaald en van een nawoord voorzien door Auke van der Woud*. Rotterdam, 010, 1991.

'Sloopend Herboren Nederland', series of articles in the journal *Buiten* (1913), 506-508, 518-519, 602-604; (1914), 20-22, 29-32, 64-67, 164-166, 172-173, 222-224, 237-238, 246-248, 263-266, 350-352, 359-361.

Das Schloss? Eine Ausstellung über die Mitte Berlins. Förderverein Berliner Stadtschloss. Berlin, Ernst & Sohn, 1993.

Rutger A.F. Smook, *Binnensteden veranderen. Atlas van het ruimtelijk veranderingsproces van Nederlandse binnensteden in de laatste anderhalve eeuw*. Zutphen, De Walburg Pers, 1984.

Wolfgang Sofsky, 'Schreckbild Stadt. Stationen der modernen Stadtkritik', *Die Alte Stadt*, 1 (1986), 1-21.

Winfried Speitkamp, 'Ein dauerndes und ehrenvolles Denkmal deutscher Kulturtätigkeit. Denkmalpflege im Kaiserreich 1871-1918', *Die Alte Stadt* (1991), 173-197.

Gavin Stamp, 'History in the Making', *The Architects' Journal* 4 (1989), 32-50.

Stedebouw in Nederland. 50 jaar Bond van Nederlandse Stedebouwkundigen. Zutphen, De Walburg Pers, 1985.

Georg Steinmetz, *Grundlagen für das Bauen in Stadt und Land mit besonderer Rücksicht auf den Wiederaufbau in Ostpreussen*. Munich, Callwey, 1917.

Stendhal, *Mélanges d'Art*. Paris, Divan, 1932.

Fritz Stern, *The Politics of Cultural Despair. A Study in the Rise of the Germanic Ideology*. University of California Press, 1963.

Nancy Stieber, *Housing Design and Society in Amsterdam. Reconfiguring Urban Order and Identity, 1900-1920*. University of Chicago Press, 1998.

Willemijn Stokvis, 'Totalitair en revolutionair denken en de avant-garde in de kunst', *De Gids* 1 (1990), 3-16.

Roy Strong and others, *The Destruction of the Country House 1875-1975*. London, Thames and Hudson, 1974.

Herman Stynen, 'Opvattingen over het herstel van de hal te Ieper', *Wonen TABK* (1983), no. 4/5, 32-43.

Herman Stynen, *De Onvoltooid Verleden Tijd. Een geschiedenis van de monu-*

menten- en landschapszorg in België 1835-1940. Brussels, Stichting Vlaams Erfgoed, no date (1998).

Bruno Taut, 'Nieder der Seriosismus', *Frühlicht* (1920), 11. Reprinted in: Ullstein Bauwelt Fundamente, 1963.

Ed Taverne, *Carel Weeber. Architect*. Rotterdam, 010, 1989.

E.R.M. Taverne, 'Bouwen zonder make-up. Acties van Oud tot behoud van de architectuur', *Wonen/TABK* (1983), 8-22.

Ian Taylor, 'European Ethnoscapes and Urban Redevelopment. The Return of Little Italy in 21st Century Manchester', *City* (2000), 27-42.

Richard Terdiman, *Present Past: Modernity and Memory Crisis*. Ithaca, Cornell University Press, 1993.

Anna Teut, *Architektur im Dritten Reich 1933-1945*. Berlin, Ullstein, 1967.

Romila Thapar, 'Tradition and Change', in: Brian Taylor, *Rai Rewal*. London, Mimar, 1992.

Keith Thomas, *Man and the Natural World: Changing Attitudes in England, 1500-1800*. London, 1983.

E. P. Thompson, *William Morris. Romantic to Revolutionary*. London, Merlin, 1977 (first edition, 1955).

J. A. C. Tillema, *Schetsen uit de geschiedenis van de Monumentenzorg in Nederland*. The Hague, Staatsuitgeverij, 1975.

Gunawan Tjahjono, *Indonesian Heritage Architecture*. Singapore, Archipelago Press, 1998.

Jörg Traeger, 'Ruine und Rekonstruktion in der Denkmalpflege. Grundsätzliches zum Fall der Dresdner Frauenkirche' in: *Architektur und Kunst im Abendland*. Festschrift for Günter Urban, published by Michael Jansen and Klaus Winands. Rome, Herder Editrice, 1992, 217-232.

Jörg Traeger, 'Zehn Thesen zum Wiederaufbau zerstörter Architektur', *Kunstchronik* (1992), 629-633.

Jörg Traeger, 'Ruine und Rekonstruktion oder Theorie und Praxis', *Kunstchronik* (1994), 288-296.

Lionel Trilling, *Sincerity and Authenticity*. Cambridge, Harvard University Press, 1972.

Jürgen Trimborn, 'Der Schlussstrich unter eine unbequeme Vergangenheit. Die Fortführung des Historikerstreits mittels der Re-Inszenierung und Schleifung von Denkmalen', *Die Alte Stadt* 2 (2001), 92-110.

Barbara W. Tuchman, *The Proud Tower. A Portrait of the World before the War. 1890-1914*. New York, Macmillan, 1962.

Alexander Tzonis and Liane Lefaivre, 'Why Critical Regionalism Today?', *Architecture and Urbanism* 236 (1990), 22-33.

Gert Urhahn, 'Ontwerpen tussen binnenstad en het IJ', *Stadsontwerp Amsterdam*. Delft, Faculteit der Bouwkunde, 1990, 109-123.

Pieter Uyttenhove and Jo Celis, *De Wederopbouw van Leuven na 1914*. Louvain University Press,1991.

Laurence J. Vale, *Architecture, Power, and National Identity*. New Haven, Yale University Press, 1992.

Arnold van der Valk, *Planologie en natuurbescherming in historisch perspec-*

tief. The Hague, Nederlands Instituut voor Ruimtelijke Ordening en Volkshuisvesting, 1982 (report).

Peter van der Veer, 'Ayodhya and Somnath: Eternal Shrines, Contested Histories', *Social Research* (1992), 85-109.

Peter van der Veer, *Imperial Encounters. Religion and Modernity in India and Britain.* Princeton University Press 2001.

Henry van de Velde, *Zum Neuen Stil.* Munich, Piper, 1955.

D.J. van der Ven, *Ken ons land en heb het lief.* Amsterdam, Meulenhoff, 1918.

Robert Venturi, *Complexity and Contradiction in Architecture.* New York, The Museum of Modern Art, 1977 (first edition, 1966).

Robert Venturi, Denise Scott Brown and Steven Izenour, *Learning from Las Vegas: the Forgotten Symbolism of Architectural Form.* Cambridge, MA, The MIT Press, 1988 (first edition, 1977).

Die verborgene Vernunft. Funktionale Gestaltung im 19. Jahrhundert. Munich, Die Neue Sammlung, 1971

Luc Verpoest, 'Neogotische Architecten en Monumentenzorg in België en Nederland. De schaduw van Alberdingk Thijm', in: P.A.M. Geurts and others, *J.A. Alberdingk Thijm 1820-1889. Erflater van de negentiende eeuw. Een bundel opstellen.* Baarn, Arbor, 1992, 175-192.

C. Veth, J.A.C. Tillema and J. Jans, *De Ontluistering van ons Land.* The Hague, Van Stockum, 1930.

E.E. Viollet-le-Duc, *Entretiens sur l'Architecture.* Paris, Morel, 1863 (volume 1).

Eugène E. Viollet-le-Duc, 'Restauration', in: *Dictionnaire Raisonné de l'Architecture Francaise du XIe au XVIe Siècle.* Ten volumes. Paris, A. Morel, 1854-1868. Volume 8 (1866), 14-34.

Shulamit Volkov, *The Rise of Popular Antimodernism in Germany. The Urban Master Artisans, 1873-1896.* Princeton University Press, 1978.

J.J. Vonk and R.T de Boer, *Inleiding tot de inrichting van het landelijk gebied.* Wageningen, Pudoc, 1989.

F.W. van Voorden, *Schakels in stedebouw. Een model voor analyse van de ontwikkeling van de ruimtelijke kwaliteiten van 19de-eeuwse stadsuitbreidingen op grond van een onderzoek in Gelderse steden.* Zutphen, De Walburg Pers, 1983.

Aart de Vries, 'Ruïnes in de literatuur', *Ruïnes in Nederland.* Zwolle, Waanders, 1997, 72-85.

Wim Vroom, 'Demping, doorbraken en de strijd tegen stedenschennis', *Amsterdam in de Tweede Gouden Eeuw.* Bussum, Thoth, 2000, 378-403.

Stephan Waetzold, *Bibliographie zur Architektur im 19. Jahrhundert. Die Aufsätze in den deutschsprachigen Architekturzeitschriften 1789-1919.* Eight volumes. Nendl, KTO Press, 1977.

Hiroshi Wagatsuma, 'Problems of Cultural Identity in Modern Japan' in: *George de Vos and Lola Romanucci-Ross, Ethnic Identity: Cultural Continuities and Change.* New York, Mayfield, 1975.

Michiel Wagenaar, *Stedebouw en burgerlijke vrijheid. De contrasterende carrières van zes Europese hoofdsteden.* Bussum, Thoth, 1998.

Christine Waiblinger-Jens, *Der Pariser Platz in Berlin von der Nachkriegszeit bis zur Gegenwart – Städtebau und Architektur.* Cologne, Kunsthistorisches Institut der Universität Köln, 1999.

David Wakefield, *Stendhal and the Arts.* Phaidon, 1973.

Kevin Walsh, *The Representation of the Past.* London, Routledge, 1991.

David Watkin, *Morality and Architecture. The Development of a Theme in Architectural History and Theory from the Gothic Revival to the Modern Movement.* Oxford, Clarendon Press, 1977.

David Watkin, *The Rise of Architectural History.* London, The Architectural Press, 1980.

J.G. Wattjes, *Moderne Architectuur.* Amsterdam, Kosmos, 1927.

Helena Webster, *Modernism Without Rhetoric. Essays on the work of Alison and Peter Smithson.* London, Academy Editions, 1997.

Chen Wei and Andreas Aass, 'Heritage Conservation: East and West', *Icomos Information* 3 (1989), 3-8.

A.W. Weissman, 'De oorsprong van de heemschut-beweging in het buitenland en ons land, benevens een overzicht van wat er reeds door werd bereikt', *Rapport der Conferentie over het Bouwkunstig Element bij de Bescherming der Schoonheid van Nederland.* Amsterdam, Ahrend, 1912.

Wolfgang Welsch, *Unsere postmoderne Moderne.* Weinheim, VCH Acta Humaniora, 1988.

Nigel Whiteley, *Reyner Banham. Historian of the Immediate Future.* Cambridge MA, MIT Press, 2002.

'Der Wiederaufbau der St. Michaeliskirche in Hamburg', *Zehnter Tag für Denkmalpflege* (Trier 23 und 24 september 1909). Stenographischer Bericht. Berlin, Wilhelm Ernst & Sohn, 1909, 79-103.

'Wiederaufgebaute und neugebaute Architektur der 1950er Jahre. Tendenzen ihrer Anpassung an unsere Gegenwart' (Arbeitskreis Theorie und Lehre der Denkmalpflege 1996), *Thesis. Wissenschaftliche Zeitschrift der Bauhaus Universität Weimar* 5, 1997.

August Willemsen, *Braziliaanse Brieven.* Amsterdam, De Arbeiderspers, 1985.

Raymond Williams, *Culture and Society 1780-1950.* Penguin Books, 1958.

Raymond Williams, *The Country and the City.* New York, Oxford University Press, 1973.

Henny J. van der Windt, *'En dan: wat is natuur nog in dit land?' Natuurbescherming in Nederland 1880-1990.* Amsterdam, Boom, 1995.

Cor de Wit, *Johan Niegeman 1902-1977. Bauhaus, Sowjet Unie, Amsterdam.* Amsterdam, Stichting Architectuur Museum, 1979.

Rudolf Wittkower, *Gothic versus Classic. Architectural Projects in Seventeeth Century Italy.* London, Thames and Hudson, 1974.

Marion Wohlleben, *Konservieren oder restaurieren? Zur Diskussion über Aufgaben, Ziele und Probleme der Denkmalpflege um die Jahrhundertwende.* Zurich, Verlag der Fachvereine, 1989.

Tom Wolfe, *From Bauhaus to Our House.* London, Sphere Books, 1983.

Arnold Wolff, 'Der Kölner Dombau in der Spätgotik', *Beiträge zur rhei-*

nischen Kunstgeschichte und Denkmalpflege. Festschrift Albert Verbeek. Düsseldorf 1974, 137-150.

Wonen in het Verleden 17e - 20e Eeuw. Amsterdam, Nederlands Economisch-Historisch Archief, 1987.

Auke van der Woud, *Het Nieuwe Bouwen Internationaal. CIAM Volkshuisvesting Stedebouw.* Delft University Press, 1983.

Auke van der Woud, *Het lege land. De ruimtelijke orde van Nederland 1798-1848.* Amsterdam, Meulenhoff, 1987.

Auke van der Woud, *Waarheid en Karakter. Het debat over de bouwkunst, 1840-1900.* Rotterdam, Nai, 1997.

Beat Wyss, 'Jenseits des Kunstwollens' in: Wilfried Lipp, *Denkmal – Werte – Gesellschaft. Zur Pluralität des Denkmalbegriffs.* Frankfurt on Main, Campus Verlag, 1993, 31-50.

Kasuku Yoshino, *Cultural Nationalism in Contemporary Japan.* London, Routledge, 1992.

Stephan Zweig, *Die Welt von Gestern. Erinnerungen eines Europäers.* Frankfurt on Main, Fischer, 1988, 90 (first edition, 1944).

H.T. Zwiers, 'Bouwkunst en crisis', *Bouwkundig Weekblad Architectura* 48 (1934), 524-525 (published in *Het Handelsblad*, 1933).

Index

A

Abma, J.   127
Adlon hotel   215
Alberts, Ton   132
Amery, Colin   187
Amsterdam   31, 35, 39, 40, 55, 57, 121, 125,
 131, 142, 161, 199
Amsterdamse Bos   75
Andreau, P.   173
Apollinaire, Guillaume   60
Apon, Dick   65
Arkel, G. van   163
Arnhem   25, 79
Athens   119, 176

B

Babylon   119
Bähr, Georg   83
Bakema, Jaap   147, 182
Bakker, Riek   127
Baltimore   144
Bamiyan   209
Bandung   172
Banham, Reyner   15, 64
Barcelona   181
Barcelona Pavilion   54
Bardet, C.J.   130
Baron van Ittersum   136
Barry, Charles   156
Baudelaire, Charles   78
Baudrillard, Jean   175
Bauhaus   67
Bazel, K.P.C. de   32, 77, 95
Behne, Adolf   67
Beirut   220, 314
Bekaert, Geert   109
Bellotto, Bernardo   202
Benjamin, Walter   87
Bensberg   19
Benthem, Jan   40
Berkel, Ben van   39, 131

Berlage, H.P.   32, 77, 95, 97, 160
Berlin   88, 156, 189, 210, 313, 314
Berliner Stadtschloss   218
Berman, Marshall   54
Berson, Henri   59
Beseler, Hartwig   101
Bestelmeyer, German   220
Bethune, Jean-Baptiste   157
Beumer, Judith   139
Bieber, Oswald   220
Blake, Peter   52, 55
Blok, Eric   136
Blomfield, Reginald   73, 185
Bock, Manfred   51
Boddien, Wilhelm von   88
Boeken, Albert   31, 64
Boer, Niek de   34
Bofill, Ricardo   181
Böhm, Gottfried   19
Böhme, Ulrich   83
Bomans, Godfried   79
Bonatz, Paul   100
Bosma, Koos   39
Boston   54
Botta, Mario   23, 36, 39, 40
Bourgeois, Victor   45
Brandevoort   193
Breda   150
Breuer, Marcel   51
Brinkgreve, Geurt   132
Brinkman, J.A.   70
Broek, van den   147
Brolin, Brent C.   52
Brom, Gerard   155
Bronwasser, Sacha   121
Brouwer, H.   152
Brownson, J.   67
Bruges   26
Brugmans, H.   97
Brussels   193
Bucherer, Paul   209

Buckminster Fuller, Richard   52
Buddensieg, Tilmann   88
Buren, Daniel   123
Burke, Edmund   167

C

Campen, Jacob van   121
Carcassonne   119
Cate, Flip ten   39
Cepezed   129
Chamberlain, Houston Stewart   71
Choisy, Auguste   68
Clark, Kenneth   158
Clemen, Paul   91, 94, 115
Clercq. S. de   77
Clunn, Harold   183
Cobb, Harry   54
Coderch, J.A.   181
Colenbrander, Bernhardt   25
Collins, Peter   176
Cologne   111, 115
Constant   181
Coomans, Jules   98, 99
Coop Himmelblau   124
Copenhagen   180
Coppé, Lucien,   27
Costa, Lúcio   29
Cremer, Jan   74
Crouwel, Mels   40
Cruickshank, Dan   187
Cullen, Gordon 185
Culot, Maurice   193
Curjel, Hans   158
Cuypers, J.T.J.   95
Cuypers, P.J.H.   97, 124
Cuypers, Pierre   125, 142

D

Daan, Gunnar   135
Dam, Cees   125
David, Jaques-Louis   78
Dehio, Georg   91, 97, 114, 203
Delécluze, Etienne   170
Delft   20, 129
Den Bosch   39, 193
Der Kinderen, A.J.   95, 97
Derrida, Jaques   47
Dessau   67
Deurloo, Ton   197
Deventer   152
Devliegher, Luc   27
Dhuicque, E.   98
Dickens, Charles   32
Dierdonk   193
Dijkstra, Tjeerd   145
Disneyland   119

Doesburg, T. van   97, 98
Doesburg, Theo van   61, 64, 70
Döhmer, Klaus   158, 178
Dollinger, Richard   100
Domkerk   117
Dommel   39
Dortsman, Adriaan   122
Drakenburg House   112
Dresden   83, 189, 202, 210
Drexler, Arhtur   66
Dudok, W.M.   97, 98
Dugardyn, A.   27
Duiker, Jan   66, 70
Duintjer, M.F.   127
Dun, Peter van   34
Dvořák, Max   19

E

Economist Building   13
Edelmann, Frédéric   189
Edinburgh   109
Eesteren, C. van   64
Ehrentraut, Adolf W.   119
Eisenhower   203
Eliot, George   78
Emden, H.M.   125
Engel, Helmut   217
Engels, Friedrich   56
Erdle, Tilmann   208
Evans, Arthur   119
Ex, Nicole   107
Eyck, Aldo van   152

F

Faisal Mosque   174
Fecht, Tom   211
Feireiss, Kristin   215, 218
Feistel-Rohmeder, Bettina   72
Fentress, James   210
Fergusson, James   157, 170
Fischer, Manfred F.   20, 87
Fischer, Theodor   100
Fischer, Wend   178
Flagge, Ingeborg   206
Focillon, Henri   169
Fontier, Jaak   27
Foucault, Michel   40, 47, 209
Frampton, Kenneth   13, 180, 211
France, Anatole   91
Franco, Jean   221
Frank, Josef   45
Frankfurt   102, 104
Frauenkirche   207
Fredericksburg   173
Freeman, Edward A.   113
Freudenstadt   101

Friedman, Mildred   128
Friedrich, Annette   206
Friedrichstrasse   214
Frugès, Henri   46

G
Gaasterland   75
Garnier, Charles   160, 170
Gehry, Frank   128
Gendarmenmarkt   214
Gendt, A.D.N. van   31, 163
Gendt, A.L. van   31, 163
Gendt, J.G. van   31, 163
Gerard, Alexander   167
Giedion, Sigfried   62, 91
Glaser, Gerhard   207
Godefroy, A.N.   31, 163, 164
Gool, F.J. van   124
Goor, C.N. van   159
Gosschalk, Isaak   31, 164
Granpré Molière, M.J.   195
Gratama, Jan   70, 160
Greshoff, Jan   79
Groningen   137, 194
Gropius, Walter   45, 52, 62, 64, 159
Günther, Hans   71
Gurlitt, Cornelius   93, 94, 114
Gutschow, Niels   101, 172

H
Haagsma, Ids   132
Haakma Wagenaar   112
Haan, Hilde de   132
Haas Haus   129
Haberman, Jürgen   49
Hackelsberger, Christoph   208
Hager, Georg   91, 114
Haider, Gulzar   173
Hamann, Richard   71
Hamburg   87, 99, 92
Hamer, W.   31
Hannema, D.   135
Hanover   17
Hartog, L.J.   151
Haus des Deutschen Rechts   220
Havard, Henri   32
Havel, Vaclav   129
Haverleij   193
Heino   135
Hellenraet, Edmond   79
Henderson, Nigel   15
Hendrick de Keyser Society   117
Hengelo   147
Hengerer, Karl   100
Hermand, Jost   71
Hermans, Louis   57

Hertzig, Stefan   206
Herzberger, Herman   26
Hesse, Herman   40
Hewison, Robert   192
Heynen, Hilde   181
Hilberseimer, Ludwig   47
Hildesheim   103, 220
Hilversum   115
Hitchcock, Henry-Russell   44, 62, 163, 164, 178
Hitler, Adolf   100, 203
Hoff, Robert van 't   59
Hoffmann-Axthelm, Dieter   213
Hofland, H.J.A.   36
Hofmann, Martin   208
Högg, E.   92
Hollein, Hans   129
Hong Kong   144
Hopp, Hanns   190
Hoste, Huib   97
Hubel, Achim   89
Hudig, Dirk   32
Huisman, Jaap   35, 125
Hulsman, Bernard   39, 40, 132
Hulst   79
Hussein, Saddam   119
Huut, Max van   132

I
Ibelings, Hans   181
Idzikowski, Adam   204
IJ   142
Islamabad   174
Ito, Nobuo   118

J
Jaffrey, Syed Zaigham Shafiq   174
Jameson, Conrad   56
Janssens de Bisthoven, A.   27
Jefferson, Thomas   179
Jencks, Charles A.   44
Jessen, Jens   218
John Hancock Tower   54
Johnson, Philip   44, 52, 62

K
Kabul   89
Kähler, Gert   314
Kalf, Jan   94, 95, 114
Karzai, Hamid   209
Keulartz, Jozef   75
Khan, Hasan-Uddin   173
Kilian, Franz   20
Kleihues, Josef Paul   211
Kleihues, Joseph   139
Klenze, Leo von   176

Klerk, M. de   97, 98
Klinkhamer, J.F.   143
Kloos, J.P.   66
Knobelsdorff, Georg Wenzeslaus   86
Knossos   119
Koestler, Arthur   60
Kollhoff, Hans   211
Komrij, Gerrit   125
Koolhaas, Rem   23, 125, 139, 181, 211
Koopman, Ton   24
Kousbroek, Rudy   127
Kouwenaar, D.   142
Krahn, Hermann   102
Kranendonk, A. van   152
Krautheimer, Richard   169
Krier, Leon   193
Krier, Rob   193
Kromhout, Willem   33
Kruft, Hanno-Walter   84
Kruit, 133
Kugler, Franz   170
Kuhlenbeck, Ludwig   71
Kuipers, E.   58
Kurrent, Friedrich   19
Kwast, B.B.   136

L
La Croix, G.F.   97
La Sarraz   64
Labrouste, Henri   68
Lagarde, Paul   71
Lakensestraat   193
Lampugnani, Vittorio M.   210
Langbehn, Julius   72
Lange, Konrad   103
Lataster, Ger   123
Laugier, Marc-Antoine   90
Le Corbusier   43, 45, 46, 54, 63, 73, 101
Le Havre   191
Lefaivre, Liane   16
Leiden   151
Leiding, Gerlinde   173
Leitl, Alfons   12
Lenin   59
Léon, Paul   98
Lescot, Pierre   169
Lethaby, W.R.   73
LeWitt, Sol   25
Libeskind, Daniel   181, 210, 217
Lill, Georg   220
Linder, Hans   20
Loghem, J.B. van   55, 57, 59, 68, 97
London   13, 179
Loos, Adolf   61, 181
Lord Salisbury   58
Lorentz, Stanislaw   204

Louis XIV   169
Louvain   97
Louvre   169
Lübke, Wilhelm   111
Luyendijk, Joris   119
Lycurgus   108
Lyotard, Jean-Fran,cois   47

M
Maarn   175
Maas, Tom   133
Maclaine Pont, Henri   173
Madurodam   146
Magirius, Heinrich   83
Malibu   107
Mansart, Jules-Hardouin   111
Marguerin, François   36
Marinetti, Filippo Tommaso   60
Mauritshuis   123
May, Ernst   56
Mebes, Paul   72, 90, 159
Meier, Richard   26
Mendini, Alessandro   139
Meurs, Paul   29
Meyer, Hannes   67
Meyer, Peter   50
Mies van der Rohe, Ludwig   45, 67
Miralles, Enric   37
Mock, Elizabeth   45
Moldau   128
Monnet, B.   21
Morris, William   90, 114, 176
Mörsch, Georg   87
Moscow   57
Müller-Menckes, Gerhard   17
Mumford, Lewis   51
Munich   19, 121, 208, 220
Muthesius, Hermann   50, 93
Muysken, C.   164

N
Nagai, Asami   119
Nap, C.   152
Nara   119
Nash, John   185
Nebuchadnezzar   119
Nerdinger, Winfried   210
New Braunsfeld   173
New York, 209
Nieuwezijds Kolk   131
Nijenhuis   135
Noble, Allen G.   173
Noordewier   132
Nordau, Max   71
Noy, Dyon   146

O

Odé, A.W.M.   77, 95
Olde Meierink, Ben   136
Ostendorf, Friedrich   51
Oswalt, Philipp   211, 313
Oud, J.J.P.   159
Oud, J.J.P.   45, 65, 67, 68, 95
Oudekerksplein   199
Oudshoorn, Cornelis   163

P

Paderborn   20
Palais Royal   123
Palast de Republik   218
Paleis van Volksvlijt   127
Palladio, Andrea   109, 167
Papadopoulos, John K.   119
Paris   111, 123, 156, 161
Pariser Platz   214
Parthenon   176
Patijn, Wytze   194
Paucard, Alain   43
Paul, Jürgen   103
Pausanias   108
Pehnt, Wolfgang   20, 45, 218
Pei, I.M.   54
Perrault, Claude   167
Perret, Auguste   191
Pevsner, Nicolaus   178
Pijpers, Edith   70
Pit, A.77
Place des Fêtes 187-189
Plake, Peter   54
Ploeg, Kees van der   9, 23, 39
Poggenbeek, W.   31
Porphyrios, Demetri   193
Portzamparc, Christian de   35
Posener, Julius   45, 55, 218
Posthumus Meyjes, C.B.   31
Poundbury   193
Prague   128, 129
Proust, Marcel 165
Pugin, A.W.N.   69, 156, 157

R

Rabinow, Paul   209
Rainer, Arnulf   121
Rais, Ghazi Mohammad   174
Raoul Rochette, D.   156, 167
Rau, Thomas   132
Réau, Louis   111
Regensburg   176
Regent Street   185
Reichensperger, August   157
Reijenga, Piet   197
Reitsma, Ella   139

Richards, James   51
Rieger, Andreas   207
Riegl, Alois   94
Rietveld, Gerrit   44, 64
Rijksmuseum   124
Rio de Janeiro   29
Robespierre   43
Robie House   54
Rokin   125
Röling, Wiek   130
Rome   88, 205
Rooy, Max van   25, 127, 137
Rosenfeld, Gavriel D.   208
Rossem, Vincent van   31, 163
Rotterdam   24, 57, 64, 95
Rue de Flandres   187
Rushdie, Salman   209
Ruskin, John   90, 109, 110, 113

S

Sackville-West, Victoria   58
Sahl, Hans   74
Saliba, Robert   221
Salm, A.   163
Sansovino, Jacopo   179
São Paolo   56
Sarajevo   314
Scharoun, Hans   45, 56
Schemann   71
Schippers, Wim T.   127
Schleich, Erwin   208
Schoppert, Peter   175
Schouten, Lydia   25
Schuller, Konrad   219
Schultze-Naumburg, Paul   71
Schumacher, Fritz   87
Schwab, Alexander   57
Schwanzer, Karl   17
Schwartz, Moshe   127
Schwarz, Rudolf   102
Scott, Gilbert   111
Scruton, Roger   69
Sedlmayr   69
Selier, Herman   143
Semper, Gottfried   40, 68, 160, 205
Senger, Alexander von   73
Servan-Schreiber   171
Shanghai   174
Siedler, Wolf Jobst   189, 218
Simmel, Georg   87
Smets   99
Smirke, Sydney   179
Smithson, Alison and Peter   13
Smook, Rutger A.F.   20
Soeters, Sjoerd   193, 201
Sonnin, Ernst Georg   93

Spengler, Oswald   71
Stam, Mart   45
Stamp, Gavin   29
Starink, Laura   57
Steenbergen, C.M.   136
Stendhal   78, 109, 170
Stephan, Peter   218
Stephansplatz   129
Steur, J.A.G van der   77, 97
Stimmann, Hans   313
Stoa of Attalos   119
Straten, J.A. van   163
Stuttgart   44, 62
Stuyt, Jan   77, 97
Sullivan, Louis   90
Swarte, Joost   25
Swigchem, C.A. van   81

T

Tanaka, Migaku   119
Tati, Jaques   187
Taut, Bruno   56, 159
Taverne, Ed   37, 95, 141
Ter Kuile, E.H.   95
The Hague   37, 123, 146, 197
Thierse, Wolfgang   88
Thijssen, Irma   147
Thucydides   108
Thumm, Martin   220
Tijen, W. van   65
Tilman, Hans   25
Toronto   174
Tournon-Branly, Marion   191
Traeger, Jörg   86
Treitschke, Heinrich von   59
Trier   92
Trimborn, Jürgen   219
Troost, Cornelis   123
Trystan Edwards, A.   40, 185
Tzonis, Alexander   16

U

Ulbricht, Walter   217
Unter den Linden   86
Urhahn, Gert   145
Utrecht   37, 44, 95, 112, 117
Utzon, Jorn   180

V

Valadier, Giuseppe   109
Vanassche, E.   29
Vattimo, Gianni   180
Vau, Louis le   169
Veblen, Thorstein   45
Velde, Henry van de   158
Venice   88, 109, 179

Venne, J.J.J. van de   151
Venturi, Robert   52
Verbeek, Hans   215
Verhagen, P.   195
Vermeulen, Paul   25
Versailles   169
Versteeg, G.   97
Viegen, J.N.G.M.A.   149
Vienna   61, 129
Viérin, Joseph   27
Viérin, Luc   27
Villa Savoye   54
Viollet-le-Duc, Eugène   33, 68, 90, 110,
    113, 120, 157
Vitruvius   167
Vlugt, L.C. van der   70

W

Waiblinger-Jens. Christine   215
Walhalla   176
Ware, Isaac   69
Warsaw   97, 204, 205
Watjes, J.G.   160
Watkin, David   73
Webster, Helena   13
Weeber, Carel   36
Weert   79
Weidauer, Walter   189
Weissenhof Siedlung   50
Weissman, A.W.   32
Welsch, Wolfgang   47
Wesseling, Janneke   123
Westeinde Ziekenhuis   197
Westminster Abbey   111, 115
Weve, J.J.   97
Whitely, Nigel   15
Wickam, Chris   210
Wiegmann, R.   156
Wieringa, Nelly   133
Wilhelm II   59
Will, Thomas   207
Willemsen, August   56
Wils, Jan   59
Wilser, Ludwig   71
Winckelmann, Johann Joachim   90
Windt, Henny van der   76
Winterswijk   147
Wirth, Albrecht   71
Wit, S.I. de   136
Wolfe, Tom   44
Workum   117
World Trade Center   209
Woud, Auke van der   164
Wright, Frank Lloyd   51

X
Xanten   115

Y
Yegenoglu, Hüsnü   221
Young, Edward   78
Ypres   97, 98

Z
Zachwatowicz   97
Zeist   24
Zijderveld, A.C.   143
Zohlen, Gerwin   217
Zonnestraal Sanatorium   115
Zumthor, Peter   151
Zutphen   77, 132, 161
Zwaaikom   137
Zweig, Stephan   59
Zwiers, T.H.   70
Zwinger   205

Printed in Great Britain
by Amazon

56059287R00156